To Roy,
Love Mom

SILENT SEASONS

SILENT SEASONS

TWENTY-ONE FISHING STORIES
BY
THOMAS McGUANE
WILLIAM HJORTSBERG
JACK CURTIS
HARMON HENKIN
CHARLES WATERMAN
JIM HARRISON
RUSSELL CHATHAM

EDITED AND ILLUSTRATED BY
RUSSELL CHATHAM

CLARK CITY PRESS · LIVINGSTON, MONTANA

Cover painting: *Silent Seasons,* by Russell Chatham
Cover design by Anne Garner

Parts of this book have appeared in the following publications:

Sports Illustrated: William Hjortsberg's "99 and 44/100ths Percent Pure,"
"The Creature from the Lower Yellowstone"; Thomas McGuane's "The
Longest Silence," "Casting on a Sea of Memories," "Twilight on the Buffalo
Paddock"; Jim Harrison's "A Plaster Trout in Worm Heaven," "Icefishing,
the Moronic Sport."

Esquire: William Hjortsberg's "The Fly Shop."

Gray's Sporting Journal: Jack Curtis's "Waltzing Andy," "Grandfather,"
"The South Coast"; Russell Chatham's "Summer, and Other Small Things,"
"Sterling Silver," "Seasons Then and Now"; Charles F. Waterman's "Ozark
and Time Passing," "Reel Cliques and Stiff Leaders."

Outside: Harmon Henkin's "Swapping."

Salt Water Sportsman: Charles F. Waterman's "Fly Fishermen!"

Playboy: Jim Harrison's "A Sporting Life."

For information contact:
Clark City Press, P.O. Box 1358, Livingston, Montana 59047

For Pat Ryan

CONTENTS

A PREFACE TO THE
NEW EDITION

The first and only edition of this book, done in 1978, went out of print with the speed of light. Interest in a reprint was nonexistent. Discouraged, I bought all the remaindered copies and hauled them up to my house at the end of Deep Creek. During the following decade I kept a few independent booksellers and fly shops inconsistently stocked.

I always believed this collection was among the best ever, and I still do. All of these stories were written during what has been called the golden age of *Sports Illustrated*—the late sixties through mid-seventies. Ray Cave was the managing editor and Patricia Ryan the articles editor. Pat Ryan was responsible, directly or indirectly, for much of the work reprinted here. She bought the first story I ever wrote, and many thereafter, helping rescue me from the unattractive poverty of life as a painter. We became friends and remain so today. It was during her tenure that all the classic pieces by McGuane and Harrison first appeared in the magazine.

Toward the end of the same era the original *Gray's Sporting Journal* appeared, becoming for a time a forum for sporting stories with a broader, more unusual appeal, as exemplified by the work of Jack Curtis.

If you view the ethic of the sixties as having begun about mid-decade and ending ten years later, then this collection is truly of that singular time of enthusiasm, idealism and optimism, and this quality is palpable and ongoing.

This new edition remains editorially unchanged from the original version. Photographs of the authors have replaced the drawings used earlier. I felt it was more important for the reader to see what the authors actually look like than what I interpreted them to look like. In 1979 Harmon Henkin died in a freak automobile accident just as his screenwriting career was gathering momentum. With this tragic exception, all the authors—and I shamelessly include myself—are today working at the top of their form.

Historically, it has proven to be nearly impossible to keep a book like this in print, while many a dreary guidebook skips happily into its tenth or twelfth printing. But someone once said, "In the breast of the fisherman, hope springs eternal," so here goes again.

RUSSELL CHATHAM
Livingston, Montana
June 1, 1988

INTRODUCTION

What we have here is a group of men who are writers, all of whom have made fishing an integral part of their lives, and who have written about it. Some have done it, to be sure, as Hjortsberg so straightforwardly points out, "for the money." We have all done it for the money because that's how we live. But there is more to it than working or playing, more than just fishing, more than writing. The parts scarcely equal the whole. In a sense each person creates for himself his own fishing mystique based upon differing attitudes and factors otherwise personally unique.

Fishing is a way of enlivening and, in its positive connotation, complicating life. It can be at times a humiliating experience, at other times an exasperating or frustrating one. At its best it is exhilarating.

There are as many ways of going about it as there are people who do it. It's possible too many judgments have been passed regarding the purity or merit of one type over another. That is why this collection of stories is not homogenous. As in any fine meal, the portions are of varying sizes, colors, textures and consistencies.

Charley Waterman is a man who makes you feel you should get a haircut and otherwise clean up your act, yet he has neither the time nor the inclination actually to suggest you refurbish your credentials. I'm not saying this with tongue in cheek: if I ever manage to get the upper hand on my glands I can think of no life I'd rather lead than the one he and his wife Debie have made for themselves.

"At one time we said that we would fish one half of the days of the year. We still fish or hunt one half of the days . . . but I find, when I start working, my problem is not making myself go in there to work, but strangely enough it's stopping long enough to go hunting and fishing."

Charley has a keen sense of humor and a fine sense of balance. "There are two attitudes toward a writer. People either feel he lives in a dirty garret and eats nothing but canned beans, or they feel he has sold something and is rich. There doesn't seem to be any in-between where you are just another guy making a living—which is more likely the case.

"Most outdoor writers at one time or another, either by design or accident, appear to believe that they are experts in a field where they are less than expert. A great many of them have been proven to be writing about something they don't know anything about. They lack the modesty to say, 'I don't know anything about this but so-and-so told me.'

"Let's say you want to shoot woodcock because you've never shot them before; and you're down in Louisiana, for example, and you've made arrangements with some guy. The guy drives up in a pick-up truck and worn out shotgun and his mean looking pointers back there that are skin and bones, and you *know* he's been doing nothing but hunting birds for years. You go out and he eyes your gun. You are on the spot. They will put you on the spot in a case like that if they can. The only way out is to say, 'I don't know anything about this but I've shot a little bit. I took it up too old to be a good shot. I'll take some pictures, and if I kill a bird I'll be lucky.' That's the only way—to be modest about it, otherwise you'll be a darn fool because you are dealing with specialists."

Waterman, in the very cleanest, broadest and best sense of the term, is an Outdoor Writer, a professional—one who can transcend the genre through his ability to shift time and place, his sheer volume of experience and his humility.

Very late on an October evening a light is on in the kitchen of Jim Harrison's house in Michigan. Guy Valdene, Jim and myself are home from a nightcap at Dick's Tavern in Lake Leelanau. The woodcock have largely gone south, or at least someplace else, so we made up for it by having four main courses at supper, five bottles of wine, any number of Wild Turkey doubles at Dick's and now, a late snack of venison with two more bottles of Pinot Noir. The floorboards creak and threaten to collapse beneath the hulks of the three fatties. Jim concerns himself with sporting philosophy:

"Hunting and fishing, twin headlights on the same rendering truck. How's that? Or: hunters are the funeral directors for Mother Westwind's children. The perch swam ever deeper, thinking about love. The sportsman had a snapshot of himself pouring a *cuba libra* into a dead tarpon's mouth. After a hard week at the foundry, Clyde and his brother-in-law Claude liked most to spear suckers in a little lake near their twin house trailers outside of Ashtabula, Ohio. They had fond memories of Mom's sucker jam. Some jars were yellow, some brown and some black, depending on their age. The best bet for white shark is an aborigine mongoloid or a whole kangaroo. If properly hooked, the kangaroo will swim for hours in ever decreasing circles. Sharks think of them as furry space cookies."

One of the few things you can be sure will stay with you after a trading session with Harmon Henkin is a lot of his tapped-out pipe tobacco around your house. Consider yourself lucky: he could have involved you in a discussion of politics.

Actually, Henkin knows as much about fishing tackle, sporting goods in general, in fact, as anyone around. His manipulation of it may have occasionally bordered on the manic and the obsessive. Finally though, the compulsion manifested itself in the definitive and redoubtable *Complete Fisherman's Catalogue.*

Now that I stop to think about it, before meeting Harmon I owned a sixty-year-old Leonard rod, a Vom Hofe reel, a Bogdan and several other classy items. But then I never used any of them, which is how I justify letting Harmon vanish with the stuff into the Missoula night.

On our last exchange I think I must have gotten the better deal, ending up as I did with a great little Winston trout rod. Why else, last July, on the hottest day of the year, would Harmon have insisted we try a little-known river that lay at the far end of eighty miles of the dustiest road I've ever seen? Why else would he have taken me there in a station wagon with a hatch back that wouldn't close?

William Hjortsberg of Pine Creek, Montana, is known to his family, friends and acquaintances by the enigmatic nickname Gatz. His large, comfortable home is set amidst broad, well-kept lawns and gauzy weeping willows. The yard, with its huge flowerbeds, enviable vegetable garden, barn, rabbit and hen houses, is tidy and manicured—the work of a compulsively neat Swiss.

One early autumn day, Gatz, the author Richard Brautigan, and I decided to make a day of it, trout fishing in Yellowstone Park. At the time Gatz owned the only car among us capable of the trip: a newly acquired Chrysler.

In Gardiner we stopped for supplies. Tackle at Park's, picnic stuff at the market and inevitably, assorted beverages at the liquor store. In the liquor store, Brautigan saw something he found unable to resist: a bottle of Jim Beam in the form of a dark blue Volkswagen.

Back at the car after fishing, in what was becoming a rather cold evening, the blue Volks came in quite handy. After we had finished, we placed it up behind the back seat and headed for home. Somewhere on Dunraven Pass an especially sharp and unexpected curve sent the little VW (outfitted, no doubt in the interest of authenticity, with real wheels) careening across the back of the Chrysler, popping the cork and spraying bourbon.

Attempts to retrieve it resulted in a fumble and another spume of whiskey. A third, and by now hilarious, grapple failed completely and the People's Car emptied its entire contents without interference onto the rug in the back seat.

"This is really going to make a big hit with Marian," Gatz said, with reference to his wife.

For months you could smell bourbon in the Chrysler. And indeed, Marian often asked, with an eyebrow cocked, when we were going "fishing" again.

For Jack Curtis fishing has never been, as it has for the rest of us, a matter of formal sport. In his den you'll find an old deer rifle or two and maybe a couple of old saltwater outfits. A far cry from McGuane's Fisher 30–06, or my four dozen fly rods and antique Hardy reels, or Henkin's Paynes and Garrisons. And his dogs, which yap at you when you drive in, are quite a different breed from Waterman's pointers.

Nonetheless, Jack lives a life as connected to nature as anyone I've ever known. It is entirely possible that in more than twenty-five years of living in Big Sur, having raised a family of four, Jack's wife has spent less time in food stores than the average housewife does in a month. The hill and the sea have it all if you know where to look.

In this section of his poem "These Days That Walked Away," Curtis shows something of the life of a homesteader on the South Coast, something of what it can be like to live in the country.

In the beginning our green boards in the wilderness,
And seven heavy horses chased us on the cliff trail
And the amateur axe's wild rebounding into sundered flesh,
In the rains the engines failed and we walked
With our children,
And at the doorway perish nine rattlesnakes
By the great rifle, the possessor of deer
And in the summer day the tame bees gather in steady
Peace the secret essence of the noon.

When the sea was still there down below the hill
House and reached in roundness glistening to the sun
Glostering up like a westering wall that sea
Or like silver gateway opening a twilit Sung garden
Where the silvered poet tongues his celadon tea
And a blue boathead whale sneezes rainbows and dolphin
Spinning lead the shanty ships down the green striped slopes
To Paradise.

Of how it was to live there at the headwaters
Of the sea, on the brow of the old broken mountain
Where the Indians traded flint for jade
Over their own bone rich black ground
And the greatest oak stands as a mastodon had stood
And where now the strawberries feed on the red man's grave
Where the orchard trees sew up the wild soil
Where we sit on the terrace at the headwaters of the sea
And swing the boys into cocky crazy laughter most becoming
To their yellow topknots flying and we are alone,
Standing high, being what we are there.

Tom McGuane once wrote in *Sports Illustrated*, with reference to yours truly, the following: "I can see my friend and neighbor, a painter, walking along the high cutbank above the river. This would be a man who has ruined his life with sport. He skulks from his home at all hours with gun or rod. Today he has both.

"'What are you doing?'

"'Trout fishing and duck hunting.'

"I feel like a man who has been laid off to be only trout fishing.

"'As you see,' says the painter, gesticulating strangely, 'I'm ready for anything. I spoiled half the day with work and errands. I have to pull things out of the fire before they go from bad to worse.' Across the river, the Absaroka Range towers up out of the warm valley with snowcapped peaks and gold stripes of aspen intermittently dividing the high pasture and evergreen forest. My friend heads off, promising a report later on."

Having lived five minutes down the road from one another for the past seven years, Tom and I have had more than a few conversations about this Life of Sport, what it is to us and how to dovetail it into all our activities.

Once, about ten years ago, Tom wrote to me, " . . . we have more thoroughly and elaborately made fishing an integer in whole lives: without which, and I mean this totally, fishing or anything like it is of no interest whatsoever. Otherwise, it is merely the province of various USA varsity clubs.

"My sense of the importance of [a friend's] fishing is based more on his sensitivity to the mystery and resonance of the fact that there are fish at all and that they come and go and run up rivers or hide under rocks or eat at night or whatever, than on the casts he might or might not make—just as Paul Klee's pictures of fishermen floating on sunken moons and upside-down fish show me he knew more about it than [a famous Professional Fisherman]."

Several things, finally, emerge as the carriage that supports this book conceptually. Not necessarily in order of importance, the first is that all the writers are at large. By this, I hope it is obvious, I mean that none of us is employed other than by that desire to do work of our own choosing and our own choosing alone. We write, and I think I'm not presuming too much to speak for all, only what we want to write, kissing in the process not one single undeserving ass.

Further unraveling the particular rope at hand, other common strands can be found. One of them is that while all of us take fishing more or less seriously, none takes himself seriously. Which leads directly to another shared denominator: a sense of humor.

Lastly, we all live in places where fishing or hunting don't have to be expeditionary. It is this, perhaps, more than anything else, that we share and that molds our approach to the outdoors. I doubt if any one of us has any real appreciation of the term *vacation*.

Speaking now for myself, I would consider a vacation from my every-day life a noxious ordeal, one undertaken only under extreme duress and insistence by friend or lover. I am exactly where I want to be not at all by accident. I take the fishing at hand in doses calculated to be an ideal measure in the fabric of the rest of my life. What degree of mental health I possess (not much, I'm told by some accounts), is due directly to that fact.

One morning while walking for the mail, McGuane was considering why a certain project he was working on in conjunction with some other people had failed. "I'm an artist because I don't want to cooperate, and I want to bite the hand that feeds me," he said.

I'll second that. One of the things that happens to a writer if he stays with the project is that he sooner or later frees himself from patriotism and politics and, subsequently, propaganda, his particular race, even his family—becoming a very universal kind of rebel, a citizen with complete social mobility.

Such people it seems, century in and century out, have frequently been devoted to fishing—in no particular form, incidentally—as a means of keeping in touch with the natural world. Sometimes it's a way of creating a compelling and intense form of solitude. In other instances it may be simply a game of chance. In all healthy cases, though, the activity—or sport, if you wish—is a positive addition to the other often less interesting aspects of life.

RUSSELL CHATHAM
Deep Creek
November 1977

THOMAS McGUANE

You can't say enough about fishing. Though the sport of kings, it's just what the deadbeat ordered. Water is as mysterious as fire: we stare into it for hours, a tendril of drool at the corner of the mouth, lips askew, with little or nothing on our minds. Time is permanently wasted as we fly into the face of reason. You can't say enough about fishing; but that won't stop me.

Angling: An American Ballet. Parts One. Oh, dat fishing! Oh, dat fishing! Me oh my! Good ole fishing. Where's the rod. Ah, here it is, hmmmm . . . Now, for a nibble. Mister Lunker say to hisself, how's about a between-meals snack! Nobody get cavities underwater! Here's somethin' looks right tasty . . . yaagh! A hook! I fears I on my way to a awards dinner!

Later: What I do with dat rod? Where I leavin' dose lures? Dat wa'nt no fish! Dat was my imagination. Hey, you up dere! Any nibbles? Shit fire! They a rat in my creel!

Wednesday, or The Birth of the Literature of Angling: Mother dog! Dat stream farther than China. Two days and no nibble. I thinks I just stay on the po'ch and reads about fishin'.

This may be a fairly curt synopsis of a complicated psychological process: the urge to stay home and read about fishing in front of a sparkling fire, as opposed to leaky waders and slime all over your hands. Few of us watching Marlin Perkins' assistant, "Jim," I believe, bucking out a twenty-foot giraffe or kicking the legendary black rhino in the shins, want to do it ourselves, whatever the assurances of Mutual of Omaha. Omaha can seem very far away to a sportsman facing the antagonized wild, firsthand.

1

Another thing to remember is that much of the literature of angling is comic in nature: the readers' drive to gloat is very large. It is hard to specify the exact nature of our thrill as, still in bed, we read of the woebegone steelhead angler, his waders full of snowmelt, tumbling down one of the frothy headwaters of the Columbia to a very uncertain future. How well I remember, as a boy in the Great Lakes region, reading of swordfishermen off the gloomy capes of Peru; they almost never "got one," if memory serves; but from time to time, an exceedingly unwelcome *Giant Squid* came over the transom and sent all the anglers speeding to the galley for draughts of rum and long chats, while the unattractive denizen of the Humboldt Current expired on deck, its suction cups all over the fighting chair.

The literature of angling, then, addresses itself to that unacknowledged side of sport, the thrill of secondhand information. Too, it enlivens our will to believe everything we read, no small gift in an age when everything is going from bad to worse.

THE LONGEST SILENCE

What is emphatic in angling is made so by the long silences—the unproductive periods. For the ardent fisherman, progress is toward the kinds of fishing that are never productive in the sense of the blood riots of the hunting-and-fishing periodicals. Their illusions of continuous action evoke for him, finally, a condition of utter, mortuary boredom. Such an angler will always be inclined to find the gunnysack artists of the heavy kill rather cretinoid, their stringerloads of gaping fish appalling.

No form of fishing offers such elaborate silences as fly fishing for permit. The most successful permit fly fisherman in the world has four catches to describe to you. The world record (twenty-three pounds) is a three-way tie. There probably have been fewer than fifty caught on a fly since fishing for them began. No permit fisherman seems discouraged by these rarefied odds; there is considerable agreement that taking a permit on a fly is the extreme experience of the sport. Even the guides allow enthusiasm to shine through their cool, professional personas. I once asked one who specialized in permit if he liked fishing for them. "Yes, I do," he said reservedly, "but about the third time the customer asks, 'Is they good to eat?' I begin losing interest."

The recognition factor is low when you catch a permit. If you wake up your neighbor in the middle of the night to tell him of your success, shaking him by the lapels of his Doctor Dentons and shouting to be heard over his million-BTU air conditioner, he may well ask you what a permit is, and you will tell him it is like a pompano and, rolling over, he will tell you he cherishes pompano like he had it at Joe's Stone Crab in Miami Beach, with Key lime pie afterward. If you have one mounted, you'll always be explaining what it is to people who thought you were talking about your fishing license in the first place. In the end you take the fish off the conspicuous wall and put it upstairs where you can see it when Mom sends you to your room. It's private.

I came to it through bonefishing. The two fish share the same marine habitat, the negotiation of which in a skiff can be somewhat hazardous. It takes getting used to, to run wide open at thirty knots over a close bottom, with sponges, sea fans, crawfish traps, conchs and starfish facing under the hull with awful clarity. The backcountry of the Florida Keys is full of hummocks, narrow, winding waterways and channels that open with complete arbitrariness to basins and, on every side, the flats that preoccupy the fisherman. The process of learning to fish this region is one of learning the particularities of each of these flats. The narrow channel flats with crunchy staghorn coral bottoms, the bare sand flats and the turtle-grass flats are all of varying utility to the fisherman, and, depending upon tide, these values are in a constant condition of change. The principal boat wreckers are the yellow cap-rock flats and the more mysterious coral heads. I was personally plagued by a picture of one of these enormities coming through the hull of my skiff and catching me on the point of the jaw. I had the usual Coast Guard safety equipment, not excluding floating cushions emblazoned FROST-FREE KEY WEST and a futile plastic whistle. I added a Navy flare gun. As I learned the country, guides would run by me in their big skiffs and 100-horse engines. I knew they never hit coral heads and had, besides, CB radios with which they might call for help. I dwelled on that and sent for radio catalogs.

One day when I was running to Content Pass on the edge of the Gulf of Mexico, I ran aground wide open in the backcountry. Unable for the moment to examine the lower unit of my engine, I got out of the boat, waiting for the tide to float it, and strolled around in four inches of water. It was an absolutely windless day. The mangrove islands stood elliptically in their perfect reflections. The birds were everywhere— terns, gulls, wintering ducks, skimmers, all the wading birds and, crying down from their tall shafts of air, more ospreys than I had ever seen. The gloomy bonanza of the Overseas Highway with its idiot billboard montages seemed very far away.

On the western edge of that flat I saw my permit, tailing in two feet of water. I had heard all about permit but had been convinced I'd never see one. So, looking at what was plainly a permit, I did not know what it was. That evening, talking to my friend Woody Sexton, a permit expert, I reconstructed the fish and had it identified for me. I grew retroactively excited, and Woody apprised me of some of the difficulties associated with catching one of them on a fly. A prompt immobilizing humility came over me forthwith.

After that, over a long period of time, I saw a good number of them. Always, full of hope, I would cast. The fly was anathema to them. One look and they were gone. I cast to a few hundred. It seemed futile, all wrong, like trying to bait a tiger with watermelons. The fish would see the fly, light out or ignore it, but never, never touch it.

During the next few months, I became an active fantasizer.

The engine hadn't been running right for a week, and I was afraid of getting stranded or having to sleep out on some buggy flat or, worse, being swept to Galveston on an offshore wind. I tore the engine down and found the main bearing seal shot and in need of replacement. I drove to Big Pine to get parts and arrived about the time the guides, who center there, were coming in for the day. I walked to the dock, where the big skiffs with their excessive engines were nosed to the breakwater. Guides mopped decks and needled each other. Customers, happy and not, debarked with armloads of tackle, sun hats, oil, Thermoses and picnic baskets. A few of these sporty dogs were plastered. One fragile lady, owlish with sunburn, tottered from the casting deck of a guide's skiff and drew herself up on the dock. "Do you know what the whole trouble was?" she dramatically inquired of her husband, a man very much younger than herself.

"No, what?" he said. She smiled and pitied him.

"Well, *think* about it." The two put their belongings into the trunk of some kind of minicar and drove off too fast down the Overseas Highway. Four hours would put them in Miami.

It seemed to have been a good day. A number of men went up the dock with fish to be mounted. One man went by with a bonefish that might have gone ten pounds. Woody Sexton was on the dock. I wanted to ask how he had done, but knew that ground rules forbid the asking of this question around the boats. It embarrasses guides who have had bad days, on the one hand, and on the other it risks passing good fishing information promiscuously. Meanwhile, as we talked, the mopping and needling continued along the dock. The larger hostilities are reserved for the fishing grounds themselves, where various complex snubbings may be performed from the semianonymity of the powerful skiffs. The air can be electric with accounts of who cut off whom, and so on. The antagonism among the skiff guides, the offshore guides, the pompano fishermen, the crawfishermen, the shrimpers, produces tales of shootings, of disputes settled with gaffs, of barbed wire strung in guts and channels to wreck props and drive shafts. Some of the tales are true. Woody and I made a plan to fish when he got a day off. I found my engine parts and went home.

One day I went out and staked the boat during the middle-incoming water of another set of new moon tides. I caught one bonefish early in the tide, a lively fish that went 100 yards on his first run and doggedly resisted me for a length of time that was all out of proportion to his weight. I released him after giving him a short revival session and then just sat and looked at the water. I could see Woody fishing with a customer, working the outside of the bank for tarpon.

It was a queer day to begin with. The vital light flashed on and off around the scudding clouds, and there were slight foam lines on the water from the wind. The basin that shelved off from my bank was active with diving birds, particularly great brown pelicans whose wings sounded like luffing sails and who ate with submerged heads while blackheaded gulls tried to rob them. The birds were drawn to the basin by a school of mullet that was making an immense mud slick hundreds of yards across. In the sun the slick glowed a quarter of a mile to the south of me. I didn't pay it much attention until it began by collective will or chemical sensors to move onto my bank. Inexorably, the huge disturbance progressed and flowed toward me. In the thinner water the mullet school was compressed, and the individual fish became easier targets for predators. Big oceanic barracuda were with them and began slashing and streaking through the school like bolts of lightning. Simultaneously, silver sheets of mullet, sometimes an acre in extent, burst out of the water and rained down again. In time my skiff was in the middle of it.

Some moments later not far astern of me, perhaps seventy feet, a large blacktip shark swam up onto the bank and began moving with grave sweeps of its tail through the fish, not as yet making a move for them. Mullet and smaller fish nevertheless showered out in front of the shark as it coursed through. Behind the shark I could see another fish flashing unclearly. I supposed it was a jack crevalle, a pelagic fish, strong for its size, that often follows sharks. I decided to cast. The distance was all I could manage. I got off one of my better shots, which nevertheless fell slightly behind target. I was surprised to see the fish drop back to the fly, turn and elevate high in the water, then take. It was a permit.

I set the hook sharply, and the fish started down the flat. I kept the loose, racing line well away from the reel handle for the instant the fish took to consume it. Then the fish was on the reel. I lowered the rod tip and cinched the hook and the fish began to accelerate, staying on top of the flat so that I could see its wildly extending wake. Everything was holding together: the hookup was good, the knots were good. At 150 yards the fish stopped, and I got back line. I kept at it and got the fish within 80 yards of the boat. Then suddenly it made a wild, undirected run, not permitlike at all, and I could see that the blacktip shark was chasing it. The blacktip struck and missed the permit three or four times, making explosions in the water that sickened me. I released the drag, untied the boat and started the engine. Woody was poling toward me at the sound of my engine. His mystified client dragged a line astern.

There was hardly enough water to move in. The prop was half buried, and at full throttle I could not get up on plane. The explosions continued, and I could only guess whether or not I was still connected to the fish. I ran toward the fish, a vast loop of line trailing, saw the shark once and ran over him. I threw the engine into neutral and waited to see what had happened and tried to regain line. Once more I was tight to the permit. Then the shark reappeared. He hit the permit once, killed it and ate the fish, worrying it like a dog and bloodying the muddy water.

Then an instant later I had the shark on my line and running. I fought him with irrational care: I now planned to gaff the blacktip and retrieve my permit piece by piece. When the inevitable cutoff came I dropped the rod in the boat and, empty-handed, wondered what I had done to deserve this.

I heard Woody's skiff and looked around. He swung about and coasted alongside. I told him it was a permit, as he had guessed from my starting up on the flat. Woody started to say something when, at that not unceremonial moment, his client broke in to say that it was hooking them that was the main thing. We stared at him as if he were a simple, unutterable bug, until he added, "Or is it?"

Often afterward we went over the affair and talked about what might have been done differently. One friend carries a carbine on clips under the gunwale to take care of sharks. But I felt that with a gun in the skiff during the excitement of a running fish, I would plug myself or deep-six the boat. Woody knew better than to assure me there would be other chances. Knowing that there might very well not be one was one of our conversational assumptions.

One morning we went to look for tarpon. Woody had had a bad night of it. He had awakened in the darkness of his room about three in the morning and watched the shadowy figure of a huge land crab walk across his chest. Endlessly it crept to the wall and then up it. Carefully silhouetting the monster, Woody blasted it with a karate chop. At breakfast he was nursing a bruise on the side of his hand.

We laid out the rods in the skiff. The wind was coming out of the east, that is, over one's casting hand from the point we planned to fish, and it was blowing fairly stiff. But the light was good, and that was more important. We headed out of Big Pine, getting into the calm water along Ramrod Key. We ran in behind Pye Key, through the hole behind Little Money and out to Southeast Point. The sun was already huge, out of hand, like Shakespeare's "glistering Phaeton." I had whitened my nose and mouth with zinc oxide and felt, handling the mysterious rods and flies, like the tropical edition of your standard shaman. I still had to rig the leader of my own rod; and as Woody jockeyed the skiff with the pole, I put my leader together. I retained enough of my trout-fishing sensibilities to continue to be intrigued by tarpon leaders with their array of arcane knots: the butt of the leader is nail-knotted to the line, blood-knotted to monofilament of lighter test; the shock tippet that protects the leader from the rough jaws of tarpon is tied to the leader with a combination Albright Special and Bimini Bend; the shock tippet is attached to the fly either by a perfection loop, a clinch or a Homer Rhodes loop; and to choose one is to make a moral choice. You are made to understand that it would not be impossible to fight about it or, at the very least, quibble darkly.

We set up on a tarpon pass point. We had sand spots around us that would help us pick out the dark shapes of traveling tarpon. And we expected tarpon on the falling water, from left to right. I got up on the bow with fifty feet of line coiled on the deck. I was barefoot so I could feel if I stepped on a loop. I made a couple of practice casts—harsh, indecorous, tarpon-style, the opposite of the otherwise appealing dry fly caper—and scanned for fish.

The first we saw were, from my point of view, spotted from too great a distance. That is, there was a long period of time before they actually broke the circle of my casting range, during which time I could go, quite secretly but completely, to pieces. The sensation, for me, in the face of these advancing forms, was as of a gradual ossification of the joints. Moviegoers will recall the early appearances of Frankenstein's monster, his ambulatory motions accompanied by great rigidity of the limbs, almost as though he could stand a good oiling. I was hard put to see how I would manage anything beyond a perfunctory flapping of the rod. I once laughed at Woody's stories of customers who sat down and held their feet slightly aloft, treading the air or wobbling their hands from the wrists. I giggled at the story of a Boston chiropractor who fell over on his back and barked like a seal.

"Let them come in now," Woody said.

"I want to nail one of these dudes, Woody."

"You will. Let them come."

The fish, six of them, were surging toward us in a wedge. They ran from 80 to 110 pounds. "All right, the lead fish, get on him," Woody said. I managed the throw. The fly fell on a line with the fish. I let them overtake before starting my retrieve. The lead fish, big, pulled up behind the fly, trailed and then made the shoveling, open-jawed uplift of a strike that is not forgotten. When he turned down I set the hook, and he started his run. The critical stage, that of getting rid of loose lines piled around one's feet, ensued. You imagine that if you are standing on a coil, you will go to the moon when that coil must follow its predecessors out of the rod. This one went off without a hitch, and it was only my certainty that someone had done it before that kept me from deciding that we had made a big mistake.

The sudden pressure of the line and the direction of its resistance apparently confused the tarpon, and it raced in close-coupled arcs around the boat. Then, when it had seen the boat, felt the line and isolated a single point of resistance, it cleared out at a perfectly insane rate of acceleration that made water run three feet up my line as it sliced the water. The jumps—wild, greyhounding, end over end, rattling—were all crazily blurred as they happened, while I imagined my reel exploding like a racing clutch and filling me with shrapnel.

This fish, the first of six that day, broke off. So did the others, destroying various aspects of my tackle. Of the performances, it is not simple to generalize. The closest thing to a tarpon in the material world is the Steinway piano. The tarpon, of course, is a game fish that runs to extreme sizes, while the Steinway piano is merely an enormous musical instrument, largely wooden and manipulated by a series of keys. However, the tarpon when hooked and running reminds the angler of a piano sliding down a precipitous incline and while jumping makes cavities and explosions in the water not unlike a series of pianos falling from a great height. If the reader, then, can speculate in terms of pianos that herd and pursue mullet and are themselves shaped like exaggerated herrings, he will be a very long way toward seeing what kind of thing a tarpon is. Those who appreciate nature as we find her may rest in the knowledge that no amount of modification can substitute the manmade piano for the real thing—the tarpon. Where was I?

As the sun moved through the day the blind side continually changed, forcing us to adjust position until, by afternoon, we were watching to the north. Somehow, looking up light, Woody saw four permit coming right in toward us, head on. I cast my tarpon fly at them, out of my accustomed long-shot routine, and was surprised when one fish moved forward of the pack and followed up the fly rather aggressively. About then they all sensed the skiff and swerved to cross the bow about thirty feet out. They were down close to the bottom now, slightly spooked. I picked up, changed direction and cast a fairly long interception. When the fly lit, well out ahead, two fish elevated from the group, sprinted forward and the inside fish took the fly in plain view.

The certainty, the positiveness of the take, in the face of an ungodly number of refusals and the long, unproductive time put in, produced immediate tension and pessimism. I waited for something to go haywire.

I hooked the fish quickly and threw slack. It was only slightly startled and returned to the pack, which by this time had veered away from the shallow flat edge and swung back toward deep water. The critical time of loose line passed slowly. Woody unstaked the skiff and was poised to see which way the runs would take us. When the permit was tight to the reel I cinched him once, and he began running. The deep water kept the fish from making the long, sustained sprints permit make on the flats. This fight was a series of assured jabs at various clean angles from the skiff. We followed, alternately gaining and losing line. Then, in some way, at the end of this blurred episode, the permit was flashing beside the boat, looking nearly circular, and the only visual contradiction to his perfect poise was the intersecting line of leader seemingly inscribed from the tip of my arcing rod to the precise corner of his jaw.

Then we learned that there was no net in the boat. The fish would have to be tailed. I forgave Woody in advance for the permit's escape. Woody was kneeling in the skiff, my line disappearing over his shoulder, the permit no longer in my sight, Woody leaning deep from the gunwale. Then, unbelievably, his arm was up, the black symmetry of tail above his fist, the permit perpendicular to the earth, then horizontal on the floorboards. A pile of loose fly line was strewn in curves that wandered around the bottom of the boat to a gray-and-orange fly that was secured in the permit's mouth. I sat down numb and soaring.

I don't know what this kind of thing indicates beyond the necessary, ecstatic resignation to the moment. With the beginning over and, possibly nothing learned, I was persuaded that once was not enough.

CASTING ON A
SEA OF MEMORIES

Because this was a visit and a return, I might have had the nerve, right at the beginning, to call it *Sakonnet Point Revisited* and take my lumps on the Victorianism and sentimentality counts, though half a page of murder and sex at the end would bail that out. But one always knew from Lit I on that if you are to cultivate a universal irony, as Edmund Wilson told Scott Fitzgerald to do, you must never visit anything in your works, much less revisit—ever.

But when you go back to a place where you spent many hours of childhood, you find that some of it has become important, if not actually numinous, and that Lit I might just have to eat hot lead for the moment, because there is no way of suppressing that importance. Also, there is the fact of its being no secret anyway. A Midwestern childhood is going to show, for instance, even after you have retired from the ad agency and are a simple crab fisherman by the sea, grave with Winslow Homer marineland wisdom. Sooner or later someone looks into your eyes and sees a flash of corn and automobiles, possibly even the chemical plant at Wyandotte, Michigan. You can't hide it.

Still, there was one thing certainly to be avoided: to wit, when you go back to the summer place everything seems so small.

You protest: "But when I got there, everything *did* seem small . . ."

Don't say it! The smallness of that which is revisited is one of the touchstones of an egregious underground literature in which the heart is constantly wrung by the artifacts of childhood.

Students of Lit I: concentrate on all that dreck on the beach that didn't used to be there, won't you? Get the usual garbage, but lay in there for the real nonbiodegradables, too. This is 1978: be sure the aluminum cans and the polystyrene crud shows up on the page. The great thing, ironists, is the stuff is really there! So, questions of falsification and literary decorum are both answered satisfactorily.

I had neared Sakonnet Point thinking, "This place is loaded with pitfalls," and I had visualized a perfect beach of distant memory now glittering with mercury, oiled ducks, aluminum and maybe one defunct but glowing nuclear submarine. And I met my expectations at my first meal in the area: the Down East Clam Special. The cook's budget had evidently been diverted into the tourist effluvium inspired by the American Revolution that I saw in the lobby. The clams that were in my chowder and fritters and fried clams were mere shadows of their former selves, in some instances calling into question whether they had ever been clams at all.

On my plate was Lit I, in parable form, come to haunt me. I knew at that moment that I had my imaginative sights. As a result, I actually returned to Sakonnet Point half thinking to see the whalers of the *Pequod* striding up from their dories to welcome me. And, truly, when I saw the old houses on the rocky peninsula, they fitted the spangled Atlantic around them at exactly the equipoise that seems one of the harmonics of childhood.

I had my bass rod in the car and drove straight to Warren's Point. There was a nice shore-break surf and plenty of boiling white water that I could reach with a plug. Nevertheless, I didn't rush it. I needed a little breakthrough to make the pursuit plausible. When you are fishing on foot, you have none of the reassurances that the big accouterments of the sport offer. No one riding a fighting chair on a hundred-thousand-dollar John Rybovich sport-fisherman thinks about *not getting one* in quite the same terms as the man on foot.

Before I began, I could see on the horizon the spectator boats from the last day of the America's Cup heading home. The Goodyear blimp seemed as stately in the pale sky as the striped bass I had visualized as my evening's reward.

I began to cast, dropping the big surface plug, an Atom Popper, into the white water around boulders and into the tumbling backwash of waves. I watched the boats heading home and wondered if *Gretel* had managed a comeback. During the day I had learned that an old friend of the family was in Fall River recovering from a heart attack and that his lobster pots still lay inside the course of the cup race. I wondered about that and cast until I began to have those first insidious notions that I had miscalculated the situation.

But suddenly, right in front of me, bait was in the air and the striped green-and-black backs of bass coursed through it. It is hard to convey this surprise: bait breaking like a small rainstorm and, bolting through the frantic minnows, perhaps a dozen striped bass. They went down at the moment I made my cast and reappeared thirty feet away. I picked up and cast again, and the same thing happened. Then the fish vanished.

I had blown the chance by not calculating an interception. I stood on my rock and rather forlornly hoped it would happen again. To my immediate right baitfish were splashing out of the water, throwing themselves up against the side of a sea-washed boulder. It occurred to me, slowly, that they were not doing this out of their own personal sense of sport. So I lobbed my plug over, made one turn on the handle, hooked a striper and was tight to the fish in a magical burst of spray. The bass raced around among the rocks and seaweed, made one dogged run toward open water, then came my way. When he was twenty feet from me, I let him hang in the trough until another wave formed. I glided the fish in on it and beached him.

The ocean swells and flattens, stripes itself abstractly with foam and changes color under the clouds. Sometimes a dense flock of gulls hangs overhead and their snowy shadows sink into the green translucent sea.

Standing on a boulder amid breaking surf that is forming offshore, accelerating and rolling toward you, is, after a while, like looking into a fire. It is mesmeric.

All the while I was here I thought of my Uncle Bill, who had died the previous year and in whose Sakonnet house I was staying, as I had in the past. He was a man of some considerable local fame as a gentleman and a wit. And he had a confidence and a sense of moral precision that amounted, for some people, to a mild form of tyranny. But for me, his probity was based almost more on his comic sense than his morality— though the latter was considerable.

He was a judge in Massachusetts. I have heard that in his court one day two college students were convicted of having performed a panty raid on a girls' dormitory. My uncle sentenced them to take his charge card to Filene's department store in Boston and there "to exhaust their interest in ladies' underwear."

He exacted terrific cautions of my cousin Fred, my brother John and me and would never, when I fished here as a boy, have allowed me to get out on the exposed rocks I fished from now. His son Fred and I were not allowed to swim unguarded, carry pocketknives or go to any potentially dangerous promontory to fish, which restriction eliminated all the good places.

And he had small blindnesses that may have been infuriating to his family, for all I know. To me, they simply made him more singular. By today's or even the standards of that day, he was rather unreconstructed, but this makes of him an infinitely more palpable individual in my memory than the adaptable nullities who have replaced men like him.

His discomfiture will be perceived in the following: he invited Fred and me to his court in Fall River. To his horrified surprise, the first case before him was that of a 300-pound lady, the star of an all-night episode of *le sexe multiple*, and included a parade of abashed sailors who passed before Fred's and my astounded eyes at the behest of the prosecution. Unreconstructed in her own way, the lady greeted the sailors with a heartiness they could not return.

After the session closed for the day, my uncle spirited us to Sakonnet to think upon the verities of nature. For us, at the time, nature was largely striped bass and how to get them. But the verity of a fat lady and eleven sailors trapped in the bell jar of my Uncle Bill's court fought for our attention on equal footing.

I hooked another bass at the end of a long cast. Handsome: you see them blast a plug out at the end of your best throw. I landed the fish as the sun fell.

I was here during the hurricane that made the surf break in the horse pasture across the road from the house. Shingles lifted slowly from the garage roof and exploded into the sky. The house became an airplane; unimaginable plants and objects shot past its windows. The surf took out farm fences and drove pirouettes of foam into the sky. My cousins and I treated it as an adventure. Uncle Bill was our guarantee against the utter feasibility of the house going underwater. And if it flooded, we knew he would bring a suitable boat to an upstairs window.

Late that day the hurricane was over, having produced delirium and chaos: lobster pots in the streets, commercial fishing boats splintered all over the rocks, yards denuded of trees and bushes, vegetation burned and killed by wind–driven salt water.

My cousin Fred and I stole out and headed for the shore, titillated by looting stories. The rocky beach was better than we dreamed; burst tackle chests with more bass plugs than we could use, swordfish harpoons, ship-to-shore radios, marine engines, the works.

Picking through this lovely rubble like a pair of crows, we were approached by the special kind of histrionic New England lady (not Irish Catholic like us, we knew) who has got a lot of change tied up in antiques and family *objets* that point to her great familial depth in this part of the world. She took one look at us and called us "vile little ghouls," which rather queered it for us, neither of us knowing what ghouls were.

I kept fishing after dark, standing on a single rock and feeling disoriented by the foam swirling around me. I was getting sore from casting and jigging the plug. Moreover, casting in the dark is like smoking in the dark; something is missing. You don't see the trajectory or the splash. You don't see the surface plug spouting and spoiling for trouble. But shortly I hooked a fish. It moved very little. I began to think it was possibly a deadhead rolling in the wash. I waited, just trying to keep everything together. The steady, unexcited quality of its movement began to convince me that it was not a fish. I lifted the rod sharply to see if I could elicit some more characteristic movement. And I got it. The fish burned off fifty or sixty yards, sulked, let me get half of it back and did the same again.

I began to compose the headline: LUNKEROONY FALLS TO OUT-OF-STATE BASSMASTER. "'I clobber them big with my top-secret technique,' claims angler-flaneur Tom McGuane of Livingston, Mont.," etc., etc.

The bass began to run again, not fast or hysterical but with the solid, irresistible motion of a Euclid bulldozer easing itself into a phosphate mine. It mixed up its plays, bulling, running, stopping, shaking. And then it was gone.

When I reeled up, I was surprised that I still had the plug, though its hooks were mangled beyond use. I had been cleaned out. Nevertheless, with two good bass for the night, I felt resigned to my loss. No I didn't.

I took two more bass the next day. There was a powerful sense of activity on the shore. Pollock were chasing minnows right up against the beach. And at one sublime moment at sundown, tuna were assailing the bait, dozens of the powerful fish in the air at once, trying to nail the smaller fish from above.

Then it was over and quiet. I looked out to sea in the last light, the white rollers coming in around me. The clearest item of civilization from my perspective was a small tanker heading north. Offshore, a few rocky shoals boiled whitely. The air was chilly. It looked lonely and cold.

But from behind me came intimate noises: the door of a house closing, voices, a lawn mower. And, to a great extent, this is the character of bass fishing from the beach. In very civilized times it is reassuring to know that wild fish will run so close that a man on foot and within earshot of lawn mowers can touch their wildness with a fishing rod.

I hooked a bass after dark, blind-casting in the surf, a good fish that presented some landing difficulties; there were numerous rocks in front of me, hard to see in the dark. I held the flashlight in my mouth, shining it first along the curve of rod out to the line and to the spot among the rocks where the line met the water, foaming very bright in the light. The surf was heavier now, booming into the boulders around me.

In a few moments I could see the thrashing bass, the plug in its mouth, a good fish. It looked radically striped and impressive in the backwash.

I guided the tired striper through the rocks, beached him, removed the plug and put him gently into a protected pool. He righted himself and I watched him breathe and fin, more vivid in my light beam than in any aquarium. Then abruptly he shot back into the foam and out to sea. I walked into the surf again, looking for the position, the exact placement of feet and tension of rod while casting that had produced the strike.

One of the earliest trips to Sakonnet included a tour of The Breakers, the Vanderbilt summer palazzo. My grandmother was with us. Before raising her large family she had been among the child labor force in the Fall River mills, the kind of person who had helped make really fun things like palazzos at Newport possible.

Safe on first by two generations, I darted around the lugubrious mound, determined to live like that one day. Over the fireplace was an agate only slightly smaller than a fire hydrant. It was here that I would evaluate the preparation of the bass I had taken under the cliffs by the severest methods: eleven-foot Calcutta casting rod and handmade block-tin squid. The bass was to be brought in by the fireplace, *garni*, don't you know; and there would be days when the noble fish was to be consumed in bed. Many, many comic books would be spread about on the counterpane.

We went on to Sakonnet. As we drove I viewed every empty corn or potato field as a possible site for the mansion. The Rolls Silver Ghost would be parked to one side, its leather back seat slimy from loading stripers.

The sun came up on a crystalline fall day; blue sky and delicate glaze. I hiked down the point beach, along the red ridge of rock, the dense beach scrub with its underledge of absolute shadow. As I walked I drove speeding clusters of sanderlings before me. If I did not watch myself, there would be the problem of sentiment.

When I got to the end and could see the islands with their ruins, I could observe the narrow, glittering tidal rip like an oceanic continuation of the rocky ridge of the point itself.

A few days before, the water had been cloudy and full of kelp and weed, especially the puffs of iodine-colored stuff that clung tenaciously to my plug. Today, though, the water was clear and green, with waves rising translucent before whitening onto the hard beach. I stuck the butt of my rod into the sand and sat down. From here, beautiful houses could be seen along the the headlands. A small farm ran down the knolls with black-and-white cattle grazing along its tilts. An American spy was killed by the British in the farm's driveway.

My cousin Fred came that evening from Fall River and we fished. The surf was heavier and I hooked and lost a fish very early on. There were other bass fishermen out, bad ones mostly. They trudged up and down the shore with their new rods, not casting but waiting for an irresistible sign to begin.

When it was dark, Fred, who had waded out to a far rock and who periodically vanished from my view in the spray, hooked a fine bass. After some time, he landed it and made his way through the breakers with the fish in one hand, the rod in the other.

On my previous nights I had gotten a fish on my last cast of the evening. I made one more tonight and got nothing. I kept casting, hoping to take a bass on my last cast. Nothing. And my time had almost run out.

It is assumed that the salient events of childhood are inordinate. During one of my first trips to Sakonnet, a trap boat caught an enormous oceanic sunfish, many hundred pounds in weight. A waterfront entrepreneur who usually sold crabs and tarred handlines bought the sunfish and towed it to the beach in an enclosed wooden wagon where he charged ten cents admission to see it. I was an early sucker—and a repeater. In some primordial way the sight seems to have taken like a vaccination; I remember very clearly ascending the wooden steps into the wagon whose windows let water-reflected light play over the ceiling.

One by one we children goggled past the enormous animal laid out on a field of ice. The huge lolling discus of the temperate and tropical seas met our stares with a cold eye that was not less soulful for being the size of a hubcap.

Many years later I went back to Sakonnet on a December afternoon as a specific against the torpor of school. I was walking along the cove beach when I saw the wagon, not in significantly worse repair than when I had paid to get in it. And, to be honest, I never made the connection that it was the same wagon until I stepped inside.

There on a dry iceless wooden table lay the skeleton of the ocean sunfish.

It seemed safe to conclude in the face of this utterly astounding occasion that I was to be haunted. Accommodating myself to the fish's reappearance, I adjusted to the unforeseeable in a final way. If I ever opened an elevator door and found that skeleton on its floor, I would step in without comment, finding room for my feet between ribs, and press the button of my destination.

At the end of a fishing trip you are inclined to summarize in your head. A tally is needed for the quick description you will be asked for: so many fish at such and such weights and the method employed. Inevitably, what actually happened is indescribable.

TWILIGHT ON THE BUFFALO PADDOCK

Dawn: a curious mixture of noises. Birds, ocean, trees soughing in a breeze off the Pacific; then, in the foreground, the steady cropping of buffaloes.

They are massing peacefully, feeding and nuzzling and ignoring the traffic. They are fat, happy, numerous beasts; and all around them are the gentle, primordial hills of Golden Gate Park, San Francisco, U.S.A. It is dawn on the buffalo paddock; the frontier is nowhere in sight.

By midmorning in buffalo country things get a little more active at street level. Out of the passing string of health nuts, ordinary pedestrians, policemen and twenty-first-century transcendental visionaries with electro-frizz hairdos that look more like spiral nebulae than anything out here in Vitalis country—from this passing string, then, a citizen occasionally detaches himself, avoids the buffalo paddock by a few yards and enters the grounds of the Golden Gate Angling and Casting Club. The club is the successor of an earlier organization, the San Francisco Fly Casting Club, which was founded in 1894. It has been located in Golden Gate Park only since the 1930s, when its facilities were constructed by the City of San Francisco.

The grounds of the club are not so prepossessing as its eighty-four-year history would lead one to expect. The clubhouse and casting pools are on an elevation that is shaped like a small mesa. The clubhouse is a single story, dark and plain, and faces the pools, which are surrounded and overhung by immense, fragrant eucalyptus trees. The clubhouse is thoroughly grown in with laurel and rhododendron, and—after street-level Golden Gate—the effect is distinctly through-the-looking-glass.

Today, as a man rehearses the ancient motions of casting a fly on the elegant green surfaces of the practice pools, he even may hear one of the stern invocations of our century: "*Stick 'em up!*" and be relieved, perhaps even decorously, of his belongings. It wouldn't be the first time. But that would only happen in midweek. On a weekend many of his fellow members will be there. Stick-up artists will go to the beach or play golf, and it will be feasible to watch your backcast instead of the underbrush.

This particular Sunday has been especially well attended. The men are wandering out of the clubhouse, where you can smell bacon, eggs and pancakes—just as you might in the cook tent of one of the imperial steelhead camps these same anglers frequent in the Northwest. They pick up fly rods and make their way out along the casting pools, false-casting as they walk and trying occasional preliminary throws before really getting down to business. At the middle pool a man is casting with a tournament rod, a real magnum smoke pole, and two or three people watch as he power casts a 500-grain shooting head 160 feet.

Between him and the clubhouse, casting for accuracy with a conventional dry fly rod, is a boy of thirteen. He is a lifelong habitué and he tournament-casts as another city boy might fly remote-control airplanes, and with uncommon elegance—a high, slow backcast, perfect timing and a forecast that straightens with precision. He seems to overpower very slightly so that the line turns over and hangs an instant in the air to let the leader touch first. He regulates the width of the bow in his line to the inch and at will; when a head wind comes up, he tightens the bow into a perfectly formed, almost beveled, little wind cheater. It is quite beautiful.

Standing beside him, an older man supports his chin with one hand, hangs his fist in one discolored pocket of a cardigan and looks concerned. From time to time he makes a suggestion; the boy listens, nods and does differently. Like most who offer advice here, the older man has been a world casting champion. When he takes the rod, you see why; the slowness of the backcast approaches mannerism but the bluff is never called; the man's straightening, perfect cast never betrays gravity with a sag.

So the two of them take turns, more or less. The boy does most of the casting, and while one casts facing the pool, the other is turned at right angles to him watching his style, the angles, loft, timing and speed of his cast.

At this point the boy is already more accurate than the older man, and from time to time he lets his backcast drop a little so he can fire a tight bow in, and score—the technical proof of his bravura. But the older man has a way of letting the backcast carry and hang that has moment or something like it. Anyway, the boy sees what it is and when the older man goes inside for breakfast, the boy will try what the older man has done—even though it crosses him up and brings the cast down around his ears. It embarrasses him. He looks around, clears the line, fires it out with an impetuous roll cast and goes back to what he knows.

By this time there are a good many people scattered along the sides of the pools. The group is not quite heterogeneous; and though its members seem less inclined to dressing up than many of San Francisco's citizens, they are not the Silent Majority's wall of flannel, either. To be exact, sartorially, there is no shortage of really thick white socks here, sleeveless V-neck sweaters or brown oxfords. They seem to be fresh out of Cardin suits—not to mention the aberrations of Gernreich, which they have none of at all. The impression, you suppose, is vaguely up-country.

My companion is a superb angler—widely known for it. He is not a member of the club and is inclined to bridle around tournament casters. They remind him of something more housebroken than fishing, and he doesn't like it. He thinks their equipment is too good, and of course it is, largely; and when they talk about fly lines and shooting heads, getting fussy over fractions of grains of weight, he instinctively feels they are letting the tail wag the dog. Nevertheless, the fisherman has something to be grateful for. Shooting-head lines, now standard steelhead gear, modern techniques of power casting and, in fact, much contemporary thinking about rod design—actions and tapers—have arisen at this small, circumscribed anglers' enclave. Still, it is difficult to imagine a tournament caster who would confess to having no interest at all in fishing—though that is exactly the case with some of them. Somewhat ritualistically, they continue to prefer their activities to practical stream craft.

My companion typifies something, too, something anti-imperial in style. Frayed lines and throwaway tackle, a reel with a crude painting on the side of it, brutalized from being dropped on riverside rocks. His rod is missing guides and has been reinforced at butt and ferrule with electrician's tape that, in turn, has achieved a greenish corruption of its own. He is a powerful caster whose special effects are all toward fishing in bad wind and weather. He admits few fishermen into his angling pantheon and, without mercy, divides the duffers into "bait soakers," "yucks" and other categories of opprobrium. Good anglers are "red hots." His solutions to the problems of deteriorating fishing habitat incline toward the clean gestures of the bomb-thrower and the assassin. And that's not all we agree about.

I sit on one of the spectators' benches and chat with a steelhead fisherman about the Skeena drainage in British Columbia. He's been all over that country, caught summer-run fish miles inland that were still bright from salt water. The conversation lags. Another member sits on the bench. "Was anybody ever really held up here?" I ask rather warily.

"Sure was," says the man next to me, and turns to the new fellow on the end of the bench. "Who was that?"

"Guy that got stuck up?"

"Yeah, who was that?"

"There were three of them, at different times."

The man next to me turns to me. "It was this guy from Oakland."

The man at the end of the bench isn't interested. The fellow next to me asks him, "Didn't he get pistol-whipped or something?"

"Who's this?"

"*The guy from Oakland.*"

"I don't know. I don't know. I don't know."

The man next to me turns to me again. "I'm not positive," he says with exaggerated care, "but the dry fly man from Oakland got pistol-whipped unless I've got my signals real crossed."

"Did they take his rod?" I ask somewhat aimlessly.

"No."

"His reel or anything?"

"No," he says, "just glommed the wallet and cleared out. It was pretty crummy."

I excuse myself. I have a new Winston tarpon and billfish fly rod I am anxious to try and I go down to the last pool, where a handful of members are casting. I am a little sleepy from the gigantic breakfast they've given me. The club grounds are on an elevation that drops off abruptly behind this last pool. There is a path going down through the heavy tree roots to a little space that looks like the banks of a stream bed. As I strip line from my reel, I notice that there are three people undulating beneath the trees down there. One is a girl wearing Levis and an Esther Williams total sun-block hat with mirrors hanging from its edges on strings. One of the men seems to be a Lapp; the other is dressed like

Buffalo Bill and his semi-rotary undulance is more frenzied than that of his companions. Occasionally he blurts "*Ohm!*" and adjusts his enormous cowboy hat with one hand that moves rather cautiously into the uproar, somehow finding the hat as it goes by on a weird parabolic course of its own. I wonder if he has seen the buffalo paddock.

Presently a girl in ballet costume leads an attractive pony into the clearing, followed by another young man with a light meter and viewing lens hanging around his neck and an enormous Bolex movie camera. He walks right past the girl and heads for us. I can see the huge coated surface of his telephoto lens, blue even at this distance, the shoulder stock of his camera and the knurled turrets that seem to be all over it. His approach becomes imposing. He looks put out.

"We're trying to make a movie," he says.

None of us knows what to reply.

"The thing is, we're trying to make a movie."

The man next to me inquires, "Would you like us to get out of the way?"

"That's right. I want you to get out of the way."

All of the casters get out of the way. The director is startled. "This will take a few minutes," he says apologetically, wanting us to spot that smile of his now.

At the end of the pool is the Pit. You can climb down into it and it puts you at chest level to the water. It is a very realistic approximation of the actual situation when you are fishing, and any fancy ideas you might develop about your casting when you are on the platforms can be quickly weeded out here. My new tarpon and billfish rod is very powerful and after a couple of hundred casts the epidermis of my thumb slips and a watery blister forms.

I return to the bench. One of the club officials is sitting there. I decide to find out if the Golden Gate outfit is merely exclusive. "It's funny," I say disingenuously, "with as many hippies as this city has, that there aren't any in the club. How's that?"

"They don't ask to join."

Inside the clubhouse, I chat with the membership. They're talking about casting tournaments and fishing—fishing generally and the vanishing fishing of California in particular. They know the problems. These are anglers in an epoch when an American river can be a fire hazard. The older men remember the California fishery when it was the best of them all, the most labyrinthine, the most beautiful. A great river system initiating in the purling high-country streams, the whole thing substantiated by an enormous stable watershed. Now the long, feathery river systems are stubs and even those are squabbled over by Cyclopean morons who have somehow institutionalized a love of useless dams.

Many of the men standing here today used to haunt the High Sierra and Cascade ranges, overcoming altitude headaches to catch golden trout in the ultraviolet zone. Probably most of them have been primarily steelhead fishermen, though some fish for stripers in San Francisco Bay.

In view of the fact that the movement of people to California in the last few decades may be the biggest population shift in the history of the world, it is amazing the fishery held up so long. But in the last ten years it has gone off fast. Ironically, it is the greatness of the fishing lost that probably accounts for the distinction of the Golden Gate Club—it has bred a school of casters who are without any doubt the finest there have ever been.

Fishing for sport is itself an act of racial memory, and in places like the Golden Gate Club it moves toward the purer symbolism of tournaments. The old river-spawned fish have been replaced by pellet-fed and planted simulacra of themselves. Now even the latter seem to be vanishing in favor of plastic target rings and lines depicting increments of distance. It's very cerebral.

There has begun to be a feeling among the membership that like music without the dance, casting without fishing lacks a certain something. And so they are fanatically concerned with the dubious California Water Plan and the rodent ethics and activities of the Army Corps of Engineers. The men sit around a table in the lodge and break out a bottle or two. They seem to be talking about some secret society, and when I listen in I discover they mean those who have bought fishing licenses in the state of California. The men propose to rouse this sleeping giant of two million individuals to keep their ocean rivers from being converted into outdoor water-ski pavilions. But an air of anachronism hovers over them. The Now Generation, the Pepsi People, seem to substantiate the claims of the high-dam builders. It appears to be true that people really would rather go around and around and around behind those Holman-Moody high-torque ski boats with that old drag-strip mushroom-can exhaust whine coming out of tuned headers and the intake whoosh of double four-barrel Rochester carburetors. But maybe some of them will see, way down beneath the polyester gel-coated surfaces of their triple-laminated controlled-catalyst slalom skis, the drowned forests of California and the long, stormy stripes of old riverbeds.

The Now Generation won't be dropping in today at the Golden Gate Club. Handmade split-cane rods and tapered lines seem a trifle dull. The Eel, the Trinity, the Russian, the Klamath begin to seem in the conversation of these men to be rivers of the mind. The ecology purists imagine the anglers as ghouls who want to hurt the little fish with sharp hooks hidden in chicken feathers. The versions overlap in new permutations of absurdity. In the park I talk with an incipient futurist who wants to know what difference it makes if the fish are lost since we can already synthesize food anyway, and I think of the high-protein gruel rock-climbers carry in plastic tubes for nourishment as our cuisine of tomorrow. Dinner's on the table! Phwablatt!

"Well," I tell the futurist, "I don't know what to say!"

The members begin to drift out of the lodge and head for the parking lot.

It's sundown in buffalo country.

If you are casting at the far pool you are inclined to switch your eye from time to time toward the underbrush. Did someone move in there?

Why delve into it? This is too agreeable. I put on a sweater in the evening and watch the diehards. The pools have gone silver. The emptiness around the few members who remain seems to make their casting more singular, more eloquent.

The whole place is surrounded by trees. Nobody knows we're in here.

WILLIAM HJORTSBERG

Like everyone else who writes for sporting magazines, I have a guilty little secret: I'm in it for the money. If getting paid for going fishing is the Eighth Deadly Sin, then the work of writing about it must be its Absolution. The opportunity to work at journalism came as a by-product of another career, that of comic novelist. Editors who liked my books offered me the chance to write for their magazines. Pat Ryan of *Sports Illustrated* was one such benefactor, and most of the outdoor writing I have done was for her.

I learned to trout-fish as a boy on Woodland Brook, a tributary of the Esopus in upstate New York. Now in Montana, I fish bigger water but am still no better than an Intermediate with a fly rod. Fishing with Experts has given me a sense of humility, very useful for both anglers and artists. Most of the stories I have done were fun to do. That's better than a paycheck any day.

THE FLY SHOP

It is a tried and true angling axiom that as a fisherman grows more specialized and refined in his pursuits, the equipment he needs becomes increasingly complex and varied. Hence, the proverbial barefoot boy content to catch anything that nibbles will make do with a can of worms and a bent safety pin, while a fly fisherman after trout totes dozens of fly patterns, lines and leaders of differing weights and diameters, as well as a variety of rods, reels, waders, vests, dressings and any number of obscure doodads whose uses can only be guessed at.

This obsession with equipment was dramatically illustrated one evening several years back when a friend suggested that all attending members of Trout Unlimited bring their fishing vests along to the monthly chapter meeting. The unannounced reason for this was a prize to be awarded to the man with the most items in his vest. I don't remember who won, but the profusion of gadgets and thingamajigs was unforgettable. My own vest was a cornucopia yielding, among other things, a surgeon's hemostat (for disgorging deeply swallowed hooks), a Pink Pearl eraser (for straightening coiled leaders), a small brass-weighted club from Hardy Bros. (known in Ireland as a "priest", its use is obvious) and a spongy sheet of amadou, a highly absorbent substance prepared from fungi (for drying the hackles of waterlogged dry flies.)

It is not surprising, then, considering this lifelong love affair with equipment, that a fisherman will spend almost as much time in tackle shops as he will upon a trout stream. And if a shop is not convenient, catalogs serve as reliable armchair replacements. Now that Abercrombie has become extinct, perhaps the most renowned purveyor of fishing tackle in the country is Dan Bailey in Livingston, Montana.

Over the years, Dan Bailey's Fly Shop has become something of an

31

American institution. As the shop produces over 750,000 fishing flies annually, chances are good that the royal coachman you are securing with an improved clinch knot to your 4X leader tippet first saw the light of day at the hands of a flytier in Bailey's. For an institution, the appearance of the place is fairly low-key. Located in a one-story green stucco building on West Park Street between Gil's Got It (a gift store) and Lentfer's Taxidermy, Bailey's has less conscious decor than the average New York City dry-cleaning establishment.

The predominant interior feature, aside from the knotty-pine paneling and numbers of mounted fish, mule deer and the world's record Stone sheep, is the Wall of Fame, a collection of several hundred wooden plaques, each embellished with the silhouette of a trout four pounds or over taken on a fly. Also inscribed are the names of the lucky angler and the fly used, together with the fish's exact weight and the location of the water where the catch was made.

Among the illustrious names honored on Dan Bailey's walls are cartoonist V. T. Hamlin, creator of Alley Oop (4 lbs. 5 oz., badger yellow, Yellowstone R.), novelist Tom McGuane (5 lbs., spuddler, Yellowstone R.) and outdoor writers Joe Brooks (5 lbs. 5½ oz., muddler minnow, Yellowstone R.), Charlie Waterman (8 lbs. 10 oz., silver Dr., Missouri R.) and Art Flick (5 lbs. 4 oz., multicolored marabou, Yellowstone R.).

The idea for the Wall of Fame had its origins back in the middle thirties, when Dan Bailey and John McDonald shared a cabin in the Catskills and traced the outlines of their larger catches on the faded wallpaper. This practice was transplanted to the West when Bailey opened his first shop in Livingston in 1938. In those days, the store was located farther up Park Street in the old Albemarle Hotel, a fanciful, turreted brick Victorian building since replaced by a squat cinderblock motel, an example of civic vandalism which the chamber of commerce prefers to think of as "progress."

The first fish on the wall was caught on August 5, 1938, by Gilbert Meloche. He was fishing the now-famed Armstrong's Spring Creek south of town and spotted a big trout rising to a pale, near-white fly. Not having an artificial to match it, Meloche captured the insect in his hat and hurried back to Livingston, where Dan Bailey went to work at his tying bench and came up with a cream-colored fly that is known to this day as the Meloche. Back to Armstrong's, clutching the new creation, raced the eager angler, and half an hour later he returned to the Fly

Shop carrying a four-and-a-half-pound brown. The silhouette was painted directly on the wall over the tying benches and an angling tradition was born.

Dan Bailey began his career as a physics professor at Brooklyn Polytech. Preferring the trout stream to the classroom, he endeavored to find a way to make a living doing what he liked best. Initial attempts involved tying oversized dry flies for use on ladies' hats sold at Bergdorf Goodman and operating a fly tying school in the back room of Lee Chumley's restaurant on Bedford Street in Greenwich Village. The Depression was not the most encouraging time for new endeavors, and Bailey soon went west.

Livingston was picked off a map because of its proximity to some of America's finest trout-fishing water. The Yellowstone flows through town; the Madison, the Gallatin and the Boulder are all nearby. At first, times were hard in the old quarters at the Albemarle, especially during the winter months when fishing was slow. Casting about for ways to earn money during the winter, Bailey bought a traveling shooting gallery from an itinerant concessionaire passing through town. At first this was a huge success, with local marksmen dropping in at all hours to bang away in the Fly Shop. Eventually, the novelty wore thin and the shooting gallery was sold to another traveler and disappeared down the back streets of time. The Baileys' next extracurricular enterprise was a whitefish business. Thirty-five years ago, the Rocky Mountain whitefish was not yet classified as a game species and could be sold commercially. Local fishermen brought their catches to the Fly Shop, which soon became a distribution center for area restaurants. The whitefish were cleaned, packed in ice and sold by the case.

The business thrived until one Christmas when the Baileys departed for a short vacation, leaving a friend in charge of operating the Fly Shop. Returning to Livingston weeks later, they were greeted by the overwhelming stench of rotting fish when they unlocked the front door. Their friend, it turned out, had been jailed for nonsupport and thousands of whitefish were left to decompose in the shop. The Baileys decided forthwith to get out of the whitefish business and move to an apartment in town.

But the days of shooting galleries and whitefish concessions are long gone. Today, Dan Bailey's employs between forty and fifty professional flytiers, each of whom is capable of producing six to ten dozen flies every day, depending upon the complexity of the pattern. The shop normally stocks three or four hundred different patterns, and boxes of exotic feathers, fur and yarn line the hallway in the tying section.

In addition to the standard traditional patterns, Bailey's will tie flies on special order to accommodate a customer's particular needs. The sample case, a tall wooden cabinet such as a lepidopterist might use to display his butterfly collection, holds thousands of these specialized patterns, each numbered and cataloged for easy reference. The case is a treasure trove of the bizarre and the extraordinary, an explosion of colors and textures that would make the palette of an abstract expressionist seem drab by comparison.

Although many of the special orders are useful and beautiful flies, not a few border on the ludicrous. Looking through the case, one comes across such oddities as a green sponge-rubber spider, a creature made of carpet yarn, and a fat white caterpillar that most closely resembles an unwrapped Tampax.

Perhaps the oddest special order ever tied by the shop was for a local rancher who raised trout in a spring-fed pond. These trout, like all hatchery fish, were fed on pellets and grew to enormous size. The rancher, an avid fly fisherman, watched with increasing frustration the pellet-gorged brutes cruising in the depths of his pond. No matter what fly he offered them (and he tried every pattern from an Adams to a white Miller), the trout refused to rise. In desperation, he asked Dan Bailey's to tie some flies that looked like pellets. Although displeased by the aesthetics of the assignment, the flytiers soon came up with a clipped-deer-hair creation that did the trick. Every year since then, Bailey's receives dozens of orders for "pellet flies" from fishpond owners all over the country.

Of course, fishing flies are not all that Dan Bailey's sells. The shop also carries rods, reels, creels, nets, waders, hip boots, lines, leaders, vests and tackle boxes. Everything, in fact, that a fisherman could possibly need and quite a few items he might easily do without. A micrometer for measuring leader diameters and a mosquito head net are among the more superfluous articles in stock. Twenty-five thousand catalogs listing most of this incredible inventory are mailed each year.

With all this, there is still room for a surprise discovery. I was in the shop not too long ago when a customer came in and spoke to John Bailey. Bailey nodded and went in back under the arch upon which hangs the largest trout ever taken from the Yellowstone on a fly, an unbelievable fourteen-pound four-ounce brown. As I watched, he opened a small refrigerator and matter-of-factly removed a covered cardboard container. It might have held cole slaw, but it didn't. I was speechless with the enormity of this revelation. Dan Bailey's Fly Shop also sells night crawlers!

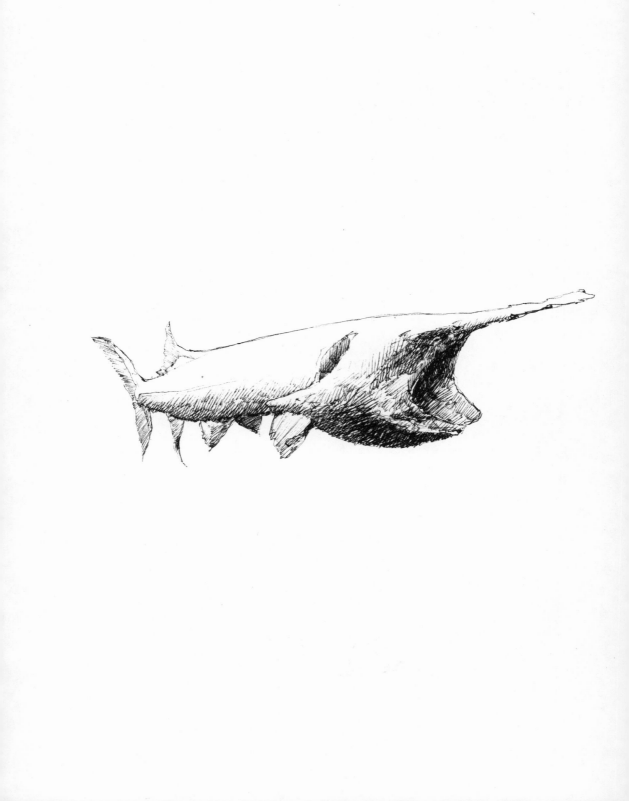

THE CREATURE FROM THE
LOWER YELLOWSTONE

A favorite theme of the Japanese rubber–monster school of cinema is the creature from the prehistoric past, some giant lizard returned out of the sea to lay waste to Tokyo. Reality is more prosaic. Next to the Loch Ness monster, the Earth's most prominent throwbacks are a number of innocuous, if intriguing, fish. The coelacanth comes first to mind, a living fossil raised accidentally from the depths in a trawler's net, but there are others as well: primitive sharks, sturgeon, alligator gar and the unlikely paddlefish.

The paddlefish is found in only two places on Earth, the Mississippi River and its tributaries, and the Yangtze drainage in China. The American version is somewhat smaller than the twenty-foot Chinese oddity, but at 100 pounds or better it is definitely not a creek fish. Pesticides, dams and industrial waste have limited the once–numerous paddlefish in more settled areas, but in the Missouri and Yellowstone rivers in eastern Montana the creature still thrives.

Intake, Montana, was the site of last year's paddlefish derby. Sponsored by the Glendive Chamber of Commerce, it ran for six weekends from late May to early July; grand prize: $150. Intake, located sixteen miles north of Glendive, Montana, is the site of an old diversion dam on the Yellowstone River; on the weekends, dozens of fishermen gather along the banks to try their luck on the giant paddlefish. A member of the Glendive Chamber of Commerce wearing a hot dog salesman's change apron wanders up and down the shoreline hawking $1 tickets to the local derby.

The fishermen stand nearby shoulder to shoulder, crowding the shoreline like a vision of opening day in a Malthusian nightmare. Several boatloads of anglers, outboards straining, buck the boiling current below the diversion dam. So many lines are in the water at once that tangled foul-ups are inevitable. "I've got one on! I've got one on!" shouts the burly fellow in the blue bowling shirt, only to reel in and find his line snarled around that of the guy four slots down, who wears garage mechanic's coveralls and a red nylon cap emblazoned with the logo KING ROPES: SHERIDAN, WYOMING. This sort of thing happens too frequently for fisticuffs or even anger and the two men reel amicably together, referring only to the Gordian knot joining them as "a sonofabitch," while their wives, sipping beer and crowned with pink plastic curlers, look on from the bank above.

The paddlefish is a primitive animal with a cartilaginous skeleton and a notochord in place of a spinal column. Its two-foot-long spatulate bill and toothless mouth give it the absurd appearance of Daffy Duck. This oblong snout is a handy tool, since the paddlefish is a vegetarian, filtering microscopic plankton from the water; it uses the enlarged sense organ to locate food. Because there are no fishing lures that imitate plankton, the only way paddlefish can be caught is by snagging.

Large treble hooks are used, often in pairs, along with fifty- to eighty-pound test line and weighty sinkers. One-inch pipe sleeves and discarded spark plugs are favored sinker substitutes at Intake. Anything that will bring the line down deep in the fast-moving current is acceptable. The technique is simple: a fisherman casts far out into the stream and drags the bottom, retrieving his line with a series of emphatic jerks, a method that incorporates all the finesse of dredging for drowned corpses with grappling irons.

Anglers accustomed to thinking of the Yellowstone as a trout stream will be disappointed with the water at Intake; it is broad and, in the spring, the color of chocolate pudding. Much too warm a river for trout here; the paddlefish's neighbors are the sauger, the burbot, the sturgeon and the channel catfish.

Still, it's a nice spot for an outing. The Fish and Game Department has provided a fishing access, complete with boat ramp and picnic tables. There are cottonwood trees for shade and the springtime hills are faintly green. It's a good place to bring a washtub full of ice and six-packs along with a portable radio and a couple of folding lawn chairs for relaxation in between snagging lunkers. This is down-home angling at its very best.

Although the paddlefish has been a Montana resident for over sixty million years, it was added to the state's list of game fish only in 1965. In spite of its unforgettable appearance, the paddlefish has been largely ignored (except for occasional mention in official records and a spate of commercial fishing around the turn of the century) from the time Hernando de Soto reported seeing the first one until 1962, when a Glendive angler snagged something weird at Intake. Within a week, sixty more were caught and word of the "mystery fish" began to spread.

Americans love the mysterious. Hundreds of Mystery Spots, Mystery Houses and Mystery Caves crowd the highways along with rock shops and reptile gardens. Ph.D. candidates track "Big Foot" and/or Sasquatch through the high Sierras. P. T. Barnum once bamboozled the nation with a crude mermaid manufactured from monkey parts and a fish tail. So the popularity of the prehistoric paddlefish should come as no surprise.

The Glendive Chamber of Commerce literature likes to compare the action at Intake with the excitement of ocean fishing (a pamphlet put out by the Beer Jug tavern says, "It fights savagely. . .exploding into the air and dancing on its tail"), but the truth is that landing a paddlefish is roughly equivalent to pulling any large weight off the bottom. A four-ply steel-belted radial might be hard to reel in, but it would not be described as a tackle-buster.

The big attraction of paddlefish, aside from the novelty, is the amount of meat you get to put in the freezer. Properly cleaned, twenty-five percent of the fish's total weight is edible, and with seventy-pounders being caught each week and a two-fish limit, one lucky day can take care of Friday nights for a year. Paddlefish have no true bones, so after the notochord and entrails have been removed along with the dark-reddish layer of flesh under the skin, it's time to reach for the tartar sauce. As with anything dubious, from skate wing to rattlesnake, paddlefish meat is said to taste like scallops.

Aside from a tide-pool encounter with a horseshoe crab (a remarkable 300-million-year-old cousin of the scorpion and not a crab at all), there are not that many opportunities to obtain a firsthand acquaintance with a living fossil. Since the first was netted in 1938, fewer than thirty coelacanths have been captured. Sturgeon are more numerous, but spreading caviar on toast is the closest most of us get to them. About the gar the less said the better; some shoot arrows at them, others prefer dynamite; no matter how they're cooked, they bear no resemblance to scallops. This leaves the curious paddlefish, the nearest thing to a trophy dinosaur a fisherman is ever likely to bring home and lay out on the drainboard: a Japanese horror movie in his very own kitchen.

99 AND 44/100THS
PERCENT PURE

In certain fishing circles, the very word "purist" is anathema. "What're you, some kind of purist?" an angler might inquire of a friend spin casting a red-and-white Daredevil spoon from the stern while he sets aside a can of lukewarm Bud and lobs a skewered shiner, still quivering from the baitwell, into a school of hungry bonita churning the oily, undulant circle of chum around the boat. Or, standing elbow-to-elbow in the rain on the banks of the Eel River during the March steelhead run, a fisherman will sum up a companion's refusal of his offered jar of neon-orange-dyed salmon eggs in favor of a homemade concoction consisting of beef suet and lemon peel soaked in sardine oil: "Never mind Charlie, he's a *purist.*" A purist is the "effete snob" of the fishing fraternity, the term having become as much of a catch-phrase as that other handy vilification, "special interest group."

Specifically, a fishing purist is an angler who prefers fly casting to any other form of the sport; it is a Mandarin choice, a matter of style. Chess and checkers may be played on the same board, with kings the object in both; but no one would argue that they were the same game. Further refinements abound; there are dry fly purists who look upon weighted nymphs and sinking lines with the same disapprobation with which they would regard a purse-seine, as well as flats fishermen who have never seen a trout stream and to whom hackles are merely what rise at the sight of incoming tarpon. A common tendency seems to be a willingness to release the catch, the philosophy of limiting the kill. This isn't to say that there aren't fly fishermen who stack trout in the deep freeze like cordwood with the aplomb of a wily worm-merchant, but, on the whole, purity means an empty creel and a continuing post-graduate course on artificials for frequently-hooked fish.

Significantly, more and more public water is being restricted to fly fishing; in many areas, the fish population, even aided by expensive stocking programs, is no longer equal to the pressure from ever-increasing legions of weekend anglers. Yellowstone Park, confronted for years every summer by thousands upon thousands of trout rotting in campsite garbage pails, has outlawed bait fishing, and many of the finer rivers (the Madison, the Firehole, stretches of the upper Yellowstone) are posted: FLY FISHING ONLY. The predictable hue and cry of outraged sculpin devotees has not yet subsided.

Still, the Park regulations permit the use of spinning tackle with a plastic casting bubble on the restricted water, as long as the lure is an artificial fly; hardly a concession to the purist ethic. There is, however, in the Deschutes National Forest of eastern Oregon, a fishing spot reserved for the purest of the pure, a lake where the limit is zero. Not only is fly casting the only fishing technique permitted, but the flies must have barbless hooks. To a purist, Hosmer Lake, with the volcanic cone of Bachelor Butte mirrored on its still surface like a Hokusai view of Fuji, is the Zen center of the art of angling.

Twenty years ago, it was known as Mud Lake. Shallow, and dense with carp, the silty bottom was continually roiled by the vacuum-cleaner feeding habits of this whiskered, thick-lipped fish. A carp may be a fine addition to a rice paddy, but it is hardly a species dear to the hearts of many anglers, so Mud Lake was selected by the Oregon Game Commission as part of an experiment in introducing Atlantic salmon to Western water.

Starting in 1951 with salmon eggs from Quebec, a state hatchery succeeded by 1959 in breeding a second generation of disease-resistant salmon. Mud Lake was treated with rotenone and tons of poisoned carp were removed. By the time the first Atlantic salmon were planted, the silt had settled and the coffee-colored lake was moonshine pure.

The first season at Hosmer Lake was 1961. A creel limit of one fish per person was permitted, but even this proved too heavy a toll, and by the second season the regulations stated that "all fish must be removed from the hook and released in the water unharmed." Over the years, the restrictions narrowed to exclude spinning reels, monofilament line (except as backing) and the commonplace barbed hook. Hosmer Lake became a purist's Mecca.

To get there, you drive thirty-five miles west of Bend, Oregon, on the

Century Drive. The snow-covered Three Sisters mountains rise out of the north and to the east stands the tapering tower of Bachelor Butte. Solid curtains of pine surround the lake, a certain finalist in any Miss American Pageant of fishing spots. But it is not the spectacular scenery which is the main attraction here; the headliner at Hosmer Lake is the aristocrat of freshwater gamefish, the Atlantic salmon.

On a day with no wind when the surface of the shallow lake is still, a fisherman can see for considerable distance through the clear water. The nearly white bottom is everywhere scribed with the vermiculations of caddis larvae, dragging their handmade, pebble-and-twig armor through the silt. Long, unwavering belly tracks of feeding fish bisect the scrimshaw. Standing in a small boat, an angler can spot cruising salmon, singles and groups, and make his cast to a particular fish.

Hosmer Lake is best described as two separate bodies of water; the upper end, serviced by the boat ramp and campsites, is deeper and appears to contain fewer fish. Although motors up to 10 hp are permitted (except when fishing), the noise of an outboard is an unwanted intrusion and the lake is really small enough to make rowing seem a pleasure. Between the upper and lower ends, where a waterway winds through tall stands of reeds, billowing clouds of green algae pass beneath the gliding boat. Occasionally, large brook trout are seen here among the reeds, the white edges of their wavering ventral fins distinct against the shadows. These trout are survivors from the days of the carp, somehow unaffected by the poison. They may be kept if caught, but are extremely wary and make for the reeds at the slightest disturbance.

The lower end of the lake is shallow and has better fishing. Small grassy islands make it possible to fish from shore out in the middle of the water, but a boat is more convenient, as the salmon, having all been caught and released so many times, are quite wary and require a bit of finding. Although there are hatches at certain times of the year when salmon can be taken on dry flies, a well-presented caddis nymph is almost always effective.

The fishing in many ways resembles the silent-stalk techniques perfected on the saltwater flats. The salmon in Hosmer Lake, like bonefish on the flats, can be seen at a distance, feeding along the bottom, and the adrenalin boost is much the same for the overanxious angler as he fumbles with his tackle, trying not to step on the fly line coiled about his feet while making the cast. Accuracy and timing are important here too, for the salmon, like his ghostly saltwater cousin, will spook immediately at any noise from the boat, and the splash of sloppy casting drives the fish away as effectively as the passing shadow of an osprey.

But when everything goes right and the cast straightens and silently intersects his probable path in time for the weighted nymph to sink to the bottom where the naturals are, then, on the retrieve, the salmon may turn, follow and take. The acrobatics of the ensuing struggle have inspired a thousand glossy sporting magazine cover paintings.

After Labor Day, Hosmer Lake is pure even of other purists; it is not uncommon to be the only boat on the water. The silence and a sense of wonder conspire to make this business of delicate, tapered rods and imitation insects seem almost mystical. This mood is further enhanced by the very special pleasure it gives an angler to release his catch.

Now that the secret of where the Atlantic salmon go when they return to the ocean has been discovered and the Danish fishing fleet seems determined to turn them all into canapés, their days as a migratory, anadromous fish may be numbered and their future existence limited to such man-made conditions as Hosmer Lake, where the landlocked salmon do not spawn but must be hatchery raised and released when mature. Unless there's more to fishing than the fillet, the future of the sport remains precarious. It doesn't take much of a purist to see that.

JACK CURTIS

Sport fishing was unknown in western Kansas before the migration from the Great Dustbowl, but when my grandfather and Uncle Bud took this child out to the Saline River to bobber catfish, I thrilled with the magic river ever so much more than with the drill of Miss Snaps, my third-grade teacher.

And lucking out from fruit picking in the San Joaquin Valley, I helped a crusty rebel run a boat dock on Shaver Lake, where there were a few bass and trout for a multitude of anxious tourists.

In the South Pacific between landings, we fished off the stern with chain and rotten meat on an iron hook for lazy tiger sharks.

After fighting a forest fire, six of us were stranded on a pristine lake in southeast Alaska. I unraveled my sweater and sacrificed my bootlaces trying to catch grayling. Except for rose hips and lilypad bulbs, we went hungry.

Then, settling down to family life, I took up suntan angling off the rocks of the Sur coast. That kind of easy fishing becomes half bird-watching. Pleasant enough.

How then do I have the *chutzpah* to write fishing stories? As most philosophical fisherfolk know, we cannot sanely escape, not yet, from our ancestral water, and our mythology agrees with our physiology. Noah sails us out of the Flood; our urine is the same chemistry as brine.

The act of fishing can be the act of catching an idea with all the energy and sophistication we can cast into the deepest mind pool. To catch the fish is to catch the insight, whether fry or whale, an epiphany as Joyce applied it to literature. The fish is a bright thought, an illumination, brought from the depths after a ritualistic preparation within nature. The fish is a flash of beauty and action enticed from an unfathomable element.

And the action is human. We are challenged by the unknown watery history behind us, and we use the sparkles of light from the darkness to keep us steady, and ready us for the unknown miracle ahead.

Thus to the writer, fishing and imagination become kin, if not identical twins, and like Moby Dick in the mind of Captain Ahab, the challenge need be honored to bring out the dimensions of men.

WALTZING ANDY

Blue as a jaybird, Shaver Lake fits into the Sierras like a breathtaking magic crystal, its miles and miles of shoreline rimmed with virgin pine forest, its air clean and sharp, its water cold enough to tuck up your Goodtime.

Where else could a man named Hex and a bass named Andy waltz furiously every spring and fall for a boy?

When you're twelve, problems come over the horizon like bulging black clouds: you're wondering if your mother really cares, if your father is someone else, if your career is a winner, if friends remember you, if Connie, the redheaded robust waitress, would laugh if you hugged and kissed her.

Hex always watched her as if she were a triple-barbed hook fringed with red feathers, and when I asked him why, he snorted and fumed until he decided I wasn't being nosy, I just needed information.

"I bit on bait like that once. Had me hooked so hard, I had to swallow the plug. A man ought to learn."

"But I saw her coming out of your cabin . . ."

His rocky jaw flinched, his blue eyes steadied on mine. "If she comes to your cabin and leaves, a man don't have to take the hook."

My father owned the boat dock, restaurant, cabins and campground on McKenzie Point, a pretty piece of landscape jutting into the lake. Wintertime, the lake froze, and there was plenty of snow for skiing.

Father and mother gambled on snow. Big Money was in winter sports. I still wonder why they worried so much about the Big Money and worried so little about their only heir, skinny, pimply and nutty with questions.

Even in that Sierra pine tree country, father wore a business suit and mother sat most of the time behind a calculator, handling the bookwork.

Hex had a pale blue anchor on his left forearm. His arm was tanned dark brown, the fine hair bleached almost white. He was not so heavy as my father, but he walked straight and matched my image of a Kentucky woodsman.

My father and Hex had served together on a destroyer a long time ago. They had been hit by a kamikaze suicide plane.

Once in a while they would drink and talk, father laughing a lot and Hex sort of nursing along the yarns, his face red as strawberries, and mother left them alone.

Before mother and father thought of Big Money, we would come up from the valley in May, unpack and set up the place for the summer season. Hex always turned up about then to take over the boat dock.

He'd paint the flat hulls green, tune up the Evinrudes and replace worn manila lines. He'd repaint the shack where we kept the rental tackle, and restock beer and candy bars, making the whole place shipshape and operational.

Sometimes in the spring, he wouldn't look so healthy, but he rarely explained and he never let it show in the steady way he worked.

"What'd you do all winter, Hex?"

"Hunted carvings."

"Where did you hunt?"

"Yucatan mostly."

"Find any?"

"No."

Once the boats were in the water and everything ready for the tourist run, we'd sit and watch the pines and the lake, hawks and sun passing over, until he'd feel the time was just right. Then he'd say, "Let's see how Andy did last winter."

The first time, of course, I didn't even know that Hex had a special bass named Andy, but when he took the barbless, single-hook spoon and cast it by the log behind the boats where no one ever fished, I was introduced.

"Named him Andy because he's an ornery fighting sonofabitch, like Andy Jackson."

Andy hit the spoon like a tiger smacking a lamb. Hex smiled as he hit back and the fish tugged and ran and tried to throw the hook. "He's alive and well, but he ain't any smarter."

Hex waltzed with him until he was played out, and Andy came in on his side, eyes bugged out, his big mouth woebegone with the spoon drooping from his bony lip.

"How'd you know it's Andy?" I was astounded that such a quiet steady man would make a friend of a fish.

He pointed at a gap in the dorsal fin, "I cut out a spine last year."

"Did it hurt him?"

"Some."

Next evening I could hardly wait. "Let's catch Andy!"

"Best not burn him out." Hex kindly and wisely included me in the picture. "He's our buddy. Being fooled and caught is a hard go."

Yes, I could understand that.

All summer Andy just lay behind the boats next to the log where nobody in his right mind would think a bass had staked out his territory. Hundreds of fishermen walked out on the ramp, rented gear and boats and went across the lake to fish, while Andy just waited there, building his strength, waiting to waltz with us.

After the tourists were gone and we'd hauled out the boats, my mother tattooing the calculator and father driving down to Fresno every morning to talk about credit lines, Hex and I sat on the dock watching the pines' rippling reflection in the lake and the sun starting to set, and then Hex said, "Let's take Andy for a run."

I fetched the barbless spoon, and Hex cast it behind the log, started retrieving, and boom! Andy hit it and went for his waltz. He seemed to be picking up new steps, because for a couple of seconds he was up and tail-slapping the water. Bulge-eyed and sore-mouthed, he came to Hex's wet hands and was released for the winter.

"Looks like he's putting on some weight," Hex said. "He oughta go three pounds."

"What're you doing this winter?"

"Australia. I always wanted a seabag full of blue and red opals."

"Make a fortune?"

"Not me, I'd just stir them up once in a while and watch them shine."

Connie the redheaded waitress started acting like a bird with a lame wing, but Hex just wouldn't follow along. He had that steady, somber look on his weathered face that he had when he released Andy.

Father worked nights now with plans and blueprints. He'd leased a mountain, and he wanted Hex to stay on and help set up the ski lifts or handle equipment rentals, but Hex countered, "You'd do better helpin' me fill up my seabag with opals."

My father stared at him with his mouth open, closed his mouth, shut his eyes and shook his head.

And then Hex was gone while I went to school in the valley. He never sent a postcard.

Next spring when he returned, he was brown and healthy, but I noticed a fresh scar in his eyebrow. I tried to show how mature I was by not asking about it. I don't think he noticed; he just said "Howdy, Jay," and started unstacking boats and mixing green paint.

"Seabag full of opals?"

"Plane stopped in Fiji." His eyes shone remotely with the bank of exotic experiences he'd been through and wouldn't ever let out. "Y'know they had ships over that way a long time. There's treasures buried in those islands by Malay pirates, never been found."

"Did you find anything?"

He handed over a hatband of seashells woven together.

"What is it for?"

"You put it around your Goodtime so the girls know you're much man."

I laughed myself silly, and Hex grinned openly, and fetching down the pole with the barbless spoon, he said, "Let's waltz old Andy."

And after the long, hard-fought contest, when Andy floated spent in his hands, Hex said, "Andy, I want you to put on a little weight by September."

Summer passed in a daze of suns and moons, renting the same tackle to the same sunburned tourists and answering the same questions. Then, in September, how fine it was to sit on the empty dock with Hex and listen to ripples slowly slapping against the boats, and the breeze humming through the pines.

"Guess it's time we ask old Andy to dance," Hex decided, and sure enough, Andy was still in his unlikely spot and aggressive as ever.

When it was over, Hex sort of patted him on his big head and said, "You just don't ever learn, do you, boy?"

Father and mother spent the winter on the run, building up the ski lodge, going for the Big Money, and I did my time in Roosevelt High School.

Hex came back in the spring looking like a dead oak. He'd lost about fifty pounds, and his pale hands trembled.

Connie fussed over him and tried stuffing him with chicken soup, keeping after him so hard he'd go out on the lake just to be alone. One day he looked at me as if he had something to say. "Boy, they gave me a hard run this time."

"Where?"

"Where there's a riverbed full of diamonds. Just help yourself."

"Did you?"

"Sure. Had a poke sack full, but comin' downriver an itty-bitty mosquito bit me. Break-bone fever."

"Where's the pole sack?"

"I passed out in the canoe, woke up in L.A. General Hospital. Nothin' left except my passport and my good looks."

"You should have stayed with us."

He laid a look on me of total disgust, as if I'd failed the simplest test, and might be irremediably stupid. "Jay, if you don't live, you're dead."

We danced old Andy again when Hex had his strength and spirit together, and as he released the pop-eyed fish, he smiled. "Look at him, he's growing. And every time he hits that lure, he's shooting the moon. I bet when he hits the air, it's heaven or hell for him."

And again, when the geese were flying and father was running down to the valley to pump up the credit, mother clicking away behind the office machines, Connie started looking sad and Hex started staring at some faraway place. I knew he'd soon be gone.

Connie changed her style. She did her long red hair up in a tight bun, and came striding around the boat shack, her fists dug in her hips and her mouth locked tight as a motor that's run out of oil, but Hex stayed out of her way, and after we'd given old Andy his September fight, we hauled out the boats and Hex left again.

I could hear the folks making remarks. Maybe they'd always made them, but I'd never listened. . . .

"He'll drag in here next spring like a bum . . . wastin' his life away . . . poor as a penny. . . ."

"Why won't he pay attention?" Connie asked no one in particular.

Snow fell early and the pack lasted late so that my father was busier than ever all winter, mother backing him up with the paperwork. They looked happy and almost prosperous that spring. Even Hex mentioned it when he came back, burned brown as teak. "Looks like they made some Big Money."

He was a little crusty at first, aggravated, and had less than usual to say, but after a couple weeks of the high country, he eased up some.

"Did you get to Costa Rica?"

"Hmmm," he sighed, deciding to get it over with, "not quite. Signed on a salvage ship instead, ended up in a calaboose in Nicaragua. Skipper sold us. They let the whores in on Friday night, but if you're broke they just laugh, and they ain't nothin' worse'n a 180-pound naked Indian female that looks like she's been pounded down to three feet tall by a piledriver, laughing at you in a hogpen you been locked in for three months."

After that long speech, he gave me a gold ring with a red stone.

"Spanish," he closed the subject. "I mean it might have belonged to Christopher Columbus.

After a few days of repairing the dock and tuning up the Evinrudes, he felt ready to take old Andy again. Same spoon and barbless hook. Same everything except we were passing another year.

Andy gave him a heavyweight fight, stronger than ever because he was bigger and angrier. And the battle was all the more exciting because Hex cared too much for the fish to ever chance his breaking the line.

He let me unhook him. "Maybe in the fall, you can give him a run." I suddenly felt as if I'd had a birthday.

The lake stayed full all summer because of the extra snow melting. Tourists crowded each other in the campgrounds, creating a slum, and Hex was quiet all through those months. I was trying to be caught by all or any of the girls flashing by, but they saw me as small fry.

The Fourth of July, a speedboat lost its driver and came zooming out of control into the swimming area. I was stunned by the noise of the driverless boat and the kids in the water screaming, but Hex was instantly a driving giant.

In one second he had the whole design in his head, dove full-clothed into the lake and did seventy yards in a crawl that made the water boil. He grabbed a bleeding, screaming girl gently as a cub, and sidestroked back to the pier, at the same time yelling at me to call the volunteer ambulance and fetch the first-aid pack. Soaking wet and lungs whistling, he bound the dangling foot and leg together with gauze, tied a tourniquet around the knee, and shot half a tube of morphine in her before anyone else really grasped the situation.

He'd always looked so slow and careful, dour and parched; then he was lightning flashing when it counted, and the girl's life was not only saved, so was her foot and leg. Next day he was settled down, carefully cleaning spark plugs.

And then they were all gone back to the tracts, back to the farms, wherever they'd traveled out of for a shot of mountain air, and I was as big as Hex by then.

"Maybe you ought to give old Andy his run," Hex said one quiet evening as Andy splashed for a minnow behind the dock.

"Me?"

"You can."

Andy hit the spoon like a streaking left hook, and announced he could outfight anyone on earth. He was a champion, taking me on. Hex had to remind me, "Easy now, remember, he's just folks." And I played him out, making him do his very best. Hex released him for me. The missing spine was growing back, but it was Andy all right.

"See you next spring, Andy." Hex pulled his hands out of the water while Andy popped his eyes and sucked in water.

"Whereaway this time?" Connie asked him.

"I'm thinking of going to the moon."

Connie rolled her fists on her hips, "You been in orbit all your life, goofy."

"Hex, we could sure use some help this winter, going to be plenty Big Money." My father tried to hold him.

"All that Big Money, and we haven't even hoisted a horn together this summer," Hex said.

Mother had new machines now, clickety-click, pastel and full of buttons.

So much Big Money, I was to be sent to a prep school.

But there was no snow that winter, the sun shone high and low every day. Father had a Going-Out-of-Business sale. All the stocks of skis and down jackets and Santa Claus caps had to be sold to people who couldn't use them. The bank transferred our mountain with its lodge and lifts and snowmobiles to someone else. Just one dry winter and we were back into the summer tourist trade, and I was back at Roosevelt High.

My father changed to gray and fat like wax, mother reduced to a sheath of nerves and heavy-rimmed glasses.

I couldn't say: change this, and it'll be fixed. Batman and Robin were not coming to help. I couldn't help father, couldn't make it snow. All I could do was unstack the old boats and hope Hex would hurry back.

He'd lost three fingers on his left hand; otherwise he was in good shape.

"How'd it happen?"

"Rotten doctor."

"Was it a shark, or a lion, or frozen in the arctic?"

"Smart ass, listen to me, just stay away from doctors."

He asked me to cast the spoon for Andy, but I had an image of Hex and Andy waltzing and shoved the pole in his hands just before Andy hit the lure. You could see the boil, the contact, and the extended moment when you know he's red-eyed enraged enough to eat the mothering spoon, and then he slowly peters out. I cupped him under water and took the hook out of his big mouth.

"He'll go four pounds now. He's grown up." Hex sounded like a parent at graduation.

All summer Connie hung around, trying to help him as if his missing fingers were a heavy handicap, and the more she mothered him the madder he got.

Finally, one morning, he said to her, "You get off."

"Why, Hex, I'm trying to help. . . ."

"Get off my dock."

She never came back to the dock, but she still dropped by his cabin at night.

I felt close enough to her and, in all my adolescent arrogance, wise enough to try to explain Hex to her. "Hex is a loner, he's like a bass. . . ."

She looked at me solemnly, a big sister, her red hair loose and draped like a falling fire to her waist. Then she smiled. She laughed. She shut her eyes and howled, she rolled on the floor and stuck her fingers in her ears.

"What the heck?"

"A bass, my ass! A cod, by God!"

That was enough to break her out of her sentimental mood for the rest of the summer.

We were winding up the season. Labor Day. All the boats were rented, all the potato chips sold, the beer box low.

Hex was towing in a disabled boat when I rented a pole to a man wearing a blue knit tee shirt that fit every fold of his belly, and white walking shorts that showed every crease in his fat knees, and climbing boots suitable for stomping.

"All the boats are out," I said.

"I just want to show my daughter how it works." The fat man smiled timidly, as if he didn't know how it worked either. The little girl was wearing a useless bikini and dripping chocolate ice cream on her bony chest.

I went down to the end of the dock to give Hex a hand in mooring.

"See honey," the fat man explained, "this is a fishing pole."

And with that he tossed the plug back of the log. He was clearing his snarled reel when Andy hit. In terror, he ran off the dock to the beach, dragging the fish as he ran, dragging him right up on the sand. When the bass commenced flopping he ran back and stomped him.

Hex turned pale, spit in the water, turned red and clenched his fists. I guess I was going through the same motions and changes. "Wait," he touched my arm, "if we tromp him, he'll sue your dad."

"But that's Andy!"

"Andy's dead and gone."

And then I realized that death was like the ruinous winter. I couldn't make it snow any more than I could put Andy back to waltzing in the water.

By then, a lady in cotton shorts and blouse was snapping Instamatics of her little girl and Andy oozing on poppa's big fat finger.

"Figure he lived more'n most," Hex said.

I wanted to cry. I wanted to roar. I wanted to blow up the road. I wanted to give Andy a decent funeral.

The knuckles on Hex's maimed hand looked like chunks of ice.

Then geese gabbled south in the darkness, nights turned shivering, and one afternoon maples flamed a finality across the vacant blue water.

Toward the end of the day of leaving, in slack twilight on the dock, a bat twists loose like ash from fire, an old owl floats across to his stand and waits. Ravens go black in green shadows. Evening star comes pale to flank half a moon closing on the setting sun. White moths waver off shoreline reeds like airborne colum-

bines, and a dusky breeze carries the gut-pumping drum of the bullfrog and the raw pitch of coyotes. There is nectar in this magic cleave of time, the same as Stone Agers smelled. When the crepuscular moment poises between day and night, the sky to the west glistens like blood, luminous as Connie's fire-falling hair. Close by the chunking of clustered boats, the lake as polished as a ballroom floor, orchestra in the forest, water and air—foxes, frogs, crickets, geese, owls— all tuning up, and then the select stillness, the Hush: night-blue tuxedos, polished piscine shapes, frosted shirtfronts. Maestro looks left, right, center, and waters reflect glittering couples waiting to dance. Smoke from a pine-knot campfire drifts over the crystal lighted chandeliers overhead, fish and moth are still, silver buckets icing champagne, a ripple under the dock, the conductor holds cosmos, balances time on his baton, ready to begin the waltz.

"Jay," Hex said, "try a cast back there with the spoon."

Without much hope, I cast back into that spot where no one in his right mind would waste a cast, and reeled in.

"Try again, wake him up."

Thinking Hex was growing feebleminded, I sailed it out again into the still water behind the log and brought it back. And he hit!

Hex almost had a visible smile on his face as I brought the small exhausted bass in. "He's more of a jitterbugger, ain't he. Looks like he'll go a pound, pound and a half."

I held him while Hex clipped off a middle spine from the dorsal fin, and let him loose.

"Andy Junior."

Hex nodded. "May take a while, but we'll teach him to waltz."

Next day he was studying an article about lost ivory in Nepal. "Man with some nerve and luck could have a time there."

"Take me along, Hex."

"Not yet, Jay."

Connie was coming by just then. She glared at him. She rolled her fists into her hips as if she were ready to paw dirt and fight. "Damn it, Hex," she demanded, "are you ever going to grow up and settle down?"

He stood lanky tall, ready to wing off for another eight months, and answered carefully, "Yes and no."

GRANDFATHER

The summer of 1929, my father grew rich selling Fords, trading oil leases, speculating in stocks, and farming marginal land. Mother had a gas stove, a fur coat, her own car, went to the beauty parlor once a week and played bridge.

In a small town in central Kansas, my father was a very big frog, and that summer when I was eight, I assumed he was so successful because he was so smart.

And because I had failed to pass the third grade, there was never any end to hearing how capable my father was compared to his lazy, stupid, stubborn son.

Why couldn't I do arithmetic? Why couldn't I read and write? Why did my classmates bedevil me?

In those days, none of the geniuses in psychology or Ph.D.s in education had discovered dyslexia; nothing is known about it now except that as many as twenty percent of children have some degree of it. Its symptoms are mirror writing, reversing numbers, awkwardness and an inability to understand the usual codes of communication. The only cure is to circumvent it with special close training.

But in the summer of 1929, it was called mental retardation or brain damage and those unlucky enough to have it were soon taken out of school and put in the back room for the rest of their lives. The educator's solution to it progressed from contempt to thrashing and, finally, banishment.

By then I was so miserable I couldn't even explain it. I had reached the point of not speaking, retreating step by step back into an impenetrable cave deep in myself, not in hate or rage, but in a stunned numbness of incomprehension.

My heart is sick when I think of the thousands of kids who were shunted off to the attic or locked in institutions as hopeless idiots when they could have led full and productive lives if anyone anywhere had understood the problem.

That summer everyone called me dummy. I stayed in the basement workshop and made little wooden boxes until my father took a look at the mess and called me all the usual names and strapped me with his belt.

Then I ran away.

I thought about hanging myself.

I didn't run very far, only to my grandfather's little house on the other side of town.

Long past tears or self-pity, I brought some clothes, a can of pork and beans and a sense of lostness and desperation.

My grandfather, a big, taciturn man, smoked a pipe and smelled of illicit whiskey, and there were many stories related in undertones about him. His reputation was so unsavory my father wouldn't let him in our house.

But I was eight and deeply troubled. I knew those glowing, secretive eyes that had seen so much must have seen something like me too, and that small, steady pussycat smile seemed to be able to encompass all the problems of mankind without turning to a frown of anger or rejection.

Whether he drank or gambled or whored around had no meaning, no significance. His economy of speech, his reserve, a dignity so full no one in town called him by his first name, was all to the good.

He carried either a short shotgun or a pistol in his back pocket wherever he went.

The town marshal understood the pecking order well enough to stay several blocks away from my grandfather, not an easy thing to do in a town of ten square blocks.

But I went to him mainly because, despite the awesomeness of his posture, I sensed he had lived through so many dimensions that he would take in a dummy.

He wore short boots, blue jeans, chambray shirts and in winter a sheepskin coat. His hair was gray and his walrus mustache grizzled, his face so corroded by many weathers that it resembled maple bark. His eyes were a deep smoky color, alight like star sapphires.

When I knocked on his door, he looked at my bag of clothes and at me carefully and said not a word.

We sat in easy silence on the screen porch. The *National Geographic* he had been reading was dog-eared and put away. He filled his pipe from a can of Prince Albert and smoked.

The sun went down, and the twilight of the long prairie slowly turned from yellow to purple.

When it was completely dark, he lighted a kerosene lamp and placed it on the oilcloth-covered kitchen table.

"Play draw poker?" he asked.

I shook my head.

He tossed a new deck of blue bicycles to me. "Check the seal and break them out."

He taught me the basics of poker that first night and we played every night after that. Our chips were kitchen matches, and we played strictly by Hoyle for blood.

After he set up a cot for me on the screenporch, he told me to go to bed. "I've business," he said, putting the pistol in his back pocket and leaving me alone.

It must have been a fine scene, him walking across town to my parents' big house blazing with light and noisy with frantic calls for a lost child. I'm sure he didn't go inside; he stood on the porch and said, "He'll stay with me for the summer."

My father must have raged because it was his nature, and my mother must have wept because that was hers, and my grandfather was firm because that was his.

And really they all knew it was the perfect solution to an embarrassing problem.

My grandfather had a way of walking that seemed discordant with his person, as if it were an adaptation, a skill recently learned. He'd spent most of his life on horseback, and only when he settled into his little house did he turn to walking as a way of moving about. He enjoyed walking, but it was never a familiar way of going, and he never bothered to learn to drive a car.

In the morning he showed me how to make up my bed, and after we had ham and eggs for breakfast, and he'd poured a slug of clear alcohol into his coffee from a gallon can and smoked a pipe of P.A., he asked, "Want to go fishing?"

I nodded, still unable to get a word out.

He looked me in the eye and nodded back.

I loved that old man at that moment more than anything in life.

He found an extra cane pole, line, bobber, hook, and he let me carry the poles and the dip net while he carried the shotgun.

His house was on the edge of town closest to the Saline River, but it was still a good mile hike along the back roads to reach his fishing spot.

He liked to stop once in a while and take in a deep breath of the grassy-smelling air. He would stand up high sometimes on tiptoe, like a man in stirrups surveying the buffalo grass and bluebonnet prairie when it was open free.

Both sides of the road were fenced with barbed wire tied to quarried limestone fence posts, which would never rot and are probably still there.

He never worried, though, about the changes of life, modernization, progress. And he never wore the air of obsolescence.

We first went to a little creek and he showed me how to use the dip net to fill a minny pail full of minnows, and we walked on slow and easy to a certain spot on the river he had selected long before. I still remember a great cottonwood log jammed into the bank where you could sit in comfort.

It was cool in the shade of the cottonwoods and black walnut trees, and a wonderful silence held over that river bend in early summer, as if nature were surfeit with sun and rain, every bird had a nest of eggs, every squirrel was happy, every muskrat fat and all the jack rabbits and cottontails madly in love.

He showed me how to bait the hook, the way to thread on sinker and bobber, the knot to tie on the end of the cane pole, and in a few minutes we were fishing, watching the bright bobbers riding the slow-moving muddy river. Nothing was said, and somehow the black massive cloud of bewilderment that had fogged over me was beginning to clear, the weight to lighten.

I've forgotten the thrill of seeing the bobber jerked underwater and my first spoken words between us, "Look, Gram!" but I remember we caught two bullheads and one big yellow catfish. We ate the bullheads for dinner, and grandfather took the catfish to the hotel and sold it.

In the afternoon we worked in his big vegetable garden. You don't really associate cowboys with gardening, but he was definitely a green-thumber, and loved to share out his bountiful produce with neighbors.

I suppose he was really bartering for the ham and eggs, because other than illegally selling catfish, he had no visible income.

In the evening after we came in from the twilight we would play poker or blackjack for an hour or so, and then he would slowly read the captions under the pictures in the *National Geographic* to me until I would nod and stagger off to my cot.

The days were so full, I felt like the satiated squirrels and birds and rabbits. My sleep was untroubled and dreamless.

Soon we were in a routine I knew and could anticipate. Waking, breakfast, cleaning, fishing, noontime dinner, gardening, supper, resting in the twilight, cards, pictures, bed. And I was trusting myself to talk again.

"What's the biggest fish in the river?"

"Channel cats. They go twenty pounds sometimes. Now, what's a jack and an ace?"

"Twenty-one, blackjack!"

Across the road from grandfather's house a great field of corn grew in long rows which the farmer tilled with a two-horse cultivator. My joy was to walk barefooted in the loose earth between the crackling growing plants, chattering to myself. It seemed then the whole field was my own universe, limitless in its growth and joy; this free and easy rambling through the avenues of corn released within me that great ecstasy of freedom experienced by artists.

Later I would try to pin down that surge of happiness in a poem:

Talking child in a Kansas tree, child
By the catfish river, leaning on grandfather's
Calcified cowpoke knees,
Where summer showers forked out the fish
And made the corn tassel and milk,
And the touch of water on good ground
Was the touch of this child
Testing the winding river bed of his sources
And his language . . .

The gray spongy doom that had been closing in on me retreated and patches of blue sky and sunshine shone through bit by bit. My strangling fear of failure visible to teachers, parents, and neighbor kids gradually fell before the faith that I could walk impressively and fearlessly any-where in town, or in the world of the *National Geographic*, where air-planes flew cross-country and over dark Africa and even over the Arctic ice.

Just when life seemed not only bearable but beautiful, I managed to find a snapping turtle in the ditch across the road. Of course I'd heard of snapping turtles and knew the smaller box turtles well enough, but I'd never been face to face with a snapper. Luckily I wasn't barefooted, because in my new-found courage I tried to nudge him with my foot, hoping he'd back up, but he hissed at me until, wholly exasperated with my bullying, he struck out with his horny beak and clamped his jaws on my shoe, just catching the tip of my big toe.

I kicked and yelled but he wouldn't let go. Finally, in total panic, I dragged him back across the road into grandfather's yard and up the steps to the door.

"I don't think cryin's goin' to wash him away," Grandfather said.

"He's got me!"

"Snappin' turtle never lets loose." He knew what he was going to have to do.

"He has to."

"Go over to the choppin' block."

He positioned my foot on the cottonwood stob, and without warning axed that prehistoric snout from its body. The snapper crawled away without its head.

"Tonight," grandfather said, easing off the shoe, "his head will fall off. Meanwhile you go barefoot."

"Are there lots of snappers around?" Fear was striking in my storming head as lightning crackles across the prairie.

"You can learn to live with them."

But I couldn't. My dreams were haunted with the mud-colored helmet-shaped turtles, their beady eyes, their spitting hiss, their savage bite.

The days were still a pleasure but the total freedom was gone. When we fished I could see multitudes of snappers in the river, their heads up, necks extended. And as the summer progressed and the river grew more shallow and sluggish, they collected in potholes and ox-bow sloughs.

But grandfather kept the routine, steady, easy, interesting and close to the earth.

"Where were you born?" I asked for no reason at all.

"Pittsburgh, Pennsylvania."

In time, he told me of how he'd gone to work in a steel mill when he was fourteen, but hated the inhuman grind so much he started walking west. By the time he'd reached New Mexico a year later, he had a horse, and hired out with ten young cowboys and the ramrod to drive cattle to Montana.

"They was just boys," he said. "Like me, they was tempered early and hard. We didn't know it, but they was fast changing times, and we were like wild horses."

"Did you ever meet Jesse James?"

"Jesse and Frank and me rode a ways together. That's enough."

I'd heard the whispered rumors of my grandfather's past and in my innocence took it for granted that anything my grandfather did would have been right and just. If he robbed the rich, he also shared with the poor.

We fished almost every morning in the same way and usually at the same spot, and in time I discovered that grandfather was pursuing a great channel cat that had broken his line months before. Familiar enough with the river and other fishermen, he was sure the big cat was still there. Without ever saying it, he was locked on the idea of landing the prize fish, not so much for glory, because he was already known as the best fisherman on the river, but because he had lost the monstrous-headed fish. He felt the eternal challenge, and he never refused a fight.

The river moved slowly as the summer so swiftly passed. Meandered potholes swarmed with snapping turtles and minnows. Crawdads constructed high towers of mud along the banks. Kingfishers flashed like blue fireballs into the potholes for minnows, and mosquitoes thrived.

We never missed a rainy morning. Grandfather felt the fish always bit better when a warm drizzle pelted the sluggish surface of the winding river.

"She flows on and meets the Arkansas, and they go together into the Missouri, now that's a fine river, and the Missouri rolls right on down to the Big Muddy, the Mississippi. How you spell it, M-i-*s-s*-i-*s-s*-i-*p*-*p*-i—and this here wheatland mud ends up in the Gulf of Mexico."

We caught fish almost every day, and each was different either in the fish or the day or the catching. And grandfather with his pistol in his back pocket would carry the gunnysack of fish uptown to the hotel and make a dollar or two, while George Veitengruber, the game warden, and Herb Wolford, the marshal, stayed up in the courthouse.

Playing blackjack one evening after he had a couple of drinks from the gallon can of white lightning, my cards were running well and my pile of matchsticks rising, and in the mellow lamplight, I dredged up a key question from the darkness of my memories.

"Did you shoot Wyatt Earp?"

"I wouldn't waste lead on such a railbird."

"Who did you shoot?"

I hit another blackjack and took his matches. He poured another jolt out of the can.

"Jack McCall was the last."

"Why were you mad at him?"

"He shot Wild Bill Hickok in the back."

"Wasn't he arrested?"

"They let him loose. Then over in Wyoming they arrested somebody they thought was Jack McCall and hung him; but it wasn't him. I tracked that sonofabitch for a year before I knew for sure."

His eyes were afire with a curious inside rage, and he spoke as if he were alone, growling to himself.

"But why was he so special to you?"

"Wild Bill was king of the gunfighters and he done me some favors. He was a good man to ride with. Too damned good for the likes of Jack McCall to shoot him in the back."

He turned his cards over and said directly to me, "This here is between you and me and nobody else."

"Yessir." I had no other answer. For sure he meant it.

"Jack McCall ran out of the Black Hills to Idaho, and I lost a lot of time finding out it wasn't him they hung, and I had a cold trail, but I hung onto him no matter all the false leads he set for me, and even had lawmen lookin' for me, but I tagged him till I caught him in a eensy-bitty town called Flagler, Colorado. He was in the saloon and wore out, and I was some weary myself, but I called him out into the street and when he went for his piece, I went for mine, and after I shot him down, I went over and kicked him right in the face hard as I could. Then I climbed on my pony and come on east."

"To here?"

"I knew it was all over the for the fiddle-footed rangers whether I liked it or not," he nodded. "It was over so fast but it was over. So I settled in here, married up with your grandmother for a while."

"Why didn't you go back to Dodge City?"

"It was all over, I said. The railroad already gone by. World changes. Today it's chicken. Tomorrow it's feathers."

"Did you rob banks and trains, have you got a chestful of money buried in the storm cellar?"

"Them are just stories little people scare themselves with. Bedtime." He leaned over to blow the light out, a haggardness of remembrance aching in his old cat eyes.

Of course, hindsight is fine. If I knew then what I know now, I'd have had the detailed story, the yarns, the whole lore, but I didn't know. I was as thoughtless and uncaring as a boy blowing dandelion fluff in a breeze.

Halfway through the summer I was reading the captions under the *Geographic's* pictures to him as he sharpened knives or cooked our dinner. It was easy and fun once I had the hang of it and nobody was pushing. The words matched the picture but I never considered how simple the process was; I just went ahead doing what I wanted to do as if it were the most natural thing in the world.

Grandfather knew what a big leap had been made.

He was drinking more and more lemon juice for what he called the rheumatism in his shoulder, and sometimes I'd notice a pallor on his face when the rheumatism was hitting him extra hard.

The rattlesnake watermelons in our garden were huge and we thumped them every day, and shared the ripe ones with our neighbors. The country gentleman corn was so sweet you didn't really have to boil it to eat, and grandfather's tomatoes were the biggest and reddest in town.

We fished every morning in the heat of August in 1929 as the river lowered and the teeming potholes separated farther apart and the snapping turtles crowded in closer and closer together, their ugly, fearsome snouts poking out of the water like ancient reptiles.

And we caught plenty of fish, bullheads, carp, catfish, but we didn't catch the big one. Grandfather by then was calling him the Old Man.

"Maybe today the Old Man will try us out."

Our colored bobbers would float on the turbid, opaque surface of the river. The cottonwoods had already flowered and sent their fluffy seed on the western wind, mulberries fell and dyed my feet purple, and the black walnuts were loaded with green-hulled nuts, and the squirrels and the rabbits, the birds and muskrats were easing through this hot month of maturation, knowing that autumn was coming, the harvest, the storage, the fullness of the cycle.

Fish would take our bait, bobbers frantically announcing the event, and each time we hoped it was the Old Man, but we were almost through the month of August before he returned.

I wish I could remember how Grandfather put me to writing fishing stories. I vaguely remember him showing me a picture of a trophy fish on a block and tackle beside a famous man, probably Zane Grey, and asking me to write the caption underneath it. He took me into it so artfully, the real breakthrough never registered. But I do remember that each day after we'd read a story in the *Geographic*, there'd be a picture and a blank piece of paper and a pencil stub for me.

In three months, from an autistic dummy he had me doing arithmetic, reading and writing, and best of all, enjoying them.

I never have enjoyed speaking, somehow feeling that I still mumble, and that I can be more honest and clear with the written word.

School was entirely out of my mind. My parents were strangers I hardly recognized. Fishing, roaming, gardening, reading, writing, card playing, the whole world opened up as mine in that summer of release in the fecund heart of Kansas.

The only thing I feared was snapping turtles. I could visualize them tearing a body to shreds with their sharp beaks the way they'd rend a hapless duck. One minute the mallard would be poking along the edge of the river, paddling and wheezing through the rushes, and the next thing, the duck would be abruptly pulled under water quick as a bullhead would pull down a bobber, and then on downstream floated feathers, attached to bones. I threw rocks at the snapping turtles' heads every chance I had.

The blue Hubbards grew to huge warty squash big as bushel baskets, and the cantaloupes and strawberries ripened to become our breakfast fruit salad, and yet in the blazing heat of August there was a scent of autumn, a new evening chill, a different breeze.

The Concords were plump and purple and grandfather invited the neighbor ladies over to help themselves, with the unspoken understanding that they would return a few jars of grape jelly. Grandfather stayed away on those days. He feared respectable women as much as I feared snapping turtles.

Doom wasn't in any breath of those fag-end days of August, not in my mind or wide-open senses, anyway. Every day was rich and sweet as a ripe cantaloupe, and I was too innocent to be aware of the changes, not only in the season but in my grandfather's strength. He was drinking a little more alcohol and a lot more lemon juice, and he moved slower when the pain corkscrewed his shoulder and paled his wintry face.

Reading became interesting, writing turned into a mirror game, a challenge much like trophy fishing. Writers kill themselves driving against their impossible ideal standards, the same as fishermen extend their strength and resources to catch the impossible fish. There at the round oak table in grandfather's kitchen was the origin of a dozen novels, anthologies of short stories, volumes of poems, many, many fishing stories. All from a kid who had practically ceased to function in the educational process. God love my grandfather.

By the first of September, even I in my careless joy could sense that little chill in the first blue light of morning, tomato plants giving up, bees devouring the sugared grapes, the shortened days.

"Sometime soon," grandfather said one evening after I'd finished reading to him, "sometime soon, you'll be going back to school, the river will rise, and the fish will grow."

"I don't want to go back to school."

"Of course."

"You never went to school."

"I did until I was thirteen."

"I don't want the summer to quit."

"Everything changes because the earth is turning. Don't wear yourself out trying to fight the changing."

"I hate school."

"Yes, but you can handle it. You're as good as the best. I'd appreciate you giving it a good lick, just to prove I know my game and my blood is strong."

We shook hands on it.

I had two weeks left, though, before returning to the big house across town, and though I tried to hoard the days, they squandered themselves.

I couldn't get enough of rambling through the tall corn across the road, or swinging in the cottonwood trees, or hiking beside grandfather to the river where the walnuts were falling and the leaves showing yellows.

"You know that big cat don't like minnies, nor crawdads, nor worms; maybe he has a hunger for a doughball." Grandfather ruminated over the subject of that big legendary catfish that had got away.

"Let's try." I was interested but not obsessed.

"Let's." He grinned that slow pussycat smile, and mixed up a batch of molasses, graham flour, anise oil and cotton. He mixed the mess with his bare hands and formed out walnut-sized balls on a tray to dry and season.

"He won't bite cotton," I said.

"He'll bite on that anise, though. He'll smell that if he's clear down to the mill, and he'll stampede upriver to swaller her down."

Morning was wet with passing showers, but the farmer was out picking his corn, sailing the ears into a high-sided wagon as the horses pulled, obediently matching his pace without any guidance, crushing each row of high stalks that had been picked, moving up and down the grand field which had once been mine.

The river was at its lowest, its flow hardly visible, its channel almost a series of disconnected potholes. It would rise within the month and then freeze for skaters.

Snappers' heads poked out of these pools like iron bolt cutters. I threw a rock at one of the pools when we unloaded our gear. The heads disappeared for a moment.

Grandfather was intent on rigging to catch the big fish, but he bothered to say, "Them snappers are just creatures that can't better themselves."

He swung his doughball-baited hook out into the river and settled down to watch the bobber. I took a spot downstream and tried to cast to the opposite bank, but my line was short, and my doughball dropped into a riffle by an ancient waterlogged snag.

Before I could settle down and watch the bobber and think of things, he hit the bait, and I felt the jerk of his strike before I even saw the bobber plunge.

"You got him!" Grandfather pulled in his line and stood to watch.

I didn't have him really. Like the snapper, he had me. He was popping the cane pole, using all the water and all his power. He sawed me upstream and then he sawed me down. I hadn't the strength to really hold him, let alone fight him, but I tried. I was yelling and silently praying, and moaning and groaning, and grandfather was saying, "Stick with it, you can do it, hang on, boy," and I was hanging on for dear life as the pole bowed under the weight of the great fish. And once he came to the top, I could see he was as big as a first-grader, big as a police dog, a giant of a channel cat. O Jesus Christ he was big!

Nearly as big as I, he was overpowering me, and my heart was sinking as I felt my weakness, the weariness of the struggle hitting into my arms and shoulders.

"Gramp," I said, hoping he would come and help, already knowing he would not.

"You can do it, boy. You have the salt."

"Gramp," I groaned.

"You have caught him, and you will beat him."

"Gramp—"

"Takes some time and nerve."

"Gramp!"

"Confidence and being ready. You're ready. Take him."

"Gramp . . . "

"Hear me, listen, you've got the salt, use it."

"Oh Gramp . . . "

"Believe me, I know you can do it."

The great fish worked me as a wild stallion works the horse catcher, as a heavyweight works a flyweight, but with grandfather's encouragement I nearly had him to the bank twice, and each time he would rise back and fling off to another depth, another position of his tethered circle.

The third time I tried to land the giant, he stood on his tail and made one more mighty leap, breaking the tip off my pole and landing in one of those hated potholes, a pool not as big as a wagon, but of unknown depth, and certainly jam-packed with snapping turtles.

"Gramp?"

"Get him!"

It was go in after him or else watch the turtles snip him into pieces.

I was paralyzed by the enormous choices, the decision that is the true crux of dyslexia. Balanced between two points, I froze on dead center and couldn't move.

The fish was flopping, crashing the pool, arching his slick body, attempting to throw himself back into the mainstream, wearing himself down into turtle food.

"Get him."

What broke that fearful paralysis in my head? I believe now that through the summer I had become identified with the doers, the action people—Lindbergh, Peary, Martin Johnson, Zane Grey and my own grandfather—and these friends were by my side, rooting for me.

Abandoning my broken pole, I shut the snapping turtles out of my mind. I had control. I knew what I was doing and that the fish was mine. All I had to do was go in there and grab him.

The water was up to my shoulders but I wasn't even thinking of water, I was taking my fish. I struggled toward him as he flipped in and out of the pothole. My hand found the tip of my pole, found the line, and I brought him close, hand over hand, ignoring the invisible beaks that would shred a helpless body. I never said a word, nor moaned or prayed. I pulled him to me. He was on his side, tireder than I, and I backed out of the pothole to the silted bank, heaving out the huge cat-faced fish, its blue and silver body over a yard long.

Grandfather handed me the club, and when I hit him behind his grotesque head, he stopped flopping and his colors lost their luminescence.

Grandfather was pale but he was game, and together we carried the champion fish back home. We were both too tired to make a show of victory.

He took a shot of alcohol first thing, and got his breath after a few minutes, and then another drink, and he was all right.

"You feeling better?"

"Fine. It's the rainy weather gets into my shoulder."

He left me and went to the neighbor lady's house to use her phone. When he returned, he said, "Let's wash him off clean, and hang him just right. I want Grant Madison to take a picture."

And by the time we were ready, Grant Madison, our part-time village photographer, arrived in his Model T with his camera and tripod.

I have that photograph of a small boy standing steadfastly beside a great fish suspended from the limb of the plum tree. In the background I think I can see the berry vines, the squash, the tall shoe-peg corn, and grandfather stands beside me, slit-eyed, pussycat smile, big as a mountain.

THE SOUTH COAST

The South Coast, to locals of Big Sur, means about eighty miles of California's central coastline stretching from the Big Sur River south to Raggedy Point.

It's a rough and steeply plunging coastline, as anyone who's driven Wonderful One, the scenic highway, knows. Its piney mountains slam like a diving seabird into the Pacific breakers. It seems to be so isolated and primitive a rock-bitten wilderness that you'd hardly think our hills were priced out of the market and that there could be enough people to wear it out, litter it over or fish it empty. But to the old-timers like me and my fishing pardner Buzz, it has become more and more obvious that the abundance of the South Coast, where we used to gather abalone, mussels and rockfish, is no more. The red abalone are completely gone, the smaller black abalone are so near to extinction it's futile to search for them. There are plenty of mussels because here they are generally over-looked as a delicious seafood, perhaps because the orange and black meat with its attached beard of coarse whiskers is somehow obscene to the unliberated. Even rockfish, like the heavyweight cabezon, or kelp bass, and bony sea trout, have become scarce.

If Buzz and I actually gave a damn, it might be a sad story indeed, but over a long period of approaching senility, we've managed to down-grade the goal of catching something below the desire to just go fishing. There's a big and fundamental difference, and it takes many years of climbing up an down the beautiful, breakneck South Coast cliffs before one may achieve this particular satori.

Most South Coasters believe the abalone disappeared because sea otters, after having been hunted to near extinction for their fur, have returned. The otters' staple is sea urchins, but there's no doubt they love the juicy white meat of the abalone, too. They dive deeply in waters where we can never go, and perhaps, as the spendthrift skin divers have done, wipe out the reserve beds of growing abalone which in time would be crowding up into the ghettos of exposed coastal rocks and sea stacks. Yet abalones and otters prospered together for centuries before man worried about either.

Now the otters up and down the coast are crowding into high-risk areas where kids of all ages with .22s plunk them off as they nap in the kelp beds, and oil spills tar them, and sewage outfalls soap and chlorinate them.

Their problem is our problem. Over the years, Buzz and I have discovered several sheltered coves where there were no crushed beer cans or coils of discarded monofilament or last week's newspapers. Many times we've climbed the sawtooth rock faces to these secluded spots and felt a sense of belonging as we cast our heavy throwlines out into the white water and cow kelp, settled back with a jug of Angelo Bertero's Zinfandel and soaked up the sun. But year by year we've been crowded farther south, probably encroaching on someone else's favorite spot. And as these years have passed, old Buzz and I have become a little more arthritic and a little thicker in the girth, so that the times we used to scramble up and down the sandstone cliffs on a climber's rope are unbelievable memories now.

Our lies are a little grander with each retelling, so that though our rope was actually only 50 feet of half-inch hemp, it has developed into a 200-foot hawser; and the many times we slipped and fell 20 feet have become legendary falls wherein we've been saved only by the grace of God having put a little mesquite bush at the right place, or a sandbank somehow washed up exactly in the proper position to loft the bodies of crashing mountaineers encumbered with sacks of sinkers and lines and wine and salami.

Our fishing and musseling on the South Coast is determined, in theory, by the tides. You can't pry loose cold, briny fresh mussels except on a low tide with a calm sea, and you can't catch a cabezon except when the tide is turning from low to high. No one knows why, but it is a fundamental verity in catching cabezon that you must have your hook there waiting on the tide-turn. Having long studied this phenomenon, we have concluded that the tide-turn jostles loose small crabs and traveling abalone from the security of their rocky nooks into the ready maws of the hungry fish.

If the surf is running high, we do our farm chores and forget all about fishing. The South Coast sea is tricky, uncaring about my life or anyone else's life or the long enjoyment thereof. Several times we have been nearly caught by that unpredictable Big Roller, nearly twice as high and heavy as any wave before it, that seems to arise out of some faraway trench to come booming at the coastline rocks. It is that one giant wave you have to watch for, especially on days when the sea is already heavy. Once that Big Roller catches you and lifts you off your warm friendly rock and takes you away, another companion wave comes along to smash you into fishbait against that same rock. It happens all the time. Each year fishermen are lost because they happened to have their backs turned just when the Big Roller came scything in.

Buzz and I have a standard set of yarns of the old days when we'd get smashed flat under tons of water, hanging on for dear life to that loving rock until the wave would recede, taking all the fishing gear and wine and salami, and leaving a couple of terrified, wet South Coasters vowing never to come near that goddamned murderous, unfeeling ocean again. That part never changes no matter how crowded the coves become with tourists and newcomer dudes. Our ocean just could care less whether it kills you or a sandflea or nothing.

I lost a good Lab retriever like that one day. And we lost our last old hogback of sea-bitten sandstone one day when someone from somewhere else bought the land and built a steel and glass house there. The screening thicket of alders and gooseberries was bulldozed out for a solid blacktop road with a gate across it, and a sign bearing the thought-provoking message, NO TRESPASSING WITHOUT PERMISSION.

I remember that they put an antiqued copper weathercock on the roof and it always pointed south.

"Good tide today," Buzz said on the phone. "Maybe we oughta go fishin'."

"Where?" I asked, knowing there was no place left to go.

"Let's look for a new place," he said after a moment.

"We've looked over everything in sight already." I'm the more conservative and responsible half of this fishing pardnership. Buzz tends to be more of a helter-skelter energizer.

I picked him up in my truck because, as usual, there's something wrong with his. The gears won't mesh, or are so tightly meshed they won't unmesh. He's never exactly sure. "Fishing takes priority over fixin','" he declared joyfully, tossing a gunnysackful of tackle and beer and wine and, I hoped, the bait into the back of the truck.

"Where to?"

"South! Hellsafire, there's bound to be one good spot left for God's own fishermen!"

We drove on past the Coastland's subdivision, on past Nepenthe's because the bar wouldn't open until noon, past Big Sur Inn, and past the houses perched here and there in the most unlikely and beautiful places, like wooden birdhouses glued to the panorama of mountains and seascape.

Each time we parked on a turn-out to look for a good outcropping below, we'd end up seeing a new house, or one being just raw-framed. There's no way to hide a house from a hideaway cove.

You need about $150,000 to buy that kind of property and build a birdhouse on it. Buzz and I have been not only unfortunate in our careers but improvident, too, taking it for granted that there would always be a place for us to fish near home. And if we'd wasted our years piling up that kind of money, we wouldn't have had time for something constructive.

We'd never really searched beyond Wild Cattle Creek because that's too long a drive for us, but feeling the hot breath of civilization on our necks, we decided to keep on going.

Two or three of the places where we stopped showed promise and we climbed down through the salt brush and iceplant to the edge of vertical cliffs that barred us from the water. One of these coves was blue as a robin's egg far below us, and no doubt it was teeming, as they say, with all kinds of rockfish, abalone and mussels; but the only way anyone could ever get there would be by boat.

We had to go on, washing down our disappointment with cold beer. Buzz was bubbling and ecstatic about the glorious sunny day, and I was grumbling about how that crowd was always out there, coming after us.

Buzz had forgotten to bring the tide book and couldn't remember what time he'd calculated low tide would be. Over the years, I've learned to pay the matter no attention because nine times out of ten he would have the damned tide figured out wrong in the first place.

"Pull off there," Buzz said, "it might just be Mr. Right."

It was like all the other turn-outs on Wonderful One, except it was just big enough to park one car.

On the left was a high red clay bank, on the right a white guardrail, and then the drop-off. We climbed out of the truck, opened another beer, scratched our ears and jawed some, not really expecting anything. But when Buzz stood tiptoe on the guardrail, his face lit up as he looked over the downslope.

"Geronimo!" He slipped and fell more from excitement than vertigo.

I climbed up on the guardrail. Sure enough. It was a slow-stepped ridge that dropped steeply to a long hogback of bare rock that arched out against the sea like a sheltering shoulder. The south side where it would be warm had several benches and ledges eroded and shaped by a million years of winter storms.

"You can't tell," I said, getting down. "There might be a cutbank or a deep gulch hid under all that tickbush."

"Not possible," Buzz declared. "Think positive. We've struck it rich."

"Why isn't there a gang down there with a picnic lunch and a roll of toilet paper already, then?" I argued.

"Because of that!" Buzz hollered, pointing at a thick hedge of bright green and red poison oak. "None of them dudes is goin' to climb through that stuff."

"Plenty of 'em don't even know it's poison oak," I said, "not until they've already busted through it all the way to the hospital."

"Never mind, Gramps," Buzz said. "Let's hit the trail! Time and tide wait for no man! God is love, and thank heaven I don't catch poison oak!"

We shouldered our packs and made a direct assault on the tangled net of poison oak, and after a few yards of nearly straight downhill, we broke loose onto a little deer trail that wound its way through the lilac that seemed to be set with sinewy triplines, and down over slippery iceplant, and through the aromatic chemise until we hit the tall thicket of tickbush. Animals going to the rocks for salt had worked a sort of tunnel through the brush, and Buzz led the way on hands and knees to the other side, where there were some pretty little red and yellow flowers blooming, and nothing much ahead except our whale-shaped ridge.

It was steep, but the steeper it is the shorter it is.

In time we reached solid sea-etched rock, and eased our way down the sloping sides of the sandstone to a ledge that was dry. We could cast off the long ledge to the south where there were good surging currents of white water, and behind us was plenty of room to run if the Big Roller ever came crashing after us.

In an eroded seam of wet rock I found a string of undersized abalone clinging as tight as they could. If we had nothing else, we might have to use them for bait someday. We surveyed our rock like Robinson Crusoes, exploring all the potentials. It was fine.

Best of all, there was no sign that any man had ever set foot on it. It was ours as long as we could keep it quiet.

We emptied the packs out on the ledge: a quart of red wine, some white Monterey Jack cheese, a new salami, a battered loaf of French bread and the fishing gear, which consisted of four throw lines made of heavy cotton chalk line, each line carrying a pair of sturdy 8/0 hooks and a sinker made of a steel washer weighing about half a pound. Years ago, I picked up several hundred of these washers when they tore down the old wooden bridges and replaced them with concrete. I had saved enough to last us.

Buzz had remembered to bring a package of squid for bait, which for him was something worth mentioning.

It was a warm, generous rock. The west breeze was shunted aside and we took our shirts off, soaking in the balmy morning, routinely cutting squid and baiting the hooks. Buzz picked a spot toward the open sea to throw out his lines, and I thought it might be better right where I was. I stripped off about 100 feet of chalk line from the wooden winder, whirled the baited line over my head like a lasso, then let her fly. The heavy sinker carried the line way out in a graceful arc and plopped down into some white water, which indicated an underwater reef where the big fish would be lurking.

That done, there wasn't much else except to hold the line awhile just in case you had a bite right off, but they weren't hitting yet. I tied the line to a finger of rock and settled back on the ledge to soak in the sun. An otter was diving in the little cove. Just offshore a line of brown pelicans came chug-chugging over the wave tops, and the cormorants were screaming at the gulls on a white-limed sea stack. Out to sea we could see several whales spouting and rolling their big bodies southward, ponderously certain, going where they always went. I wondered if they ever felt crowded, whether they ever kept or tried to keep a secret little cove for themselves, whether they settled for less and less as they grew older.

Buzz scratched the gray hair on his Buddha belly and squinted his eyes against the sea glare. I sliced off some cheese and tore loose a chunk of French bread.

"Some folks just don't know what a good fishin' spot is," Buzz said comfortably. "Main thing is we don't tell anybody about this one."

He scratched at his beard and considered what he'd just said and amended it: "Less'n we bring a couple girls down. Lots of girls'd welcome a chance to come to a nice place like this."

I laughed. "Who you got in mind?"

"Well, I don't just know offhand," Buzz grinned, showing his worn down teeth. "It's kind of a long step for most of them beavers on my route."

The throw lines surged on the slow waves. The heat was beating against the rock, bringing out the good sweat on our broke-down torsos. Buzz and I had separately done some ranching in our younger days, but we'd also drunk a hell of a lot of whiskey, wine and beer, and pursued a vast number of ladies, as well as fishing some, so that we were not exactly in the peak of condition any longer.

"I bet there's some powerful big fish in that cove." Buzz opened the wine bottle, took a slug and handed it on to me. "Remember that cabezon I caught that had the big rock in his belly?"

"I remember him. I think I remember it was me that caught him," I said.

"Goddamn it," Buzz said unexpectedly. "My kids don't know nothin'. They don't know even how to rockfish."

Hard to say just what glinting tangent Buzz's mind might travel.

"How come you drink so much?" I asked, turning around so the sun was roasting my back. "Goddamn, it's been a long rainy winter and I'm white as a fish belly."

"I drink because I don't want to know how the day is goin' to end," Buzz ruminated, as if he'd pondered the question many times and knew the answer. "If I woke up in the morning and saw a schedule of work, lunch, and drivin' home and dinnertime and TV and off to beddy-bye, I'd just crawl under a rock. I drink so somethin' different will happen that I don't expect. I want all my days unpredictable."

I used to take my own kids and Buzz's kids out on the rocks for abalone or rockfishing, but now they'd rather drive fast cars around the curves of Wonderful One. They always make fun of old Buzz and me going fishing as if they knew something we didn't already know. That's how they are.

As if we hadn't fished off the rocks for a half a century and seen the Big Roller rising up after us.

The otter had his mate out there now. She'd just swum around from the next cove and she had a pup in her arms. We didn't say much, we just watched her feeding the pup in the surge and swell. "That's like livin' on a waterbed," Buzz said after a while. "Ever get any on a waterbed?"

"Sure," I said. "I tried one out once. But I think if I had my choice, I'd rather be a parachutist. Wouldn't that be something: floating down through the sky with a lady parachutist?"

"I never considered it," Buzz said. "Maybe we ought to try one out. I'd hate to miss something."

"You know, they say in Scammons Lagoon one male whale will kind of hold and steady the cow while the other bull tops her and breeds. They say they are just crazy down there at Scammons Lagoon, leaping up out of the sea into the air sixty, ninety feet long. Lots of folks go down there and take pictures of them."

"You think we caught any fish yet?" Buzz asked.

"Too soon. Tide hasn't turned yet. We'll catch us a sackful when the tide turns."

The hot sun was burning into our hides and moving some of the old juices again. We were half asleep, listening to the sloshing waves and smelling salted rocks and kelp, and thinking about how great it was to have this day in this place and, maybe a little smugly, that hardly anyone really knew what a human pleasure it was.

"About time?" Buzz murmured out of the hot blue sea-dream.

The wind was changing toward the south and freshening. The sea had picked up a long chop.

We pulled at our handlines and, as expected, they were all snagged on underwater rocks. "Hung up," Buzz swore grimly. "Ain't that always the goddamned way!"

There was nothing to do but pull until something broke. As the lines came free, they were missing hooks or weights or the whole rig.

"I'da swore there was lots of fish in these waters," he said.

"There is. I know there is," I said. "I think we just caught the wrong tide. Next time we'll get the tide table figured out, and now that we know where we're going, we'll be hauling in the big ones."

"At least we don't have to lug anything up that hill," Buzz said agreeably.

We coiled up the ruined throw lines and stowed them in our packs. The sea was blue as turquoise; the chop like silver fretwork.

We finished the wine and put the empty bottle and wrappers in our packs, and left the bait and leftover lunch for the gulls.

Buzz put on his shirt and hoisted the pack. "Maybe we didn't catch much, but we sure found the spot," he said. "I hope we can make it last forever."

I followed him as he leaned against the steep, hard rock and climbed up toward the highway. We could see the cars going by like hard-shelled bugs way up there. They were driving as hard as they could.

The Big Roller. The sheltering rock. The South Coast. Trying to fit it all together, I know what I'm talking about, but I don't know if anybody's listening.

HARMON HENKIN

Though some self-righteous evangelical preachers of the gospel of angling push the notion that the sport is conducted in a sublime and rarefied atmosphere, to me it has no greater claim to spiritual purity than sex, dope or any other recreation in contemporary America.

Fishing is an integral part of this society's social fabric, and since this society is based on the grossest sorts of economic and cultural inequities, there's no reason to believe it would be immune from these distinctions. Angling can become a concise mirror for observing the nation at play, as significant a phenomenon as observing it at work.

Over the last few years I have become more and more interested in the sociology and internal policies of the sport, leaving to others the perhaps more gratifying task of describing how, when and where they catch fish.

My own angling is basically a personal act in which a hundred or so times a year I roam the streams and rivers of Montana, valiantly attempting to prove it is impossible to catch a very large trout on standard dry fly patterns.

Though fishing is itself a wondrous pastime, I find myself more and more fascinated by my other role as participant-observer, as the social scientists say, and look on the sociology of angling as an untapped field. Since the bourgeoisie loosened its grip on the sport over the last few decades, it has become more democratized, and the types who inhabit its world have become less homogeneous and more interesting.

There are the outdoor writer-publicists in places like Henrys Fork, always trying to impress others with their skills; the hyper-hustlers touring the tackle shops like insurance salesmen, pushing this product or that earthshaking fly pattern; and the self-proclaimed aristocrats who believe a wool sweater and cane-rod collection gives them status.

It's these people who give the sport its current flavor, an ambience distinct from any other period in the 500-year written record of the sport, and it's these people who continue to spark my interest in writing about the nuances of fishing. If the whole business were merely about Man versus Fish it would be intriguing enough, but as a larger social presence, it is overwhelming and engrossing.

SWAPPING

"Cut the small talk. I didn't drive halfway across Montana to hear about the weather."

A cruel smile creased my lips as I watched him squirm. Reluctantly, he eyed a rifle propped in a corner of the room, a beautiful .257 Roberts, built around a 33–40 Mauser action and finished with a Circassian walnut stock. His wife paced nervously. It wasn't the first time she'd seen this happen. She knew how it would end. I had him.

"Isn't there some other way?" His voice trembled. "How about taking a saddle or maybe even a horse? That'd square it."

"No chance," I shot back. "I've waited two years. It's gotta be the rifle."

Glancing at the rare, chromed Smith & Wesson .44 magnum in front of me on the kitchen table, he stood up cautiously and edged toward his rifle. My hand slid toward the pistol.

"Alright, you bastard." He turned and faced me. "But you have to throw in some more shit. And good shit, too."

I dug into my bulging pack and fished out a glistening Rollei 35 and a Hardy Perfect fly reel made in the fifties when they really built them.

His eyes were wide.

"Both of 'em?" I ventured.

"Yea. But I want your North Face 60/40 coat, too. Deal?"

His hand flashed across the table and grabbed mine.

"Deal!"

He poured two shots of Wild Turkey to celebrate the successful consummation of our umpteenth trade in six years, and another triumph of frontier barterism over American got-to-be-newism.

Currently about twenty people make up my hard-core extended trading family, and lots of others hang around the edges waiting for the right piece of merchandise to turn up. The group is not socially vertical but absolutely horizontal. No distinctions are made on the grounds of wealth or achievement. Who has what and who wants what is our sole operating principle. Our "members" cut across the socio-economic gamut and include writers, ranchers, photographers, foresters, food stampers and even a few actors who take a piece of the swap action while summering in Montana. The ex-owner of the .257 Roberts? Well he's one top screenwriter and a fairly successful rancher to boot. He could buy all the sporting goods he wants and maybe the store itself. But what fun is there in walking into a shop and handing over an American Express card or money? No style. No ritual. The clerk just tallies up the price and that's that. So we trade.

We have such different and varied lives that there is a continuing ebb and flow of goods through the circle. When someone returns from an extended trip, say to Europe or the East Coast, the others, living in scattered locations across the state, begin milling around like a cowboy cargo cult waiting for the manna. And since trades are not always one-on-one, involving parties up to the fourth part at times, the telephones will be ringing from Tinkers to Evers to Chance: "If I give you that and he gives you this, will you give them the things that I just hafta have?"

There are some things that have to be understood about this sort of swapping. The object is not to come out financially ahead. That would be like winning a chess match by smashing your opponent in the head with the board. As I say, our swapping process is a matter of style, of ethics that often border on the metaphysical. You want to get the best deal you can but you don't want to screw the other person. Advantage and disadvantage in a trade accrue from the intrinsic value of the merchandise rather than anything as vulgar as a price tag.

In our hard-core circle, scoring financially bespeaks of base philistinism. Semi-honorable people like us don't hustle one another in deals. Montana isn't Hollywood, after all. You know if you "won" a trade by the sum total of the "ooohs" and "aaahs" received from interested parties who hear about the action.

I became aware that it was really possible to get something I wanted for something I didn't want shortly after exiling myself from the more advanced sector of capitalist economy on the East Coast to the more primitive version in the Rocky Mountains.

In Maryland I had done a little trading, mostly of fishing tackle. But the other person usually wanted their attorney to draw up a contract covering how many points they retained if the Japanese spinning reel they were swapping turned out to be an antique from the sixteenth-century dynasty and whether the warranty they got on your rubber worms was complete or limited.

My first job in Montana was doing trout and elk journalism for Missoula's daily, and I was getting tired of hauling around my Mamiya 2¼ x 2¼ twin lens reflex camera. It weighed just slightly less than the ship that brought it to market.

One day the paper carried an innocent-looking classified ad: "Alpa 35mm camera for sale, lenses and accessories included." I had drooled over those Swiss gems for years.

I called the guy and we chatted. He didn't seem the least bit interested in quoting me a price, but he did invite me over to take a look. He lived in a modest house outside town and was a soon-to-retire Forest Service employee. Old-time traders like him, I figured out later, use the "For Sale" classified of Montana newspapers the way massage parlors use the pages of the L.A. *Free Press*.

He escorted me immediately into his den. It was stocked nook and cranny deep with all sorts of cameras and fascinating outdoor paraphernalia. In a half-open closet I spied a veritable arsenal of rifles.

He sat down in a comfortable chair without even gazing at the Alpa and its accessories, parked next to him on a small coffee table. He lit his pipe and we discussed articles I had written, Indian water rights, mackinaw fishing and man's fate. Not a word about the Alpa.

Finally I interrupted.

"Uh, can I see the Alpa?"

He handed it over and excused himself, walking out of the den, which gave me time to look it over. A fine piece of machinery! Then he came back and sat down.

"Uh, that's a pretty nice camera you have," I ventured, knowing even as a novitiate not to commit myself too early in the game.

"Yea, it sure is," he responded as befits a master.

"But you notice those nicks and scratches in the black finish? On both sides. There's a loose screw on the 28mm lens, too." (Knock the merchandise.)

"They don't hurt anything."

"Can you get an Alpa fixed in Montana?" (That line once saved me $100 on an English Ford in West Virginia.)

"Nope. Can't get any camera fixed in Montana. Got to send them to Chicago or somewhere."

"Oh, well. What do you want for it?"

"What do you have?"

"A little money."

"How little?"

"Maybe about two hundred and fifty. In a couple of days, anyway." I knew that was about half what it was worth.

"Oh. You must have something else. Everybody does."

I paused and thought of my shares of man's worldly goods.

"Well, I have this Mamiya two and a quarter, a Winchester thirty-thirty and yea, a mountain tent and there's a twenty-two pistol, a Ruger, and I just bought an old Land Rover."

His eyes sparked. "You say, an old four-wheel-drive Land Rover?"

Well, he didn't get the Land Rover but he did get my camera, pistol and tent. I got the experience and the Alpa.

I walked out of his house a born-again consumer. But like many a convert I went overboard, dreaming about the big score. My commodity forebearers who tramped across the Great Plains and into the mountains 150 years ago probably dreamt of hustling the Blackfeet or Crow out of every last beaver skin and buffalo hide the tribes had. At that moment I wanted to be part of this long and dishonorable American tradition. It seemed the only way I was going to get all the gear I wanted but could never afford to buy as a coolie journalist.

Thus, a week later, I returned to this guy's trading cornucopia eager to latch on to one of the fine and, let's be honest, valuable guns squirreled away from his decades of swapping. Easy pickings, for a city slicker.

But it was like dating a coed in the fifties. He wasn't promiscuous. Top-quality goods were being kept for the right guy, and that wasn't me. All I had was a fly fishing outfit and $25 cash. It got me an old Winchester, a turn-of-the-century .22 rifle we figured was worth

$100—the same as my stuff. But I had only paid $25 for the rod and reel. Heh heh.

I then embarked on a crazed trading spree. It was hunting season, and I traded rifles almost daily, dreaming not of giant antlered beasts, but of more and better rifles. Once my ammunition supply got so far behind my trading zeal that I was carrying bullets for a rifle I had disposed of a week and four guns before, and had none for the rifle at hand.

But it was working. I had parlayed my initial $25 investment into a beautiful Mannlicher-Schoenhauer 30–06, a great all-around hunting rifle worth about $450. My fortune multiplied in a few short weeks in my spare time, as the matchbook says.

Then I heard about the king of the traders, an old grizzled geezer who not only had a wondrous gun collection but was viewed by the other swappers as Monty Hall is by Let's-Make-a-Dealers.

I went visiting. We spent the normal hour or so chit-chatting and I tried to avoid his decidedly beady eyes. Then we got down to business.

He went through a standard repertoire of Winchesters, Remingtons and other banalities, always careful not to let me too close to his cavernous gun room. He brought me guns one at a time.

But I was positive there were untold goodies in there and I knew from his total lack of expression that he was just dying to get my Mannlicher.

Finally he retreated into the darkest recess of the gun room and got it: "Just to show you. Would never trade it. Was my father's."

My God, it was lovely. Michaelangelo must have formed and finished the stock, Cellini the metalwork. It was undoubtedly the Kaiser's personal stag rifle. And worth a thousand for starters. It was the ultimate. I had to have it. But of course I didn't show a trace of emotion.

To make a long afternoon short, he got the Mannlicher and a $200 check which I had to rush off to cover, and I got his daddy's gun. After convincing the bank I needed the $200 to send my sister who was locked in an Albanian jail, where she had been imprisoned for trying to bring free enterprise to that country, I zoomed to my gunsmith. He was getting tired of my incessant, "How much is this gun worth?"

"Well, how much is this one worth?"

"Has a beautiful stock."

"How much?"

"Great metalwork. Wish I could do stuff like that."

"How much? How much? How much?"

He looked it over carefully inside and out.

"You mean as a collecting piece or as a shooter?"

"Huh?"

"Somebody changed the caliber and did a terrible job. They probably picked it up from a Kraut as a souvenir after the war, took it back home and monkeyed with it in the basement."

"What the hell does it shoot?"

"Damn if I know. Never saw anything like it. Some kind of wildcat thirty-five special."

"Can you buy that shell?"

"Can you buy happiness?"

"It's ruined as a collector's piece, too?"

"Nobody wants a gun with a sex-change operation. If you really wanted to shoot it, I'd have to put a two-hundred dollar barrel on and that'd look awful on a quality gun like this."

"What's the best money I could get for it?"

"If you found the right guy, maybe a hundred. I'd give fifty for it as a wall-hanger."

Into each life a Hindenburg must fall.

Thus I became a quasi-gentleman trader, realizing, as have so many before me, that for every shrewd person there is certainly one shrewder. Also, I realized at this point that trading for profit is a full-time occupation, like running a pawnshop. Trading for the use value of something seemed like a part-time endeavor that was at least semi-honest. The contacts with like-minded Montanans that became my trading circle were made. If you can't buy the stuff you love, love the stuff you buy and swap for the rest.

The styles of the individual traders in the circle are as varied as the swappers themselves. Some of them, normally tough business dealers in their professions, get just too coy for words. They need soft sounds and understanding smiles before they'll give in to your proposition and surrender their goods.

Others are like hard-bitten old hookers. Never a word about their sentimental attachment to a piece of equipment comes from their lips. You meet their price in goods and they'll give you anything they've got. That's the McCabe and Mrs. Miller syndrome.

Some sorta love to trade but it scares the hell out of them. One trendy poet (almost a literary folk hero who counts his royalties like the grains of sand in Death Valley) has a paranoid style that offends all but the most callous. In one extended session, on a par with an expense-paid vacation in the Black Hole of Calcutta, he took overnight to decide whether the Hardy fly reel and other minor goodies were worth what his beat-up .22 was worth. And this was after we had gone back and forth through the intricacies of the trade countless times. I thought he was going to have a nervous breakdown. He did everything but call his agent to find out if my fifty-dollar stuff was worth his fifty-dollar stuff. If trading weren't at least partially a sport unto itself, I would have given him the reel just to relieve his angst.

But at least he didn't begin by insulting my goods. That's another gray area in trading ethics. It's perfectly moral to point out scratches and blemishes and to try gently to denigrate the quality of merchandise. But you should never blatantly insult it with the kind of snotty barbs you get in piss-elegant bike shops when you tell them you pedal a Gitane and it doesn't have campy parts and the clerk makes you feel as if you were on welfare.

The basis for our trading is quite simple. Someone has something you want more than something or some things that you already own. At other times, however, we trade for the hell of it, I guess because we don't have anything more exciting to do. Sadly, most newcomers, weaned in our cash-and-carry culture, have a hard time catching on. If you sweetly offer one of your trinkets for one of theirs, they immediately figure they're going to get screwed.

These initial feelings are admittedly justified. We all know that this is the most God-awful *caveat emptor* society on earth, where even a $7,000 Oldsmobile fresh from the factory can be inhabited by an alien engine from a Chevy. And who knows what's inside those glossy pieces of imported gear hawked in discount houses that never seem to last long enough to make good on guarantees.

The term "horse trader," as it derived from the nineteenth-century West, doesn't earn the novice's confidence either. He was the guy who fed his animals locoweed to make them lively before dumping them on the dude from Philadelphia. It takes patience and understanding to convince the novitiates that trading is merely an exercise in personal property redistribution, a rudimentary form of socialism between friends.

Nobody in our group could even begin to make a partial living from our game, shaving a nickel here, a dime there. It's a time-consuming process. You could do better working at McDonald's than shuffling the oversized mammals and camping gear and fishing tackle that are the stock in our trade. Though the paraphernalia that changes hands can be worth anything from a couple of bucks to maybe a thousand at the rare outside, value has no correlation with the length of the deal. I once spent an entire day trying to convince a potential swapee that my $5 used fly box was equal to his $5 used cartridge holder; a $500 gun deal was made one night last spring in a blink of an eye.

Sometimes, if someone is ultra-hot after an object the owner really values, we institute the Safety Valve or Grandfather Clause, which is as close as possible to having a new shotgun and shooting it, too.

Someone has a beautiful Loveless knife you want, for example. After making your best offer to the guy, who isn't very anxious to get rid of it but is wavering, you add: "You have first chance if I want to get rid of it." Since few things are ever kept for extended periods, this can be quite reassuring.

It seems that this clause, which I invoke occasionally, is akin to baseball's Reserve Clause, since in a sense you retain ownership theoretically of something forever, having the right to forbid future trades. But the Supreme Court has not ruled on this issue yet, and its constitutionality remains in doubt.

We all have at least a modicum of knowledge about the goods we trade, so most often things are traded as is. What you see is what you get, sort of. But at other times a mighty scream will arise after the gear is found to be patently defective. This happens most often with cameras, stereo equipment and other electronic gear. The scream is an automatic deal nullifier, but it rarely happens.

There are, of course, twists and turns to this aspect of trading. Two years ago I picked up a vintage Hardy fly rod from an unknowing tackle shop for a song, dance and $15. I traded it immediately to a friend who has a real weakness for such angling artifacts. I wouldn't guarantee the rod in any way, shape or form. He wanted it as a bargain quite badly and gave me $30 worth of stuff, ecstatic since the rod in good shape was worth $100 and he had the technical expertise to refinish it at home.

Alas, he couldn't resist fishing it once first. On his third cast the rod snapped neatly in half below the middle ferrule. He certainly did lots of whining. But what could he expect from a thirty-dollar, forty-year-old cane rod? Bad luck, I called it.

But then a couple of years ago I paid $200 to a supposedly reputable dealer in "previously owned tackle" for a Paul Young rod. But something looked funny about the rod, an opinion shared by another member of the circle. We called the dealer, and after some sharp questioning he admitted the rod was really a Heddon—an inexpensive mass-produced rod from the 1930s—that had been wrapped by Paul Young. Fraud, I called it.

As the value of the dollar has fluttered downward in the past several years, the value of high-quality used goods has rapidly increased. Collectors, speculators, hoarders and wheeler-dealers dominate and try to monopolize the second-hand markets for guns and fine fishing tackle, establishing inflated prices for them. Thus things are so desperate that people have even forged bamboo fly rods, supposedly made by the master cane builders of the thirties, forties and fifties. And the collecting mania has become more irrational as the general quality of goods has declined. Every stratum of society wants its investment bargains. If the richest people are collecting gold artifacts, the next group on the economic rung can't afford the real thing and take to silver or brass. The bottom rung is stuck with plastic ashtrays and cigarette lighters.

Prices for most used things have zoomed up and there are lists for previously owned almost-everythings that are avidly pored over by dealers. The profits for these dealers depend on buying low, creating a big market, then selling high—as in, for example, the energy crisis. But that's how we equipment freaks get abused. A climbing rope isn't an investment to us. It's a way of getting off a mountain, a tool. Ditto with cameras, guns, fishing tackle and camping gear. All tools.

Something is worth what the other person will give up for it, more or less, depending on desire and/or need. Sure. That can vary from trade to trade, since a piece of gear may go back and forth any number of times over the years. But it's greedy to keep exact notes on market fluctuations: "When you traded me that sleeping bag last year, they were selling for a hundred and twenty and now they're a hundred fifty so I want those snowshoes and one hundred dollars." Boo. We are not interested in prime interest rates.

Of course, some pieces of equipment are so exquisite that an unofficial declaration is made to keep them within the circle even though at times nobody really wants them. There is a delicious-looking wood-handled pocketknife made in England that is often thrown in as a maraschino cherry in deals. But though this sweetener looks incredibly useful, it's much, much too heavy to be carried around and winds up in someone's desk drawer waiting for its next turn to be traded. It has remained in the group since I bought it at Randall's Knife Company in Orlando, Florida, five years ago.

Lots of the stuff is bartered from person to person until it is unofficially declared boring. At this point it is put away by its owner whose feelings are bruised by the lack of interest, or else traded to an outside party for something with more use or barter potential. Sometimes we will pick up something simply because there is someone in the group who will be hot for it.

Having our own group also gives us the added bonus of protection against professionals and rustlers, like putting our covered wagons in a circle. We have to at least co-exist with each other as well as merely swap, so our greed is tempered by conditions, as Prince Kropotkin would say. The professionals who live by buying cheap and selling not so cheap often have no such scruples. They are here today and gone tomorrow. And they know exactly what things are "worth," and can skin us down nicely on equipment that if kept as an investment would certainly have lined our pockets.

Winchester Model 70s from before 1964, when the company changed production procedures and cheapened the quality of the rifle, have doubled or tripled in value in a few years, mainly from collectors' pressure. We let lots of them drift out of the circle at cut-rate prices, not realizing how much their value had increased. The people who got them did. Old Leica cameras from the late twenties through the forties are also a hot collectors' item, but in our sublime innocence we used to throw them in as minor deal sweeteners the way a roadside café will toss in an extra piece of Wonder bread with its stew. Most of them eventually found their way outside the group, worth as much as ten times what we asked for them. A Garrison fly rod—fewer than 900 were ever made—was finally passed out of the circle (because of its, at best, mediocre action) by me for around $500 worth of tackle. That was only a year and a half ago, and the damned rod lists for around $1,000 now. Because of such corrupting influences, we try these days to temper our practical knowledge of equipment with financial knowledge; not fanatically, but nobody likes to get taken. And by now, most of the circle is quite expert in one or more facets of outdoor gear, including such arcane subjects as single-shot rifles, Leonard fly rods, pack saddles, single-lens reflex cameras and the like.

Downright frenzied activity started a couple of years ago when I returned plush from selling a book in New York, loaded down with all manner of things I picked up in the big city and outlying suburbs. I came back by Amtrak and made an initial trading stop in Livingston to divest myself of a shotgun, then a short hop to Bozeman, where a beautiful Garrison fly rod left my possession. Next was trade-center Missoula, where lots of things were involved in boggling multiparty swaps. Last stop was Hamilton, where a doctor friend wept until he got a Leonard fly rod for some junk or other. I felt like the Johnny Appleseed of commodities by the time I got back to my St. Ignatius cabin.

In the ten years I've lived in Montana, I've owned every major brand of rod, reel, camera, camping gear and reasonably priced gun. And I've learned a bit about all of it because I've used all of it. But far more important, some of my closest friends have come from the ranks of those who at first were merely owners of something I wanted. These were the people who had the pretty fly rods or fancy guns which we talked about on our way to discovering something far more valuable.

WHITEFISH

The old men come back each winter, singly and in pairs, numbers diminishing with time, to reclaim their rivers. They trudge through powdery snow or frozen fields to the banks of ice-clogged waters and while away the short days in pursuit of whitefish, certainly the proletariat of the trout family.

The younger working-class residents of western Montana ski, play with Tinker Toy snowmobiles, or do whatever else outdoor fashion is dictating this year; but these commodity-oriented pursuits require greater energy, mobility and, for sure, expense. The older people are mostly getting by on piecemeal pensions, Social Security and sometimes just handouts. They don't have a full range of options.

Semi-slick advertising agencies trying to lure affluent tourists to Montana don't waste their time boasting of the subtle joys of standing beside demi-iced-over rivers in midwinter or the still frigid days passing for early spring in the Rockies. The glittery out-of-staters who invade Montana's famed trout streams in the summer are back in their temperature-controlled urban environments now. Their delicate casting techniques and intellectual approaches to angling are being sublimated into catalog fantasies and Zen contemplation of streamside tactics.

Everything slows down on these rivers in winter. The tourist arrivistes wouldn't recognize the off-season tempo of the waters they visit in summer, but the slowing metabolic rate of these old-timers, in their sixties, seventies, and even eighties, seems perfect for this season, when most mountain life-forms are hibernating. The lethargic tempo of the whitefish with its gentle, nibbling strike is perfectly in tune with the pace of its pursuers and the season.

These men are the kind who have remained close to the land and whose lives are intertwined with its still-young history. When I asked one how long he had been fishing a particular stretch of the Clark Fork river, outside Missoula, the answer was a terse "Seventy years." Western Montana has been settled, in any meaningful sense of that word, for only 100 years.

This winter fishing is a truly indigenous angling form, and the old-timers who developed it—long poles, peculiar flies and strange baits— are still around, still practicing and perfecting the sport. They are mostly retired from the basic industries of the region: forestry, mining, rail-roading and nickel-dime ranching. They're the ones who didn't strike it rich, didn't get a chance to retire in Florida or Arizona. As lifelong friends, they return to these rivers almost daily to fish their familiar beats as consolation for not being a winner in life's Gong Show.

Though these men fish year-round, in summer the old-timers can be lost in the rush of anglers. It is only in the long winter that they have the waters pretty much to themselves, and being alone in this season when things seem to stand still, these men acquire their proper perspective.

Both they and the fish they seek are marginal, a capital crime in America. The species is the main pariah of the salmonid family, of which the bright-colored trout is the most hustled-after member. Cursed with a disturbing resemblance to a sucker, these brown-looking fish were dubbed "Bottlenoses" by Lewis and Clark. In the tongue of the local Salish tribe, whitefish are *Xoyu*—meaning puckered lips—and Indian legend has it that their small, circular, downward-pointing mouths came from falling off a ladder in the sky.

At any rate, whitefish have little of the grace and sleekness of their much-pursued cousins who occupy the same waters and have generally the same feeding habits. Whitefish are treated with the same genre of contempt in the West reserved for carp in the East. After mutilating a seventy-five-cent dry fly, something they relish in summer, many a whitefish has been cursed and tossed into the bushes to rot, by an angler anxious to get on with trouting.

But the old men who have known whitefish for decades are better judges of their value. It isn't only because whitefish are fair game in most rivers all winter, while trout have a closed season which makes them desirable to old veteran anglers. These men claim that whitefish caught in winter have a very firm flesh and, despite being more bony and having more fat than trout, are on a par with them when baked or pan-fried.

But much more advantageously, whitefish, which can run as heavy as five pounds and will average a pound in the bigger rivers, are in a class by themselves when smoked.

Over the decades the whitefishermen have developed the techniques of smoking them to almost a culinary art. When gently cured over hickory or birch chips, they have a delicate flavor not available for less than $5.95 a pound in New York. A staple in all the old-timers' homes are small jars of either wet or dry smoked whitefish, invariably offered as hors d'oeuvres. Accompanying the snack are tales of the unique way in which they are prepared in home-built smokers made from old refrigerators or whatever else is lying around.

So it is a combination of choice, recreational necessity and dietary delight that gets the old men out on the rivers beginning in December, when the weather turns cold enough to school the fish up in deeper water away from the shallows and ends of pools where they summer.

Though in its own way this winter fishing is as complex and ritualized as fly rodding for trout, whitefishing has very little in the way of a written history, remaining part of the old oral tradition of sport. Through years of standing on gray days on banks overlooking dark waters, these men have learned the best ways to catch whitefish, and if you want to learn, you have to go to them as primary sources. There are thousands of books on trout fishing, but when the literature of angling mentions whitefish at all, it is as addenda, saying they readily take flies and spinners in summer.

The tackle and techniques which make expert trout or bass fishermen are of little avail now. This angling's traditions have been developed over the years by trial and error, and to master its intricacies is a time-consuming process, requiring more patience and concentration than most of the younger generation of Montana anglers are willing to give a pursuit they consider, at best, a pastime between trout seasons.

Each of the old whitefishermen, like any angling virtuoso, has his own idiosyncrasies, of which he is possessive and proud. This is not the kind of sport with big breakthroughs. No graphite rods or turbine engines have come along, and no one is likely to invent a wishbone offense for whitefishing. Watching the old men slowly work the river, one is reminded more of their Parisian counterparts, who endlessly fish the Seine for an assortment of smallish fish, than of other forms of high-powered American angling.

Instead of the shorter specialized fly and spinning rods used during the regular season, the old-timers prefer long poles made of traditional cane or telescoping fiberglass from ten to sixteen feet long. In the nineteenth century, when some of these men were born, long poles without reels were standard gear for those without the wherewithal to purchase the then relatively new casting gear. It was essentially the same tackle that had been used for the first 500 years of the sport. With the increased specialization, popularization and lowering of the price of angling tools over the past decades, the cane pole became anachronistic. Except for small boys and old men, the casting rods of the various genres were superior.

But for whitefishing experts, the long pole remains the most efficient weapon. With temperatures rarely stretching into the forties and often below freezing, reaching out over the ice to open water using a tall pole is far easier than making casts with a short rod.

Some of the poles, which cost around ten dollars, have the guides and cheap push-button spinning reel merely clamped on with electrical tape. The narrow guides on regular rods will often freeze shut in winter after a few retrieves of wet line, but the short casts required with the long poles minimize the problem.

Most of the fishermen use a delicate porcupine-quill bobber to keep the bait flowing near the bottom, and to give a silent signal when a whitefish is gently tasting the offering. There is a great deal of finesse required to determine exactly how many of the tiny split shot are needed, and exactly how far between the hook and the float they should be put to get a natural drift. Whitefish don't exert themselves much to satisfy their slowed-down winter appetites, and a few inches can be the difference between twenty fish and a skunking.

It is in the choice of bait where fishing individuality among the old-timers becomes most manifest. The two general types are the maggot-and-fly combinations and the insect-larva favorites.

A familiar sight in tackle shops on winter mornings is the old-timers purchasing their sixty-cent plastic vials filled with sawdust and maggots before going out to the river.

The maggots are hooked by their tails, if you can speak of maggots as having tails, to specialized whitefish flies tied on small No. 16 and No. 18 hooks. In the lexicon of flytiers, these creations are Palmer-tied, clipped-hackle nymphs, usually snelled with six inches of nylon leader material, looped at the end to make it easier to attach them to the light monofilament line in freezing weather.

Though it couldn't have been more than fifty years ago, exactly when these flies became a separate type from other trout flies is beyond memory. The old men aren't sure. According to the weathered anglers, these single-colored bright flies, sold in myriad tints, are what initially grabs the attention of the fish. In summer, whitefish will strike a bare fly, but in winter it requires the addition of the delicious maggot to succeed.

Discussions between wintertime anglers as to the correct fly color are at least as ferocious as those between summertime anglers over which sort of trout pattern is most effective.

"If a green one doesn't work, always switch to a brown fly," says one whitefisherman who has been playing his skill on the Bitterroot River for fifty years. "No. No," says another one who has worked the same stretch of river for the same period. "Start out with a yellow fly and put on a black one if you don't take any fish in an hour."

The debate rages and it is only the temporary success of one variation over another that settles the point. But the results are often reversed the next day or even in the next hour, so, as in most other angling points of disputation, things are never really resolved.

However, for many of these old men still willing and able to make the necessary effort, the fly-and-maggot combinations run a far second to live insect larvae. The capturing of the nymphs is a sport within a sport which, according to one agile angler in his seventies, is almost as much fun as catching whitefish. The rivers are waded, itself an adventure in winter, with the fisherman carrying a sheet of screening material or a large kitchen strainer. The netting is held downstream on the bottom, and using the feet in a shuffling dance, rocks and gravel are dislodged, sending the larvae downstream. After a few of these underwater maneuvers are completed, the angler takes his haul ashore.

Though they know nothing about academic entomology, these men know what larva takes fish best. They scrutinize the netting like members of a museum field research project, placing the larvae thought of as being superior bait into a Band-Aid can or like container, and tossing the others back into the river where they will hatch out as caddis, stone or mayflies next summer to the delight of fly fishermen.

They usually favor the large nymphs in the stone-fly family, and most especially those which have moulted their hard casings. These nymphs, whitish in color till the transition period is over, are probably the same kind of delicacy for fish that soft-shell crabs are for residents of the East Coast.

When questioned as to why they prefer a certain nymph, only slightly different in coloration from the others, the men fall back on their empirical tradition, telling of years past and of whitefish caught on exactly this kind of bug.

One of the real legends is the trick of storing a maggot or helgramite nymph in the cheek, to keep it thawed and lively on days when the thermometer is really plummeting. The notion of putting maggots in one's mouth might not please the crowd at Elaine's, but medically it is not unhygienic, and the old-timers accept the practice casually as part of the sport.

As they fish, the old-timers, dressed snugly in woolen coats and pants, stocking caps and rubber boots, talk to their angling partners in the short sentences that are part of the Western tradition. "Yeps" and "Nopes" make up most of the conversation. They respond to questions only verbally, eyes always fixed on the moving water and the all-important bobbers.

Friendly enough, and always willing to deal with even the most naive questions, their fishing takes precedence. The fish are important to them, and to their nonfishing friends and neighbors. Whitefish are an important piece of nutrition, especially during these bad economic times, and the giving away of the fish to others is a method of gaining social esteem among their peers, and gives them a chance to socialize in the process.

When the fishing is good, they can fill their baskets or rucksacks quickly. Since the fish are usually schooled up in holes, a limit can be taken in an hour or two if the whitefish are hitting. But when things slow down, the anglers dip into their bag of tricks, roaming the banks from hole to hole, sometimes venturing out halfway across a deep, ice-coated river, alert to colors and sounds indicating weak coatings.

On relatively warm days, favorite whitefishing rivers such as the Clark Fork, Blackfoot and Bitterroot are best fished early and late in the day. In midday, chunks of ice break loose from the shoreline and float downstream, making the fishing rough.

When a cold snap freezes the rivers solidly, a winter storm suddenly hits, or the fish just won't have anything to do with them, it is usually just a short trip home. Many walk to their favorite stretches. There is good fishing in the Clark Fork and Bitterroot within the city limits of Missoula and Hamilton.

It is mainly the young who are impatient, believing that the white-fishing is better on the other side of the snow-covered pass. Few of the old men will travel more than a few miles to fish, preferring the waters they have always fished and known best.

Many more people go after whitefish during the warmish spring days before runoff muddies the water, but these are mostly fair-weather anglers who rarely develop the perseverance to take their quarry consistently.

Even though they seem to like companionship, for most of the old-timers whitefishing is something done alone. Being alone much of the time is part of being old in this society. But the solitude of whitefishing is not the same thing as the loneliness of the urban old. These anglers, many of whom are the sons and grandsons of the first settlers in Montana, are at home along these rivers. They have fished here all their lives, earned their livelihoods here and, now that they are retired, they can still retain a measure of dignity and a sense of worth, fishing away the winters of their lives in an area where they have their roots.

Even if this form of angling dies out with the passing of that generation, as seems likely, it will have served its purpose for these men. You need memories to while away the hours, and the young don't relate to the world in that way any longer.

As one explained when asked why he ventured out on a frigid afternoon to catch whitefish: "It's about the only way I can have another day of enjoying life."

NEW BREED

"Five years ago I would have demanded he be shot." Raymond Pearson, age twenty-five, keeps his eyes casually fixed on Coneyville Rapids up ahead, mentally planning a safe course for his fifteen-foot fiberglass McKenzie riverboat, a long way from his birthplace in Jersey City.

The dudes, a neurosurgeon and his wife from St. Louis on their first float trip on the tricky Madison River, have stopped casting Bitch Creek nymphs and are nervously watching the white water.

"Yea. It was just a few weeks ago. There I was, taking out the president of a big-time war industry, showing him how to catch fish and enjoy Montana."

The boat hits the choppy, rock–clogged rapids and is dancing past the standing waves. Pearson easily keeps it on the straight and narrow just as if were the everyday occurrence that it has in fact become for him in the past couple of years.

"I wound up really liking him. Out here he was a nice guy. That's one thing about being a fishing guide. It brings out the contradictions in me."

We're through the rapids now, and the couple smile reassuringly at each other.

"Hit the left, the left!" he shouts at them, and obediently their graphite rods begin arcing in the direction of a calm eddy along the port side of the boat. Dual miniature plops as the big, weighted rubber-legged imitations of a stone-fly nymph hit the water. Then a second later:

"Nail it, doc!"

The surgeon leans into the rod, jerks the tip back, and is fast to a brown trout his inexperienced eyes hadn't seen hit. The couple has had trouble hooking fish. They've been floating five hours and have landed only three of the couple of dozen fish that have struck at their flies. Pearson wants him to land this one.

He digs deeply into the strong current with the large wooden oars, driving the boat onto a narrow sandbar, grabs an oversized net and leaps smoothly to the bank.

"At least I got something from three years of high school basketball," he laughs, scooping up a beautifully marked sixteen-inch trout and handing it over to the doctor, who beams at his wife for a moment before unhooking it and gently placing the brownie back in the water.

Pearson smiles, too. He likes it when his clients don't have to be prodded to release their catch. That's a strong part of his environmental ethic, and a strong sense of ecology is very much a part of the new generation of guides beginning to work the West.

He looks around at the cloud cover that's starting to break slightly in the south. The dudes have had a hard time controlling their casts in the gusty winds the Madison Valley is infamous for. Maybe it will calm down a little later in the afternoon.

"Lunchtime," he announces, and begins rummaging around in the large cooler underneath the middle seat.

"Ah. Braunschweiger. The people's meat. Not like the piss-elegant gourmet meals some fancy outfitters are serving, but it's only eighty-nine cents a pound and delicious if you don't read the ingredients. The worse the fishing gets, the better the lunches they give out." Everyone laughs.

Fat sandwiches made with whole wheat bread, tomatoes, Monterey Jack and home-made mayonnaise are passed around, washed down with red wine and Oly Beer in recyclable cans. The clients are youngish and enlightened and the conversation is light and wide-ranging: politics, monogamous relationships in a postmonogamous society, the energy situation and trout fishing in America.

The woman looks at the orange-and-black Bitch Creek dangling from her 8½-foot fly rod as she munches on her sandwich.

"That's really a good fly pattern, isn't it Peggy?" Pearson asks, leaning against the boat, waders folded down to his waist.

"Yes. Except for that stupid name."

"Bitch Creek? Yea. It's sure sexist, but the fly was named after a creek up in the mountains where somebody first used it, so you'll have to blame whoever called the creek that. The management takes no responsibility."

Sexism! Imperialism! Ecology! Scarcely the basic concerns of earlier generations of fishing guides, who were mostly concerned with getting their customers into fish and keeping them out of danger.

But times have changed, and even if the last decade didn't turn America British racing green, as Charles Reich and others had hoped, at least it did leave an avocado tint, swirling lots of young heads around in the process.

It really shouldn't come as any great surprise that some counterculture types have taken up guiding tourist trout anglers in the Rockies. After all, you have to make a living somehow, and one of the basic notions of the post-sixties dropouts was that the cities were hopelessly corrupt, and a retreat to the country was one of the only available forms of personal salvation. And while they may not have found salvation, they have found enough saving graces to make the occupation worthwhile for an ever-increasing number of urban expatriates.

"Many fishes bite, if you gots the right bait," sang Taj Mahal and, echoing the lyrics, many of these expatriates now living on the edges of the economic system continue to search, if not for the right bait, at least for the right pattern to give them something interesting to do in wonderful surroundings.

Chuck Kneib, with a big bushy beard and tough-looking features, seems like one of the mountain men who settled this area of western Montana 150 years ago. He's sitting on a large boulder on the shore of the roaring Blackfoot River as a yellow raft filled with clean-cut University of Montana students bobs past, female voices shrieking in mock terror.

"I was majoring in geology at Missoula, switched over from Missouri. We were out on this field trip. The instructor was burned because none of us recognized this one group of rocks. 'We're trying to raise geologists for the mining companies and you don't know a phosphorial formation,' the teacher said. I didn't want to be channeled into one of those polluting huge corporations, an oil company or mining outfit, so I dropped out and now I'm a fishing guide."

A decent-sized trout is rising in the middle of the channel as Kneib ties on a big, bushy dry fly.

"I grew up in Saint Joe, Missouri. My dad's a truck mechanic and used to take me out hunting and fishing all the time. I can always remember hating the cities and loving the woods. Missoula's too big for me now.

What's it got? Thirty, thirty-five thousand people and growing uglier all the time. I didn't get into fly fishing for trout till I moved out here three years ago, but it wasn't too hard to pick it up after all the bass fishing I'd done in the Ozarks. I'm still learning, though."

He stands up, strolls a few yards down the bank and begins letting a little fly line out through the guides of the glass rod he built. He false-casts carefully toward the fish some fifty feet away. The fly drops naturally to the surface of the water six inches from it. As the deerhair caddis passes, the trout lunges, but in the heavy rush of clear mountain water Kneib misses the strike. He shakes his head. "Win some, lose some."

"After I dropped out, I just fished for six months till my money ran dry. I got a job surveying up in the hills, then got into commercial fly tying, but the store owners rip you off. They pay four dollars a dozen for your flies if you're lucky, and sell them for ten."

So Kneib drifted into guiding visiting anglers in the summer and picking up some extra money trapping in the winter, mostly coyote and beaver. "There are too many coyotes around these days, and it's better environmentally to trap them and sell the pelts than to let the government and ranchers use heavy-duty poison that kills everything."

He usually takes his customers down the Smith River, which he works with a friend. It's a gorgeous stream, running through an almost roadless chunk of cattle country in north-central Montana, with some of the best rainbow and brown trout fishing in the state. The sixty-five-mile float requires an arduous dawn-to-dusk five days, bringing him in closer personal contact with his clients than most other guides, who normally have one-day outings.

"Some of the dudes I've taken out have been okay people anxious to learn about a world different from the one they live in, but other ones treat guides like we're a lesser species of animal. Since a lot of them are rich, they act as if the fish should jump into the raft out of respect, but that kind usually can't cast or read the water."

Kneib spots another fish feeding across the river and begins nimbly jumping from rock to rock to get into casting position. This time he nails it, landing an eighteen-inch rainbow after an intense few minutes of struggle. He releases the fish, then rocks it back and forth in the current till it regains strength enough to swim hurriedly away.

"Yea. Lot of times it's only glorified babysitting. Some of the dudes are totally incompetent in the woods. They can't even light a campfire, and if it's cool or rainy they get bummed out. Their whole lives have been spent in seventy-degree air-conditioned or heated comfort."

He blows on his fly to dry it off before making a few long, aimless casts, more for the casting practice than in any hope of catching a fish.

"We get some strange birds, too. Maybe the fresh air gets them off or something. There was this one Englishman who went rushing out to the river bare-ass, just wearing tennis shoes and a polo shirt. I couldn't believe it. Too bad there weren't any big horseflies around."

Like his guiding peers, the twenty-five-year-old Kneib is suspicious of his clients' claims of being ardent conservationists.

"They pay lip service to ecological philosophy, paying membership dues to Trout Unlimited and other groups, but they'll sometimes have little dollar signs in their eyes, with visions of subdivisions and prime real-estate development property, as they float along. The outdoors is where they come for a couple of weeks a year. It's the indoors and the money that really attract them."

If these new guides have any unifying ideological principle, it's a strong commitment to their natural environment. "A lot of the men who started guiding thirty, forty years ago, when things out here were virginal, haven't really noticed the changes. The pollution and development has happened slowly, not dramatically, but it's more obvious to us newcomers," said one. Though many, like Kneib, consider themselves apolitical, none minces words when it comes to the mountains and rivers all of them have come to love. They have little patience when it comes to what they consider the hypocrisy of the traditional sportsmans' groups, run mainly by and for the upper economic classes.

"Rich liberals want to save the fisheries out here," says Pearson, "but they also see the 'necessity' of tearing up the northern plains for coal to power their electric toothbrushes. They understand the problem, but are too hooked on the system to fight. Old-line conservationists, in groups like Trout Unlimited and the Fly Fishing Federation, push for smaller creel limits and for catch and release programs, and I think that's a good thing, but they don't need the meat. They can afford that minor ethical luxury. Overfishing a river doesn't ruin it. It just makes the average size of the trout smaller. The profit motive is what wipes out a river. Subdivisions along a river bank are a middle-class phenomenon, and traditional conservationists don't condemn that kind of private property."

Radical ideas? Maybe. And since most of the other guides working the

Madison River are conservatives, if not actually reactionaries, doesn't Pearson get a lot of flack?

"No, not really. I'm younger than the other guides, so maybe they figure it's okay to be outspoken when you're young. They're not real friendly toward me, but they're not unfriendly either. We sometimes sit around in the Longbranch down in Ennis and down a few beers, but the only politics we talk are environmental ones. They know I'm on the left, but what we have in common is a fear about the future of the Madison, and they're just as worried about that as me. The people around here will listen to just about anything if it makes sense and might help save the river. Without the trout and the tourist fishermen, Ennis and the whole river would economically dry up and blow away. We're all going to have to work together at some level for our common survival."

Eighty miles away in southeastern Idaho, twenty-three-year-old Jerry Seimes paddles his canoe across the lower end of the softly gliding Henrys Fork of the Snake River, perhaps the best piece of light dry-fly fishing water open to the public anywhere in the country. He guides mostly on the Ranch, as a five-mile stretch of the spring-fed river, owned until this year by the Harriman family of New York, is known nationally. Outdoor writers have been publicizing the Ranch heavily, and anglers from around the country flock here to test their technical skills in fooling the at times ultra-wary rainbows that can easily range up to five pounds.

Seimes has been meticulously working Henrys Fork for six years now, and knows its nuances better than almost anyone else. It's tough fishing, and there's a premium put on being able to present a tiny fly imitating whichever one of its many mayflies is hatching from the rich water. It's a sort of Princeton Institute of Advanced Thinking for fly anglers, and most newcomers come away empty-handed, wearing piscatorial dunce caps.

The chunky trout are dimpling the surface as they feed on a tiny trichorydes mayfly, locally known as a black-and-white, but Seimes suggests I put on a cinnamon ant pattern.

"I'm from Winona, Minnesota. My father's foreman of an iron-pressing factory there. I have a degree in drama and speech from the state university, but I've always been into fishing. There's pretty good brown-trouting in Minnesota, but nothing like Henrys Fork."

We're approaching a house-sized boulder along the far bank of the river. He points at a small indentation in the rock where it's undercut.

"That's one of the few places on the Ranch where the rainbows both feed and live. Mostly the fish hide out in one place and travel into the current to feed. Lots of ants fall in from the boulder. Trout love to eat them. Maybe it's the formic acid."

The water is high this season and it's hard for me to spot the small fly on the surface from forty-five feet, especially since I've forgotten my Polaroid sunglasses which cut the glare so well. But Seimes acts as binoculars for me. The eyesight of most guides is amazing, but of course they have to train themselves to know when a fish has hit when their clients don't. It's part of the job.

"Strike," he says.

I miss. He shrugs.

"Cast at that second niche, ten feet farther down."

I do, and almost instantly I'm into a solid rainbow that Seimes tells me was around twenty inches after it easily snaps the 6X tippet, which has a two-pound breaking point.

"I think the social relationships on Henrys Fork are different than on the big rough rivers like the Madison. This is a much more intellectual kind of fishing and the kind of clients I get are much more technically oriented, or at least think they are. Sometimes I spend a couple hours trying to get into position to cast to one big fish. Patience is more of a virtue here."

We're floating lazily downstream again, and I'm idly casting a trichorydes imitation at the smaller fish.

"What I like to do is teach my clients the practical applications of the various theories of fly fishing that are effective here. Despite what some of the experts say, there are lots of different techniques—dry flies, nymphs, terrestrials like the ant and even big streamers that will take fish. There's been too much of an emphasis on fly pattern lately and not enough on basic angling skills."

I hook an eight-inch rainbow that's as unexcited about the process as I. From a healing cut on its lip, the fish has obviously been caught and badly released before.

"Yea. This place has lots of social prestige for some anglers. I see lots of one-upmanship. The kind who sit around reading all the books on fly fishing and think they know everything about fishing. Their theory has outrun their practice."

I nod in agreement. Sometimes the talk in Henrys Fork Anglers, a fly shop near the Ranch, sounds like an old-fashioned Mass, with fashionably dressed anglers dropping the names of various and sundry insects in staccato fashion.

Seimes had a card made up that reads, "Jerry Seimes, Gillie."

"It's serious and a joke, too. Gillies were the fishing servants of the old upper-class English fishermen, and I'm a sort of manservant to upper-class anglers, too. But I've really enjoyed the role so far."

Seimes is as close to a perfectionist as any guide working anywhere, knowing the literature of the sport, the tackle, the techniques, and has even had some success as a tournament caster, a separate but not equal skill. However, he doesn't know how much longer he'll guide.

"Being a professional takes something out of it for me. I love the world of fly fishing, but when it's your bread and butter it loses some of the excitement. The relationship between me and the fish is mediated by the financial aspects of it."

Unlike the previous generations of guides, the newcomers have mixed feelings about spending their lives as guides, agreeing with Seimes's complaint that it can taint the sport. It isn't an original complaint, however. Around the turn of the century John Waller Hills, a British angler-author, warned against making a living from angling for the same reasons that Seimes outlined. But of course it was easier for Hills to make such pronouncements since he was independently wealthy, like most English anglers with access to the better waters of the Isles.

"It's a great job for at least a few years," says Pearson, who has a political science degree and was accepted to law school a couple of years back, but opted for the river instead. "Fly fishing is a nonexploitative pursuit and I'm living what I consider the good life out here, even though most of my dudes wouldn't agree."

He, his friend Karen and three other people share a homestead first settled in 1868 in the dramatic hills rising above the river. They raise whatever vegetables they can during the short growing season and swim in the spring-fed ponds that fleck the leased property.

"Lifestyle," he says. "That's the key to why I'm here. We eat the whitefish we catch and have smoked at forty cents a pound, and they pay four ninety-five a pound in New York. Friends from around the country are always dropping in for visits and we have pretty much everything we need, a stereo, a radio and no TV. Most of the stuff that people spend their lives accumulating is jive."

But he worries about the ominous sign of rich newcomers who are starting to buy up the fifty-mile-long valley, posting No Trespassing signs on the property they may visit only two weeks a year.

"When I float wealthy people, potential absentee landlords who show interest in locking up a hunk of the Madison, I try to scare them away. The winters are murder, the bears are vicious and the rednecks will get you with the rifles in their pickups. Worse comes to worse, I tell them, the Hebgen Lake dam is going to burst during the next earthquake and wipe everything out, including real estate values."

It's for sure that Pearson, Kneib and Seimes won't ever make enough money from their guiding to buy up any of their favorite rivers, even if they were philosophically inclined to do so.

The economics of guiding are pretty blunt. Many of the older guides in the area who have become successful, such as Bud Lilly and Pat Barnes, two ex-schoolteachers from the Gallatin Valley, have made it basically because of the well-stocked tackle shops they've opened and the reputations they've nurtured over the past decades. Loyalty to a particular guide is common among clients—unless they get skunked too often. But the hassle of running a small business isn't everyone's idea of blissing out in post-Horatio Alger America, and none of the young guides wants a future sitting behind a counter dealing dry fly dope.

Pay for guides can vary tremendously, depending on how their operation is organized. Since most trip contacts for newish guides come through tackle shops, guides try to attach and ingratiate themselves with one or more of the better outlets in the area.

It usually costs a dude around $75 to go out on either a float trip or a walking excursion to a river or lake. Two people are usually nicked about $100, and a third ups the ante to $125. That doesn't sound too bad, but some of the shops that do the arranging take twenty percent or more for arranging things. The fishing season at best runs from Memorial Day to slightly past Labor Day, and except for the really elite guides, you don't have customers every day. Beginners may just have a client or two a week and longish periods of economic drought as well. There are lots of cancellations because of nasty weather and the like, and ever-increasing God-awful expenses.

"I'm lucky," says Pearson. "I work mostly out of Ed's Tackle Shop in Ennis and the owner, Ed Curnow, is a good guy. He doesn't take anything for the setups. I can make between twenty-five hundred and three thousand for the season, but out of that comes the regular small expenses—gas, lunch, fishing equipment and the big items like my boat, trailer and four-wheel-drive Toyota Land Cruiser, which I need to get around in the back country.

Most river guides favor the big McKenzie boats, made either of wood or fiberglass. They're the safest craft and the best to fish from on the roughest rivers, where an inexperienced dude could topple a canoe or tear a hole in a raft. The boats can cost as much as $1,200 stripped, and $1,600 equipped with such goodies as a casting station, extra-comfortable seats and a storage bin. Seimes can get away with a canoe for much of his work on the Henrys Fork, but it is a smooth river without much danger. Big rafts like the ultra-expensive Avons, which cost as much as a McKenzie, are used on the Smith River by Kneib, but they only have a life expectancy of a few seasons before the rubber gets a little shaky.

"It's getting to be an expensive business to get into," says Kneib.

Over the past few years some big-time outfitters have set up on some rivers, hiring equipmentless guides at a salary of thirty-five dollars a day or so to handle their customers. Those high-rollers use mostly very young apprentice-level guides who don't have the capital or contacts to set themselves up as independent entrepreneurs.

Insurance is another problem for the guides interested in protecting their equipment. "Last year I took out a policy on my boat," says Pearson. "It was cheap. About thirty-five bucks for the season. Three days later I was starting to run the Alberton Gorge on the Clark Fork. It's probably the roughest piece of water in the state. The boat just crumpled. My two passengers got tossed out and made it ashore. I got swept down eight miles, four after my life jacket got torn off. I don't know how I survived. My body temperature was eighty-eight degrees when they got me to the hospital. The insurance company didn't want to pay off. It was a real battle before I got my money, and then they cancelled me immediately. Now I'm on my own like the other guides."

Despite the difficulties of making ends meet, these angling Natty Bumppos don't want to take big game hunters out in the fall.

"They're a bunch of losers," says Kneib. "Drunks who get mean and crazy when they haven't killed anything. I love to hunt but on my own, away from anything else human."

Pearson, who did a little guiding for out-of-state elk hunters, agrees. "I quit after the first group. They were strip miners from West Virginia. Big executives who wanted to treat everything in the hills like it was a piece of bituminous coal. Very crazy guys. I thought I'd wind up getting shot before it was all over. I don't need that kind of grief. Big game hunting attracts the weird types.

"Fishermen are weird, too, but in a harmless way. I think the kind of person who hires a guide has changed some. This year I took out a guy who described himself as an ex-beatnik. He told me wild stories about Jack Kerouac and the old days in San Francisco. But now he's relatively rich and guilty. I also took out this young flashy guy and his buddy. He said he owned a National Hockey League team and lots else. They had enough coke on them to get the entire Madison Valley ripped and busted, but had a good time fishing. I don't see how they could even find the river. I think this new kind of dude is looking for a guide hip enough to appreciate him. I don't think it would amuse the old-timers around here to take out coke-sniffing, dope-smoking customers. It'd blow their minds."

Pearson points out that the trend in the Ennis area has been from local guides who grew up on the river, learning everything about its moods and secrets in the process, to traveling professional angler-guides who come in just to make money and do some fishing. "We have college basketball coaches, dynamite blasters and every other sort guiding down here this year. They just take a few months off from their regular jobs to work the Madison. They don't have the same sense of place about the Madison or Montana that we do. The West is our home full-time, not just for the summer. For them it's just a healthy, outdoorsy job."

To a degree far heavier than on other rivers, the Madison River guides have a very rigid hierarchy, ranging from the old-timers who've been working it for as long as fifty years to newcomers like Pearson. The guides have to acknowledge their place in the guiding universe, but with the right contacts they can rise quickly, with accompanying esteem in the post-fishing bull sessions. The prospect doesn't excite Pearson very much.

Like the emperor's new clothes, the ultracompetitive aspects of fly fishing are a well-known secret, a residual macho element from the old days that won't go away. Many guides break their butts trying to get their often incompetent dudes into as many big fish as possible, cashing in on the rewards with more clients and big tips. This is something else Pearson doesn't get too excited about.

"I took out these two rich wheat farmers from Kansas during the salmon–fly hatch. You know, those huge stone flies that get every big fish in the river moving when they emerge. I gave the guys my regular catch–and–release rap. How trout were too valuable a natural commodity to only be caught once. 'Screw that,' they said. They were paying me one hundred bucks and were going to damn well fill their cooler with dead fish carcasses. I knew it was going to be lots of trouble as soon as we pushed off from Varney Bridge. Huge browns were rising everywhere. Anybody, living or dead, could have caught their limit of ten. I was real polite to them. I even tied their flies on, but I must have been shaky or something. The knots I tied kept on breaking off for some reason, and I had a lot of trouble controlling the boat when they had fish on. They hooked a couple dozen fish but only landed two to take home, probably for fertilizer or something."

He smiles and reminisces some more.

"Yea. This is a strange business. This dude from the East drank a beer and threw the can into the river. I caught up with the can, grabbed it and beached the boat, then read him the riot act about littering. He really looked guilty, like I was going to pop him or something. About an hour later he ate an orange and threw the skin on the bank. I didn't say anything, figuring it would rot, but he must still have been stinging from my lecture. 'Don't worry, son,' he said, 'orange peels are biodetergible!' Environmental consciousness comes hard for most Americans."

Kneib gets as much pleasure convincing people to throw fish back as does Seimes, though the creel limit on Henrys Fork is much tougher than on Montana waters, where the Fish and Game Commission still believes it's the nineteenth century and the buffalo herds are on the other side of the hills. None of the guides has any real objection to someone keeping a fish or two to eat, but what they hate is the waste of fish that symbolizes the waste of resources that has characterized this country for 200 years.

And so they guide and earn a modest living trying to teach understanding and appreciation of a relatively untouched world to a mostly wealthy clientele who live suburban and urban lives, alienated spiritually and physically from the vacation paradises they visit for a week or two a year.

"I'm basically a loner," says Kneib, "and sometimes the work drives me up a tree with frustration, but if I have to guide to stay outdoors I will. No oil company is in my future."

Seimes says the same thing in different words. "Henrys Fork is my home river and I like that concept. Being able to observe a single river day in and day out during all its moods is a special sort of pleasure for me, and that's why I guide. I could make money other ways, but this way I've been able to spend six years on Henrys Fork."

Pearson likes to tell the story of the beer company executive who was floating the river with him, drinking a goodly quantity of his company's product as they went. The beer was being nationally boycotted because of its Pleistocene labor practices. Pearson repeatedly turned down the client's offers of a can. As the day proceeded, the guy began giving him strange looks as a hint of what the rejection was about dawned on him. "You're not part of that stupid boycott, are you?" he asked. Pearson grinned and nodded. "Out here? You're spending your life on this beautiful river away from all that political crap and you're boycotting beer? It doesn't have anything to do with you!"

"You're wrong," Pearson said. "As beautiful and isolated as this place seems to you, it's part of the real world with all of its problems, and if we don't treat all of it as one interconnected thing, neither this river nor anything else will be around much longer."

That's why the young guides are here. They accept that they're part of the real world, but they're still far enough out of the mainstream to get a nicer, more relaxed view than any of their urbanized peers, scrambling to get somewhere, will ever have.

CHARLES F. WATERMAN

For better or worse, fishermen read a great deal, and some of their cherished works would have received stock rejection slips if produced about any other subject. Fishing writers deal with a rather small corner of the world's works, and probably aren't being followed by Pulitzer scouts.

Anglers' sunrises are represented as more brilliant than those seen by milkmen or grain-combine operators, but no matter how gaudy the prose, a great many fishermen will accept it because it's *their* sunrises good old So-and-So is reporting. The more familiar the subject, the more the joy.

There are some wonderful nuts-and-bolts fishing writers; for that matter, fishing-tackle catalogs can be pretty interesting too. It may be harder to learn fishing than writing, and maybe there's more luck in the latter.

There are a few real authors who just happen to be fishermen, and I'd probably read their stuff if the subject were glass blowing or soil analysis, neither of which interests me very much. And if one of them happens to be doing a subject I'm interested in, I've struck it rich.

Frank Woolner can steer his typewriter from a New England hillside to a European red deer crossing a foggy road, and I shall follow him willingly, but if a plain nuts-and-bolts recorder did that, I'd swear he was just getting off the subject. Russ Chatham and Charles Dickey might stick some sociology into their fish biology, and I'd go along. Roderick Haig-Brown holds me on a tight drag, although I keep telling myself I don't see anything special about what I'm reading, thus proving I'm a novice analyst of such things.

No matter how yellowed the pages, Izaak Walton can't keep my attention. Washington Irving was better than a green hand with colorful copy, but when he tried to write fishing stuff, he bombed. There is a lip-curling term among those who labor in the outdoor-writing trenches—"me-and-Joe stories."

That simply means straight narrative of experiences, sometimes cute, generally with close friends. When I read something by a me-and-Joe writer and find a bit of real color in it, I am instantly jealous, because he's not supposed to know about such things and is out of his classification. Ray Bergman did me-and-Joe with a flair, and I think it's more than years that make people collect his works.

There are a few outdoor writers who refuse to be literary, saying they get paid just as much for straight stuff typed fast without a second copy. Of course, it is a shock to find one of them has turned out a perceptive novel I can't understand.

There are a number of what I call "trout writers," most of whom come from cultured backgrounds I have never visited, and nearly all of whom reach poetic heights with angling trivia. I won't name them because I refuse to be faced tomorrow by one of them I have negligently omitted. There are about a dozen and they're good at their thing, although some non-trout-fishermen would say much of their stuff is mawkish.

Some of the world's great authors on other subjects are fishermen on the side, and when they drop in a page or two of it they do a wonderful job. I always wonder how they'd be on a straight fishing piece, but I probably won't find out. Could they handle 3,000 words of bluegills or bullheads?

For example, Hemingway's offshore fish were supermonsters to be challenged by supermen. Smaller fish, to him, were incidental to more important things. He dealt with the bigger things of life and death, and it is probably tougher to make a mark with yellow perch. Anyway, it makes me feel better to think so.

Some "straight" writers on fishing subjects must be either experts or charlatans, a requirement dispensed with for literary souls. When I was peddling my first efforts years ago, I listened jealously to praise of a well-known author of fishing stories.

"But can he really fish?" I probed.

The answer covered it all.

"Who the hell cares?"

OZARKS AND TIME PASSING

The two men didn't talk very much and every day they built another johnboat and painted it dark red like an Ozark barn. When the paint had dried they put a chain on the bow of each and slid it into the James River at Galena, Missouri. The planks soon swelled tight and the boat was ready to run the river and come back on a flatcar.

There were green johnboats, too, but the first ones I saw were barn red, and I assumed that was the true johnboat color. It was more than fifty years ago, and the origin of the boat's name was already forgotten. I asked an Ozark kid of my own age why they called them "johnboats," and he said he wasn't sure but he had an uncle named John and maybe that was the reason. I doubt it.

Those flatboats were pretty simple. There was no raised transom for an outboard motor in those days, nor any oarlocks; just a board seat in the stern for a paddler and another in the bow, more to hold the boat together than to sit on, I suppose. They nested together pretty well, piled on flatcars and then on trucks in later years.

They still make johnboats in the hills, but nowadays they're mostly aluminum and fiberglass, and factories smelling of resin and paint turn out glossy bass boats that run fifty miles an hour. They would have been apparitions on the old James River. The new bass boats flash across the big impoundments and study the bottoms with clicking, whirring things—they show the old and silent riverbeds where the johnboats slipped along half a century ago. The big lakes are lined with resorts and homes today; but then, except for the occasional town, there were only a few houses along the old rivers, most of them presiding over little rocky hill farms.

The first of the White River dams I saw was the Taneycomo at

Forsyth, downstream from Branson, and even fifty years ago there were resorts there. Tour boats would show you the lake, with everything named after characters from Harold Bell Wright's *Shepherd of the Hills*, which had its setting there. Now there's a Dogpatch, U.S.A., a little farther south in Arkansas, with characters from much later literature.

The big johnboats were sluggish under homemade paddles of the mountain men who guided them down the smallmouth rivers for a day, a week or even more at a time, but they rode the rapids softly, taking the steep waves below the "shoals" in measured thumps. There were two casters to a boat, seated on folding canvas chairs, and the guide on his burlap cushion of spare clothing, with room even for a modest sideswipe with a short rod.

A few of the guides fished themselves, and their choice of stubby tubular-steel bait casting rods—sometimes less than three feet long—evidently began with the convenience of laying the weapon aside quickly when the paddle needed attention. Sportsmen in khaki might use split bamboo, but a hill-country guide in bib overalls and felt hat used short tubular steel, and so did kids who mimicked him. "Takapart" found its way into the names of some of the reels to emphasize their simplicity, and well into the thirties many did not have level wind. I recall admiring the Meisselbach "Takapart," but my own reel was a Shakespeare Precision. Braided silk was the plugging line of vacationing float clients—smooth-casting, but needing to be dried after use. The guides and I used crochet thread, which seemed to work about as well and cost much less.

There was no doubt about the favorite bait casting lure along the James and White rivers. For years it was the Peck's feather minnow, referred to simply as "Black Peck" or "Yellow Peck." It had a spinner in front of a weighted head and a long feather body, often with a pork rind attached to the single big hook, or the occasional trailer hook.

I still have an old Tom Thumb casting plug, a fast-wiggling little diver with metal "lips" both front and rear, and when I first began fishing on James River, it was second to the Pecks' in popularity. The fly fishermen used the Callmac bass bug, the Tuttle's devil bug, Tuttle's mouse and feather minnows like the Wilder-Dilg.

News traveled fast among river fishermen, even if its interpretation was questionable. One evening, two float boats came downstream to Galena, both with heavy strings of smallmouths, one of them a four-pounder, and all but that one fish were caught on the Yellow Peck. The big one was caught on a Black Peck and the general store at Galena sold out of Black Pecks the next morning. Those river smallmouths run bigger in memory than in fact, and I am surprised that the yellowed snapshots show them so small.

I was not an Ozark boy. I was raised on a flathead farm in southeastern Kansas almost 100 miles away, but an unreasoning passion for the river began during a family vacation there, with the Model T Ford and white canvas tent, sightseeing in the "mountains."

I was less than ten years old, but I had a craze for fishing, not just a healthy love for the outdoors but an obsession that has lasted until after I should have grown up and accepted more productive pursuits. My father did not fish, but tolerated my weakness regretfully, and was ashamed that I would somehow get back to the James River during much of school vacation when I should have been helping with the farm work. I was ashamed, too, but I must use the word "obsession" again. I slept on the riverbank and cooked poorly balanced meals over an old stump soaked in kerosene.

I had taken very few real river floats with guides, but I soaked up the river scene and fished mostly alone, wading in overalls and casting the Peck and the Tom Thumb, or struggling for half a day upstream with a johnboat to enjoy an hour of bliss floating downstream like the vacationing businessmen. I would cast frantically as I drifted, reeling too fast most of the time so that no inch of water would be wasted. That was in the late twenties, and it wasn't until the thirties that I used a fly rod much.

All of the smallmouth rivers were fickle. In spring, when most of the heavy rains had finished and the water, still cool, began to clear, there would be times of excellent fishing. Low, warm water could turn the fishing poor in midsummer, and guides would paddle continually in the slow stretches, and would often have to drag and shove the loaded johnboats over the gravel bars. With fall came the reddened oaks, flocks of ducks that flared over a float boat as they came upon it suddenly in a river bend, and energetic bronzebacks with enmity for Pecks and Tom Thumbs.

The smallmouths were "black bass," and the largemouths caught in sloughs off James River and in the slower, wider parts of White River below, where the James emptied in, were called "linesides." The occasional walleyes were "jack salmon" and the rock bass were "goggle-eye." Many years later when I returned to the rivers I found the small-mouths called "brownies."

Once, as a reward for some now-forgotten high school triumph, my father paid for a full day's float with a guide, downstream from Galena, and went along to watch, not knowing that I had become a better caster than most guides. I'd worked at it harder and longer.

I had not slept the night before and was suffering nerve-wracking anticipation. When the boat actually began to slide downstream and plopped over the steep "shoal" with the big boulder just below Galena, I somehow managed to produce a mammoth backlash, a supertangle I can still see, and prodded it helplessly with quivering fingers while the guide threw his lure over shadowy chunk rock and against willowed banks. I had no spare reel and I heard the guide land two fish and remark condescendingly that I could use his outfit, while my father asked if he could help me. It was a long time before I untangled the mess, my parent's worried sympathy hanging over me like a rain cloud, and it now seems incredible that such a little mishap could be so important. All that expensive fishing time lost was catastrophic, and when I finally straightened in my canvas chair the sweat of humiliation ran down my neck—but it was then that I saw the muddy creek pouring in from the right. It had rained the night before somewhere back in those hills, and the creek water boiled into the James River, leaving a sharp line where it met the clear river current and turned downstream.

For some reason I had neither a Peck nor a Tom Thumb on my line—but whatever the forgotten reason, the choice of a jointed Pikie minnow had been made with deliberation. I threw it at the juncture of bright river and muddy creek, and the big smallmouth came storming up and took it crosswise in his jaws, lunged in a half-jump and went down in clear water where I could see his gyrations, a blur of twisting fish and flashing plug, distorted by curling currents. When he was in the boat my confidence came back.

And then I could do no wrong, the plug breaking the little eddies above the shoreline rocks and against the drowned willows, the gentle bulges over the upthrust boulders and the foamy vees of undecided water at the edge of the rapids. The burnished fish came out from underwater shadows in quick streaks, sometimes in twos and threes. They sometimes turned about the plugs before they struck. I remember them much larger than they must have been.

"He casts just as good as I do," the guide said, and then admitted he had been keeping score.

Then, "He puts it up there against the bank better than I do," he conceded, and although the guide was a mediocre caster, I can recall no greater angling triumph. It is true that he used the paddle a bit, but the day's score was so one-sided, I'm sure I would have caught more fish, even if he had cast full-time. And my father, who had suffered through my fishing addiction, could see I had at least become reasonably proficient at a game the niceties of which had never before occurred to him.

But when the day of glory had ended and I was back splashing the side channels and tugging on waterlogged johnboats, priding myself in my casting of three-eighths-ounce lures, I met a wading hill-country boy with a great string of smallmouth bass he had caught on a gigantic "Dowagiac" torpedo plug with five big trebles and two spinners and twenty-five-pound line on his Montgomery Ward reel. I doubt if I ever equaled that catch.

It was the long float trips that made the Ozark rivers famous, the parties made up of several fishermen. There might be a commissary boat as well, to carry the camping gear and cook, going mushily with little freeboard. The man with the commissary rig would paddle on through and set up camp on a high bar, ready for the guests' comfort when they arrived in late afternoon—a procedure that was still followed much later when most of the fish to be caught might be rainbow trout. For the charm of floating remains in the hill country, changed though it may be by engulfing progress, the rivers shortened by great impoundments painted like blue dragons on Missouri and Arkansas maps.

But in those days of fifty years ago there was instant wilderness when the boat rounded the first bend. The home landing was probably a little town, mostly unpainted, but with a false-fronted store or two and a neat church, the streets of gravel and generally tilted. And if the float began in early morning, there would probably be mist on the river, so that a cat-fisherman running his trotline or limb lines might seem suspended in dark silhouette as the boats went by. Some said the fishing wasn't good until the mist cleared, but it wasn't always true.

Later generations of float fishermen would frequently see whitetail deer at the water's edge, but when I first went to the rivers there were few deer in the hills, and I never saw one on James or White river then. There were nesting ducks in spring, gray squirrels in the oaks, and barred owls to startle a kid under a tarpaulin at night. Always there was the wood smoke as there is today, sometimes in faint blue wraiths through the valleys.

Although their presence was not obvious to a man engrossed in casting a plug or fly rod streamer, the hill folk lived near the rivers, if not on their banks, and the rocky roads strayed from cabin to cabin. Here and there would be a steep trail coming down to the river and probably some kind of boat, often a sort of caricature of a johnboat. At evening there might be the sound of an axe in some unseen clearing and, inevitably, the call of a hound. Later, the tired fisherman in his blankets might hear the rising and falling tones of a distant coon pack, crossing ridge and hollow, and the next thing he sensed would be wood smoke, coffee and bacon, with the mist on the river not yet burned through by the sun.

Float fishing became big business and some of the companies were famous. Perhaps the best known of all was the Jim Owen outfit at Branson, and I sent Jim Owen the first angling telegram I ever wrote—carefully counted words to learn how the fishing was—and I can quote his answer:

> *River high but catching some fish.*
> —JIM OWEN.

Almost everyone tries to go back and no one will admit that things are better, for always something has been lost. I fished Lake of the Ozarks when it was new, and after I had caught some largemouth bass, a smallmouth took the popping bug against the shoreline and went deep, then to be netted by a St. Louis surgeon named Tremaine who could cast and paddle a canoe with hardly a pause at either.

A world war later I went back to Galena after many of the dams were built, and I could not find the place where I camped below town, near "Mighty" Barnes' service station. I was not sure of the spot where Charley Barnes, the famous guide, let me help him with a trotline.

Then, when most of the familiar rivers down in Arkansas had been backed up, I floated the Ouachita and the Buffalo for bass. I caught trout below a dam or two, but I always felt hill rivers should have smallmouths instead. Then, the last time I returned, I tried to get back the whole thing.

It was one of only a few uncrowded smallmouth stretches left, and I would do it in the grand manner, I decided. There was no big boat company there, but I found a man with a johnboat, even if it was made of plywood and smaller than the old ones, and I found a guide who had been very drunk for several days. I wondered if he could paddle all day, but he did, while I waved a fly rod from dawn until dark. I caught some bass and a great many sunfish, and I don't know if the fish were as a big as those of my youth or not. That night the man who owned the johnboat picked us up in a shiny truck, but somehow I guess I had expected a snorting old Model T, or even a mule with a flatcar. I was very tired, and it struck me like a blow that I was fifty years old—and even that was quite a few years ago.

Of course, there are float trips today and perhaps they are better, for the equipment is, and those who float on their own are partial to canoes. And since most of the bass rivers have been swollen into reservoirs, I am sure there are more bass than there ever were when I cooked over the old stump. Many of the old cabins with rough stone fireplaces are long drowned, along with the rocky roads that led to them, and the people who build homes along the lake shores wouldn't have room for their bass boats on a mumbling little river.

And of course there were not enough bass for the thousands of later vacationers. Perhaps it was best to leave only some token stretches for the folks with canoes. I don't know if I'll go back or not.

FLY FISHERMEN!

I have observed fly fishermen for forty-four years and report herewith in the interests of research. Most of the names have been changed to protect the guilty.

By illustration, Jeff is running for Congress, and it would be a political stab in the back to use his real name since no true saltwater fly fisherman would vote for him after learning he uses an automatic reel; the fact he is a fly fisherman would lose him the spin-fishermen votes; and the nonfishing public would turn away after learning he fritters his time at angling. See?

There is nothing wrong with an automatic reel in many situations. It has considerable merit when fishing the South Florida canals, which is where Jeff uses it, but I think his is a prototype for the first experimental model. He can take it apart in the dark and frequently does, and even when it is running perfectly, its take-up sounds like a beach buggy stuck in a pile of scrap iron.

Jeff and I were fishing on the Florida Keys and, fishy-smelling and stained with salt water, we dropped into what we thought was a scruffy lunchroom for a hamburger. In the Keys you should be more careful than we were, because some of the fancier places disguise themselves and this was one. Busy lying to each other about fishing, we were seated in the center of the crowded dining room, wet pants and all, before I saw we were in the wrong place and an upswept French-type waitress with a little frilly apron had handed us menus the size of the table.

Jeff, who has the kind of voice a congressional candidate needs, supported by an unusual accent, never glanced at the menu but ordered a can of Three-in-One oil, and the waitress, who had big eyes anyway, scampered back into the kitchen for a conference. They'd probably already heard the order back there, because there had been dead silence from all the other patrons since we entered. Now there was a discreet scuffling of chairs as everybody shifted to see us better, and Jeff whipped out his original automatic fly reel, pushed back the orchid centerpiece and dismantled the thing on the tablecloth with the dexterity of a shell-game operator.

The only hitch was that the spring somehow tossed a small part on the floor, and Jeff pursued it on hands and knees under a nearby table, where he recovered it among a forest of nylons. He and the waitress got back to our table at the same time and she regretted there was no reel oil in the place, a surprise to Jeff, who said it was very unusual in pear-shaped tones that could have been heard on nearby U.S. Highway 1.

He announced calmly that he would repair his reel without oil, and proceeded to do so while everybody's lobster thermidor got cold. I do not recall what we ate but, restaurantwise, things were almost back to normal when Jeff finished the job and touched the reel lever for a trial run.

The old clanker howled, "Whuzzeeee-whap!"

Somebody dropped a dish of Key lime pie and there was a tinkle of falling silverware. I went outside and I guess Jeff paid the bill. He said the reel was fine again.

The Florida canals are a good location for a study of fly casters, and when you fish the roadsides you have to watch your backcast as it is easy to flip a leader around a convertible from Newark or a semi-trailer from Tampa. After years of practice you learn to throw a backcast through the traffic.

I misjudged some time back, when the snook were hitting small bait against the opposite bank and the wind made a low backcast necessary. I saw this station wagon coming at about sixty-five miles an hour and it was towing an outboard boat with motor attached. I decided on the spur of the moment that I could let the car by but, nevertheless, my backcast could be tossed over the boat. I never thought about the possibility of adverse air currents, and one of them sucked my line down and wrapped it around the motor. I've lost many a fly by similar errors, but that was the first time I got the *line* hung. There was about 150 yards of strong backing and I was unable to slow the station wagon.

In fact, I was unable to let go of the line that was playing through my hand, and if anyone tells you any fish goes as fast as a station wagon towing a boat, he's a damned liar. The reel thawed pretty badly, but I threw the rod and reel on the ground and jumped on them so the backing broke off at the spool. My hands were in bandages for a while.

If you happen to have that line, I can identify it. It is a bright-orange weight-forward No. 10 and there is a little blood on the running part.

I have learned a lot from canal fishermen, part of it by direct confrontation and part by peering through gaps in the saw grass.

When I was fishing beside a fellow we'll call Rocky, I noted that he was catching roughly eighteen fish to my one, although the snook were blasting wildly just across the narrow ditch. I asked him why and he said I had to throw the fly clear into the grass on the opposite side and pull it out past the fish, which he said were facing the grass and herding the bait against it. I did and started catching fish same as he did.

Next day I came back to the same spot and started in confidently, but I couldn't catch anything while Rocky was cleaning up again. Again I inquired.

"Hell, man, you gotta change things now," Rocky said. "The fish are facing this way today!"

Science.

Fly fishermen are primarily men of strong character and firm allegiance. I was fishing for spotted weakfish with a fellow we'll call Cuthbert, and his favorite fly was a frightening streamer he called the Purple People Eater. We were standing on a seawall and the small specks were thick, but Cuthbert wasn't doing too well. I'd caught eight fish on a popping bug, and as far as I could tell he hadn't had a bump on his pet dingus.

Finally he caught a single undersized trout and ran over to show it to me.

"Man," he said, "that old Purple People Eater sure gets 'em. Do you want to borrow one?"

Faith.

Another guy, whom I shall call Ted Smallwood, has special fishing methods. To make it interesting, we'll pretend he owns a fishing resort on the Southwest Florida coast.

He and I and a fine fly caster I'll call Buddy ran an outboard boat for twenty-some miles to a place where Ted said the snook were tearing it up in a mangrove creek. When we got there, the winds had changed the tide and water was so high it was impossible to cast back under the mangrove bushes where snook live.

I rowed and Buddy cast beautifully from the bow. Ted, who was in the stern, announced he would fish a little too, although he said he didn't care much about it, and since he didn't have his rod he would borrow the one I had been using. Since it was a sleek little 8½-footer belonging to my wife, and Ted doesn't exactly use a feather touch in salt water, I had some misgivings, but there wasn't much I could say.

Flipping his fly like a master, Buddy hadn't raised a fish, but Ted started catching them right away. He'd slam the streamer into the bushes and then yank it away with a lot of swamp-rat rhetoric, shaking the whole loosely attached shoreline. At first I though he was just dumb and awkward, but I finally realized the snook were coming out to see what was going on and would clobber Ted's fly. He was about as stupid as a shot–stung pintail drake.

I was about to tell Buddy what was going on when the boat slid over a network of sunken logs some twelve inches under the surface. As we passed them, Ted made a series of hangup jerks in the mangroves and a big snook rose silently from the depths of the log jam about seven feet from the boat and gave us a cold, delinquent stare. Ted dapped his streamer near the fish's nose and it disappeared in his mouth, whereupon Ted set the hook violently in what I figured was an impossible situation. But again the swamp fox thought he knew what he was doing.

Ted, who looks like an overaged Ram tackle, just lifted up on my wife's rod and hung on. His huge forearms bulged and the sweat ran down his nose. The leader tested twelve pounds and the whole snook weighed fourteen, but I don't know what his front eighteen inches would scale and that's the part Ted held out of the water until the snook gave up. The rod made funny creaking sounds but it never gave way. I dropped both oars over the side, and after Ted released the snook we went back to the dock.

My wife said there was something wrong with her rod.

"It must be softening up," she said. "It needs a lighter line than before." So she gave it away and got a new one.

An experienced fly caster can throw a reasonably good line with a hoe handle, but he invariably decides on a particular type of rod which he swears is better than anything else. Possibly it is a very short, stiff one and possibly it is a long, soft one that requires a tall fisherman to prevent the tip from dragging the ground.

Generally, the accepted test of a fly rod is how far you can cast with it. This is equivalent to judging a new sedan solely by its maximum speed, but fly fishermen are not ordinary people.

Now there was the salesman we'll call Hubert. He sold all kinds of fly rods, but he was hooked on one type—stiff as a poker and about the same length. He could do a good job with it, and carried on a perpetual demonstration on the lawn, in supermarket parking lots and at various fishing camps.

Though this rod had definite advantages, it was not a distance stick, an obvious fact Hubert refused to recognize despite all sorts of concrete proof. Such earnestness in fly fishermen is sometimes confused with pigheadedness.

Now one day Hubert wheeled his car up to a crowded fishing resort and staged a demonstration before a crowd of people who were interested in fly fishing and, since I happened to be present and had known him for a long time, Hubert invited me to try some of his rods.

Several models were already strung up, and I chose a medium-length job that would throw a line farther than Hubert's pet with no effort whatever. I took some pleasure in doing this, knowing all the time that Hubert could do the same thing if he'd just lay down his freak stick and pick up a more standard rod. The audience viewed Hubert as if he had just washed ashore, and walked back to their cottages.

But the next day he was back and somehow got a crowd of prospective customers together again. He then rounded me up and invited me to do some more casting with him. Figuring this cluck was a born patsy and maybe just a little stubborn, I consented, and when Hubert unlimbered his wading staff type of rod, I simply reached into his car and took out the same stick I'd used the day before.

Hubert laid out a fair length of line on the grass and, without moving it and in an unnecessarily loud voice, challenged me to equal his cast.

I tried but nothing happened. Overnight the creep had substituted a peewee-level trout line for the big saltwater taper the rod required. I looked about me but saw no sympathy in any face, so I walked away, leaving Hubert lecturing on the merit of his stub stick.

Crafty.

I went fishing with a fellow who said he thought he needed a new fly outfit. It was getting to be too much work, he said. Maybe he was just getting too old for fly fishing, he said, but he had trouble keeping his backcast up and wasn't getting sufficient distance.

We had a good spot to work for some rolling tarpon, so I slid the anchor over and got ready to cast from a stationary boat. My friend, whom we'll call Jack, was ready first, and just as I was about to work out some line, I hit the deck because of an unearthly noise that apparently came from nowhere.

The sound was a sort of whistling whirr, higher pitched than that of a low-level aircraft, but somehow mechanical and a bit unearthly.

I looked up at my companion, but he was placidly watching his bug. It would bear watching.

Although Jack wasn't so much as twitching his rod tip, his bug was leaping out of the water, buzzing about the surface and throwing little geysers. It went "putty, putty, putty," and it went "ploop, ploop, ploop!" and it gradually slowed to an occasional convulsion and lay still.

Jack picked it up and again came the whistling whirr over our heads, again came the cast and again the bug went, "putty, putty, putty," and "ploop, ploop, ploop!"

"What in God's name is that?" I quavered.

Jack didn't answer for a minute, because a small tarpon sizzled around the thing at high speed. He rolled wildly, bulged under the fly, splashed his tail on the surface and came to a quick halt, breathing hard, about three feet from the bug. The bug then gave one last ploop, flipped a few drops of water, quivered and lay still. The little tarpon spun around and darted up a tidal creek, leaving a distinct wake.

"Well," said Jack, "this bug is run by rubber bands. When I make my backcast the wings wind up and the bands get tight. Then when I throw it on the water the bug works all by itself, but it is kind of hard to cast and maybe that is my trouble."

I asked him if he had caught anything with it.

"Well, no," Jack said, "but it sure makes the fish act funny."

Dr. Clutch was a real whiz on spotted weakfish and he never talked a great deal about his methods, some of which were clinical in their approach.

Smitty ran a fishing-tackle store and a doggoned good one. He was a fine fisherman and a careful student of method, passing on helpful facts to appreciative customers. When Dr. Clutch came in and told Smitty the trout were hitting and he needed company on an impromptu fishing trip, Smitty was eager to leave the store to the hired help and get with it. Smitty figured he might learn something.

It was a bit sudden, so Smitty left the store in his blue suit with his fly rod under one arm and a plastic box full of streamers and popping bugs in his fist. It was to be a wading trip, and since Smitty didn't have his usual waders at the store, he grabbed a new pair of chest-highs out of stock.

The doctor had his mind on fishing and drove pretty fast with a sense of urgency. He loaded Smitty into his outboard boat and took off across the flats with the kicker singing the blues and hitting about every other chop.

Now the doctor's system of fishing for saltwater trout was to locate a nice patch of grass and go booming up to it in the boat. When a short distance away, he'd cut the throttle and the skiff would squat, pushing a big wake into the grass. The wave would stir up the hidden baitfish and some of them would dart out into the open, whereupon the trout would start swatting them. The doctor would by then be out of the anchored boat and laying a streamer fly among the busy fish. Good stunt, but he didn't explain it to Smitty.

Well, Doc zeroed in on a lush patch of grass while Smitty was sorting out his improvised tackle. The boat whizzed up to the right distance and Doc chopped the engine and bailed out in his waders with his fly rod in his hand in three feet of brackish water.

Smitty is not stupid. He figured the boat had caught fire and got out too—in his blue suit with his new waders under his arm.

Not everything is known about fly fishermen. As the researchers say, further study is indicated.

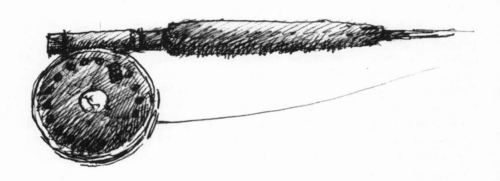

REEL CLIQUES AND
STIFF LEADERS

My bitterness about the harmless snobbery of trout fishing requires no detailed analysis. I believe it started with my near-failure in two Latin courses. At the time, I saw little use in a language that had failed to meet the competition and had died out on its own, and my barely-passing marks were acts of pedagogical charity.

Ironically, I nearly flunked Latin because I went fishing when I should have been studying. It never occurred to me that my angling life would be blighted by such a foolish choice. And although I have caught quite a few trout in the intervening years, I have never learned to hold up my end of the conversation where current trout anglers gather and invariably call bugs and things by Latin names. I visualize the system as a small pool of trout surrounded by a great wall of semantics.

I should have seen what was coming during my first day of trout fishing many years ago at Roaring River State Park in Missouri. Before meeting my first trout I had spent some years pursuing black bass with a fly rod, and in my early thirties I assumed trout were just fish with spots. In fact, I had read that biology held the bass to be a more advanced form of life than the salmonids.

Those were hatchery trout in Roaring River and there were great crowds for weekend fishing, the first casts being signaled by a gunshot at dawn. An old friend, Jack Gowdy, who had done some trout fishing in Michigan and a great deal at Roaring River, told me my best bet was to stand just below a tiny dam and cast a spinner and fly into the gentle boil before the opening shot had stopped echoing through the Ozark hills. Before daylight I could barely make out the freshly planted rainbows massed below the little dam, and when the shot came I got a pretty good one on the second cast, having missed my first strike. It was the only fish I caught all day and I put it on a chain stringer. As the light grew, I found I couldn't catch any more trout, so I turned away to find another spot, meeting the first fully equipped trout fisherman I'd ever seen.

Of course I'd seen pictures of them, but I had to stop and stare a little at the hat with all the flies stuck in it, the well-stocked vest and English waders, the leather-trimmed wicker creel and the varnished landing net. The man stared back at me and my stringer in disdain and said, "My God!" softly to himself. I stifled an impulse to stick a boot into his thick middle and rightly told myself that I was better equipped for bank-fishing than he was.

Fully equipped trout fishermen look funny to non-trout fishermen. I had hoped that the gaudy bass fishermen's jumpsuits with advertising patches would take the heat off, but waders and vest still lead the comedy parade for laymen. I'll tell you how I know.

While fly fishing for Florida shad (equivalent to spearing suckers, by most trout fishing tenets) I happened to wade into the St. Johns River with just what I'd wear and use while trout fishing. There was a steady parade of trolling outboard boats, and trollers have never learned that what they say to each other over their motor noise can be heard for a great distance. Anyway, although I took the first gibes gracefully, a few hours of X-rated remarks and dirty names got through my skin and I looked for a more private place to fish.

Although the names used could have been heard in almost any alley, the prevailing theme—and one I believe may be true—was that most people wearing such gear think they are better than other people.

The uppity demeanor of trout fishermen is in direct contrast to the approach of bass fishermen, who make considerable pretense of illiteracy, regardless of their educational background. A trout fisherman describes his prey as a "gleaming shard of crimson and silver." A bass fisherman says he hunts "hawgs" and hopes he can "gouge some of them big ole sows." There must be something in between.

Fly fishing for trout bubbles through a continuing turmoil of ethics, codes and cults, but these are largely a matter of semantics. I still think if you could couch dynamite caps in the correct terms that they might be acceptable. Take the dry fly and wet fly business. For many years the dry fly fisherman considered the wet fly fisherman little better than a seiner. Then some inspired soul fostered use of the word "nymph," and we had a whole new set of standards. For a while the nymph was respectable only if fished upstream, but that didn't last long. For that matter, a lot of dry fly fishermen turned around and started wading downhill.

Twenty years ago the Woolly Worm was not respectable, and I recall the wife of a purist dry fly man who referred to it by spelling it out.

"We never use those words in our family," she said.

Then, just when the nymph fishermen became accepted and started developing a select snobbery of their own, I went fishing with one of them. I was thinking in terms of nothing larger than a No. 16, but this fellow uncased his Leonard bamboo and tied on what looked to me like a Woolly Worm—with a sinker. Swish! Splut! He caught a big trout and explained to me that his nymph *did* resemble a Woolly Worm to some extent, but that he had tied it with some special hair, making it a nymph.

So then the nymph, however Woolly Worm-like, was highly respectable. And you could take a plain, ordinary wet fly, crop its wings a bit and call it a nymph and avoid stigma. Then Sylvester Nemes squared everything off with a book called *The Soft-Hackled Fly*. It is a fine book on wet fly fishing, but Mr. Nemes played it cool when he didn't begin with those words. He put everyone at ease, too, by explaining that a wet fly with very soft hackles breathes in such a way that it could be any one of a number of nymphs.

As a youth I recall reading about dropper flies and a "cast" of three wets, and I can quote faithfully. The author said, "but it is better to employ only two, and one is all the expert uses."

I read the other day that there is now going to be a return by the elite to more than one fly at a time. Since everything else has gone the limit, I foresee casts of flies that resemble trotlines—if the law allows. It may be that your skill will be measured by how many flies you can cast at once without snagging your waders, for today your prestige in some circles is gauged by the distance you can throw a sinking head.

At about the time I heard of the nymph being accepted as distinguished from a "wet fly," I began to hear a lot about the wizards of the Letort in Pennsylvania. That's a tough creek with some highly skeptical trout, and I think its masters are among the best fishermen in the world—but since mayflies (fill in the Latin name) haven't been too thick there, the Letort people started imitating ants, sow bugs and crickets. They had to come up with their own code of ethics because artificial crickets would be scorned on some waters. Charles Fox and Vince Marinaro are properly revered, but some of their flies don't fit the standards set on some waters.

Although the true resident fishermen of the Letort never upstaged me, I had been put in my place several times by satellite anglers who had found me grubbing along on less "hallowed," less "revered" and less "storied" waters of the provincial West. Twice, however, it was my turn to grin with leering satisfaction at the treatment given to "Eastern mastery."

The first time concerned a beautiful ant imitation which employed tiny bits of cork as flotation and which produced satisfying glugs from trout living west of the Mississippi. When I drew it on a paper napkin for the edification of a Rocky Mountain fishing peasant, he squelched me with the statement that he didn't want to hurt my feelings but that he "fishes only with feathers and hair."

The other triumph of the masses came when I fished my first day on the Letort and was using a Letort cricket, dry. I was standing on one of the little casting walks installed by Charles Fox and was about to give up, having slaved much of the day over various broad brown trout tails which waved at the edges of the Letort's fertile beds of vegetation. I had caught no fish and was about to give up on one I'd worked over for twenty minutes when I heard a splash at my elbow and, upon looking about, saw a brown trout heading back toward the bottom.

I did not cast to him because he was too close for that, but I got my rod turned around and dunked the cricket down so that it sank about three feet from my waders. The trout came back out of the slightly milky Letort depth, looking like an open mouth with fins. I saw a retarded gleam in his eye as he grabbed the sinking cricket in a rush. It is gratifying to know that such an idiot trout lives in the "fabled," "storied" and "revered" Letort.

In recent years I have noted that Arnold Gingrich must have been right. He wrote of the New York Anglers Club that " . . . the list of its members' writings would serve as a practical guide to the angling literature of its time and place with very few conspicuous or noteworthy omissions."

That's been quoted before, and whether the Easterners are the only capable trout writers or not, the "New York view" is about the only one that gets set down as "classic" trout writings. Many authors who have been successful in other fields have learned that the Easterners have a lock on acceptable trout literature, and since Easterners seem to be the principal readers of it, the publishers go along. I recall the nasty crack of a Westerner who said a two-foot stained-glass window in New York would get more editorial comment than a year of South Dakota sunsets.

And although the Eastern trouters (generally classed as "New Yorkers" by those from a bit farther west, regardless of where they actually live) keep saying that trout fishing has produced more fine literature than any other sport, I'm afraid that many a "classic" trout work might not be good enough to see print if written about something else, say, moonshining or clam digging.

I am sorry to note (having had that trouble with the language) that the Easterners are teaching Latin to Western fishermen. But the Westerners are entitled to it, having taught the Easterners to cast. The steelheaders were double-hauling and firing shooting heads for years before most Easterners had heard more than a rumor of such goings-on.

It didn't take immediately. Twenty years ago I heard well-known anglers say that the use of sinking lines was not fly fishing at all. Today I find quite a few bloody-eared Easterners learning to chunk leadcore.

Of course, the fly fishing aristocracy is not confined to the East, and I have heard California anglers who dropped names with sodden thuds along miles of streams from Colorado to Alaska. The "names" of fly fishing have no idea how many close personal friends they have.

Since the folks in the circles I move in tend to have redder necks, I know only a few Famous Fly Fishermen. But I have been pelted with their names by many anglers who could not cast thirty feet and who freely confused whitefish with grayling.

I did once happen to know one of the greats who was around a bend from me. And I was approached by a pair of well-equipped fishermen who said they were old fishing partners of his and asked if I knew where he was staying, as they wanted to see their old buddy. I was in a bad humor for some other reason, so I told them he was just around the bend and to come on, we'd go find him. Since they'd obviously never seen the guy in their lives, they simply fled in the other direction.

It is in equipment that snobbery is at its happiest (remember, I never said it was bad—just prevalent).

The automatic reel, which is a wonderful tool for small, brushy streams, keeping valuable line from ruination, simply doesn't belong with the old-school tie. I have here a plaintive letter from a young angler who wants to know what is wrong with his automatic. None of the great fishermen, he says, uses one. I am having a hell of a time answering him because where he fishes the automatic is hard to beat.

There's a revival of bamboo fly rods, many of the most expensive ones being sold to fishermen who would do just as well with green catalpa— but then I suppose some Ferraris get no farther than the supermarket. Bamboo has its rightful place in the lighter tackle, of course. But if you have a "storied," "revered" and "hallowed" name on it, the quality can be distinctly secondary and still bring a high price.

No one doubts the elegance and efficiency of bamboo in some spots, but there are some classes in which it is outdone by glass or graphite. I had nothing to say when a new heavy-duty bamboo model was demonstrated by its promoter, alongside glass taking the same size of line. The cheaper, lighter glass stick cast farther, easier and with better control—all of which the salesman conceded readily—but he said there were bamboo lovers who would prefer to suffer with the wood.

We inherited our dry fly fishing from Britain about ninety years ago, and shortly afterward the Americans built bamboo rods that wiped out the British sticks in all kinds of competition. But the magic of English equipment still clutches us. I once had a splash-on in a troutfishing movie and the producer made me borrow an English reel. More class, he said.

Although no one doubts the workmanship of the finest British reels, some of them are, frankly, a bit delicate. Drop one on a rock and it is through turning. And, frankly, a sloppier fit will stand more dirt and abuse. I have considered a lettered sign for my U.S. reel saying, "I have an English reel at home."

I am entranced by the rituals of rod testing performed by the elite in various tackle shops. I have observed the double-handed, horizontal whipping motions and the one in which the tip is pressed against the floor. I have been awed by the test in which the rod is laid on a counter and its vibrations counted after the tip is flicked. The results are reported in engineering terms with which I am unfamiliar.

I am planning a test which won't tell anything about the rod but is sure to get me recognized as a quality trout angler. I plan to put the rod across both of my shoulders back of my head, the way laborers in some foreign countries carry yokes with a bucket on each end. But I shall not hang buckets on the rod. I shall turn my head so that one ear is against the stick and then I shall reach out with one hand and flip the tip and listen intently to the rod shaft. In rehearsal I have not heard anything, but it sure looks scientific.

I know a dealer who is all for the various rod tests. He says that they don't have much to do with how a rod will fish, but that any rod which stands up under all that abuse can't be all bad.

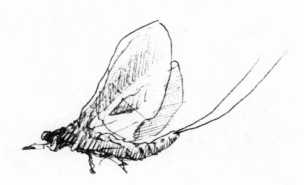

JIM HARRISON

I think it's generally ill-advised to make statements about something you love. Statements are for politicians and they are notoriously bad lovers, according to recent evidence. But here I am making a statement which I prefer to think makes me a bad lover rather than a politician. Fishing has kept me sane since I was five, a matter of thirty-four years, also an arguable statement in light of recent severe nervous breakdowns. But fishing has tried real hard. Recently I fished badly and with little energy in Michigan, Pensacola, Cozumel and Durango, Mexico. It goes in streaks. Often we fear serenity. We think it's going to make us die. The Japanese have always thought the fishermen, farmers and wood-choppers had a corner on serenity. The Chinese think so too, at least I can say so as they're off in a corner by themselves and aren't likely to complain. I agree with our brothers of the East. Few of us shoot our-selves during an evening hatch. Fishing makes us less the hostages to the horrors of making a living. In some Jungian (Carl, late of Switzerland) sense it returns us to the aesthetics of the ancient art of gathering and hunting our food. It is a time warp we may step into for a little peace. That's why there are so many churls and knaves in competitive forms of fishing. They don't know this. Most of them should be fishing bull gar with grenades. So much in our time makes one want to stand in a river or go to sea in a boat, notwithstanding the recently formed Gay Anglers Alliance of San Francisco. Fishing is the most wonderful thing I do in my life, barring some equally delightful unmentionables, and not disregard-ing gluttony and booze. It's in the top five.

A PLASTER TROUT IN
WORM HEAVEN

I admit I woke up grousing; a lick from my Airedale pup Hud, named Hud to offend all people of good taste, did little to improve my mood. I reached up to the radio from the floor where I must sleep forever, since a 1,000-yard tumble while bird hunting savaged my spine. A newsman was reporting the accidental death of Herb Shriner, my favorite boyhood comedian. A girl in New York City once told me I talked like Herb Shriner. It takes many generations of rural indigence to make a Herb Shriner voice, long evenings of pinochle around a kerosene stove trying to pick up Chicago on a ten-dollar radio. There was a light rain against the windows, and I thought of a statement once made by a statistics nut to the effect that Michigan receives less sunlight than any other state.

I walked out to the barn and tried to look at Lake Michigan—on a clear day, few though there may be, you can see over thirty miles, way out beyond the Manitou Islands. And the hills are conceivably full of the sound of music. Because of the obtuse presence of the media, I often think of myself as living within a giant, beautiful, scale-model cigarette commercial. I sang a few bars of "It's Great to Live in the Great Lakes Country." The landlord looked at me quizzically from a tool shed. I waved. No time for embarrassment. I was going to a festival.

There appear to be a lot of small hat sizes around here, I say to myself, perhaps unfairly, entering the hotel bar in Kalkaska (pop. 1,475). One learns to mistrust locations where even a good hamburger is not available. But the drinks are extremely large and cost only fifty cents. Getting drunk here would be punching inflation right in the nose. The man sitting on the stool next to me in the crowded room announces himself as a former marine.

147

"Once a marine, always a marine!" I reply, attempting to placate his obvious hostility. The same may be said of Harvard graduates. They simply never let you forget.

Then the marine says, "If you don't love it, leave it," quoting the great Merle Haggard tune and eyeing my rather trim Pancho Villa mustache. His lips are flecked and stained with one of those nostrums used to combat stomach acid.

"Leave what?"

"The U.S. of A."

"I *looovve* it," I say, rolling my blind eye counter-clockwise, one of the few skills I picked up in college.

"Damn ajax," he replies, drinking deeply. Beer drizzles down onto his faded fatigue shirt.

"Do you favor the cattle prod as a fishing weapon?" I say, taking out my little steno pad and turning to him on the bar stool. He shrugs and leaves.

I reflect on the pioneer spirit and how it made our country what it is, and the odious Bumppoism that emerges for events like the National Trout Festival. The slogan of this year's festival, the thirty-fourth annual, is "This Land Is Your Land—This Is My Country," which is typical of the sort of hysterical chauvinism and contradictory rhetoric one finds in rural hardhats. At Jack's Sportshop, where the fish in the contest are to be weighed in, flag decals are for sale. It brings back all those articles I've read in the past twenty years celebrating the sportsman as a modern conquistador:

WE FIST-FOUGHT HITLER'S LUST-MAD LUNKER TROUT

"It seems that I was asked to go up in the High Lonesome with Bob, Bob Sr. and Bob Jr., partners in a Dairy Whip—insurance—real-estate—kapok-flailing operation in a little town next to the Big Woods in our state. We left at dawn after a hearty breakfast of fresh country eggs, country flapjacks, country bacon and country toast, all washed down with many cups of hot black java. I sat in the back of the nifty camper with the three white police dogs that would be used to guard us against those terrors of the local woodlots, porcupines. The dogs were named Rin and Rin Tin and Rin Tin Tin to keep things simple. Next to a holstered .357, Bob Jr. wore a machete that he claimed made an excellent fish priest. We were towing a boat and an all-terrain vehicle and in addition had brought along four trail bikes, a dozen varmint rifles of various calibers, fishing gear and a case of good old snake bite medicine . . . yuk yuk yuk. . . ."

This might be called the brown-shoe-white-sock syndrome and is, I fear, the predominant attitude of fishing- and hunting-license buyers.

In what might be called the town square of Kalkaska, except that nearly all of the town is on one side and the railroad tracks are on the other, there is a statue. Not a Confederate general, a Union general, an Indian chief, a bronzed howitzer or a limp tank. It is a trout. I am told that it is a brook trout, and it is nearly twenty feet high. Curled and flexed, its enraged plaster strikes out of the smallish fountain at an imaginary giant fly, or more likely a worm dangling from worm heaven. Actually the fish looks like a cross between a smelt and a moray eel, or a sick alewife with a tinge of green creeping along the dorsal and the dread death spots beginning to appear.

But that is not the point. People passing on Route 131 may glance to the right and see the fish and muse aloud, "This is fishing country." The trout is continually bathed by water jets, but today there is a malfunction in the fountain. I cross the street with Cliff and Clint to see what's wrong. Clint Walter is to receive the Citizen of the Year award and is a benign and dedicated conservationist. Cliff Kimball is the president of both the festival and the Chamber of Commerce and is an unabashed booster. It seems the pump hole for the fountain is filling with water and if something is not done immediately the electric motor will short out. Cliff says it took a lot of pancake suppers to build this trout shrine. In small towns in Michigan, and probably elsewhere, pancake suppers, perch fries, ox roasts, chicken-gizzard barbecues, square dances and raffles are used to raise money for statues, PTA tea services, bank uniforms and school trips, like sending the senior class to Chicago or to Milwaukee on the *Clipper*. Anyway, the fountain is fixed after some tinkering. Emergency ended. The fountain will spray throughout the festival.

The fire whistle blows and Cliff and Clint hasten off, both members of the Volunteer Fire Department. The bandstand, with its red, white and blue bunting, is deserted. I climb up the steps and walk to the microphone. My chance! There is a crowd slowly assembling for what the program calls Youth on Parade, with floats, pets, clowns, bands and attractions. I feel like the dictator of British Honduras and have a dark desire to bray some nonsense, such as, "The trout on my left is rabid!" or "The war is over!" But I recognize my urge as literary and blush.

I spot a man I watched a week ago in Leland snagging steelhead with gang hooks, a custom a bit more stealthy and subtle—and popular—than old-fashioned dynamite or gill-netting. I could yell at the oaf and expose him, but then the point would be missed on the gathering crowd, which now numbers at least 200. Cliff mentioned that approximately 70,000 people would be here or "in the area," as many as attend the Shenandoah Apple Festival but not nearly as many as are said to attend the Traverse City Cherry Festival. There are fibbers afoot in the heartland.

It is a glorious day, the mildest opening of the trout season to come to mind. A few years ago I sat huddled on the banks of the Manistee with a mixture of snow and sleet flying in my face, my hands red and numb from tying on streamers, and the guides on the rod icing up every few casts. The first day always seems to involve resolute masochism; if it isn't unbearably cold, then the combination of rain and warmth manages to provide maximal breeding conditions for mosquitoes, and they cloud and swarm around your head, crawl up your sleeves and down your neck, despite the most potent and modern chemicals. Early in the season the water is rarely clear, making wading adventuresome. The snags and deeper holes become invisible to a fisherman. You tend to forget that stretches of familiar water can change character within a year's time—last season's safe eddy below a pool measures a foot above the wader tops this spring, surely the coldest, wettest foot conceivable.

I walk over to the Chamber of Commerce office and have coffee with Cliff. He is pleased pink about the weather. Questioned about the crowd possibilities, he replies obliquely. He says that Kalkaska is the smallest town in Michigan with a full-time Chamber president. He allows as how his duties are so pressing, he does not have time for trout fishing— perhaps a little pike fishing later in the season in the Upper Peninsula when "things slow down." I reflect on this. It would be hard to create a slower village. Driving around Kalkaska County, you are reminded of those Jonathan Winters routines involving a hound with a bald tail sleeping near a gas pump and chickens scratching in a bare yard. But such places have an undeniable charm nowadays. Much of the popularity of country music is surely due to nostalgia for those drowsy days when "we didn't have much, but we had fun."

The village is beginning to fill. Some of the people are farmers in bib overalls on their traditional Saturday visit to town with their pickups full of sacks of feed and groceries. But there are many out-of-county and out-of-state license plates, and the bars and restaurants are full. I talk to dozens of people, and their reasons for coming are varied, ranging from "I never missed one" to "I like the parade" to "a chance to visit the hometown."

Everyone seems to know everyone else, but this is the sort of camaraderie caused by good weather and the prospect of a parade. It occurs to me that nothing really happens at a festival, no daring feats of excellence, but that no matter how artificial the point of celebration might be, these events provide entertainment, an excuse to go someplace, a break in what up here is the arduous process of making a living. Now that much of our countryside is less intensively agricultural, festivals compete with county fairs in popularity. A great number of misplaced farmers have gone south to the factories of Flint, Grand Rapids, Lansing and Detroit, and they look for any excuse to return to the country with their aluminum campers and pale city children dressed in what are considered locally as outrageous costumes.

I decided to take a short tour of the streams to see how the fishermen are doing. There are three reasonably good trout rivers within twenty miles of Kalkaska: the small Rapid, the medium-sized Boardman and the large Manistee. In addition, inside of a two-hour drive you can reach the Pigeon, Sturgeon, Black, Au Sable, Betsie, Platte, Pere Marquette and Pine, plus innumerable smaller creeks. A large stretch of the Au Sable has been brought back from relatively degenerate conditions by an organization called Trout Unlimited, which is the fly fisherman's court of last resort. This provides adequate fishing for all but the most adamant whiners, among whom I number myself.

I was horrified in Livingston, Montana, last year to hear Joe Brooks, the famous angler, say that Michigan fishing was fine. After all, I had traveled nearly 2,000 miles to hit the honey buckets. There is no question that the streams are not what they were, say, before 1955. The reasons are usual ones—newly developed resorts, cottagers, road builders, oil interests, industrial effluents, virulent pesticides.

None of these need cause irrevocable damage, but getting government aid is difficult. Other forms of fishing—trolling for lake trout and coho salmon, for example—have a larger constituency and command a larger share of the money and the attention of the state's Department of Natural

Resources. And so the charter business is booming and the boat manufacturers are happy. Large coho and Chinook are being caught in quantity, and it is difficult to begrudge their advocates the fun of catching them, though trolling seems to be a desperately boring form of fishing. The coho, however, have disturbed the steelhead fishing by jamming the mouths of rivers emptying into Lake Michigan with spawning fish in their death throes.

All the fishermen encountered on the Boardman complain about the warm and sunny weather except a young boy who has three nice browns, about fourteen inches apiece. Most of the anglers are using worms, and none flies. I drive over to Sharon (pop. two or three, seriously) on the Manistee. The story is the same—too much heat and light. It has often troubled me that, no matter, truly cunning fishermen invariably catch fish. Their methods must be plastic and unconstrained, perhaps unsporting. During July and August on the Boardman, when I mostly catch spiritless hatchery fish, a few crafty old men catch large browns by chumming the stream with quarts of grasshoppers, then placing a small hook to make one of the bugs a fatal meal. Though effective, this seems, to my way of thinking, a bit low.

Ernest Hemingway fished the Boardman as a young man and complained in a letter home that the swiftness of the water made wading difficult. I think this was part of the novelist's imagination, because there were, even in his time, four dams on the last twenty miles approaching Traverse City. The final two-mile stretch is now murky and exudes a shameful stench. And it is not simply a matter of saying that things "aren't what they used to be," which is neither helpful nor interesting. I am privately in favor of the death penalty for any form of pollution not speedily rectified. If you are keen on trout fishing, I advise that you log thousands of hours a summer, because the signs, short of radical ecological surgery, point to its demise.

When I return from my streamside tour around noon, Kalkaska is choked with people, though a wombat most assuredly can choke on a single kernel of corn, and I have no idea how many people there are. I park in a shady residential district and walk the five or six blocks to the center of town. The lawns are neat, the houses modest but in good repair. What do people do? Take in each other's laundry and throw festivals? Our land is full of incomprehensible wonder, and nay-sayers should be raspberried.

152

On Main Street, Cliff is up on the bandstand in a boater and a string tie. Hank Snow's country music blares from a public-address system that tweets and howls and screeches, drowning out the lyrics. Cliff makes some garbled announcements. He is a mixture of booster and carnival barker. I remember he once lured the International Sled Dog Races to Kalkaska for the slow winter months.

Perhaps in an age heavily flavored with the artificial and the often very distant spectator sport, a celebration of trout or dog is a good thing despite the heavy dosage of sheer hokum. A Silent Majority spring rite laced with streaks of yokel patriotism.

In front of the hardware store there is a kindly old man who tells me that many years ago a rainbow weighing over twenty pounds, caught at Bailey's Rapids, won the contest. Bailey's Rapids is a stretch of the upper Manistee near Fife Lake and not far from town. I have fished the area with some eagerness. It is unlikely that this fast, shallow stretch of water can offer good fishing much longer; too many cabins have been built on its banks in the past decade. The waters will inevitably degenerate from seeping septic tanks.

I feel melancholy reading the Official Program, which announces such events as a canoe race, a Grand Royal Parade and one last item, a Buick Opel Paint-in. I plan avoiding the latter but allow my mind to revolve wildly around its possibilities. I begin to think numbly of the many small communities in Michigan that throw one sort of festival or another to draw dollars before winter sets in. (Climate may soon be no hindrance; a few months ago there was a snowmobile festival.) We have a Bean Queen, a Strawberry Queen, a Cherry Queen, a Smoked Pickerel Queen, an Alpenfest Queen and a Red Flannel Queen from Cedar Springs, whom I am to meet later today. The new Trout Queen is Pat Christian, an appropriate name for a lovely girl from the north country. I wonder if in the swine provinces of Iowa they have a Pig Queen. Or if somewhere in our country there is a simple Queen Queen. And do they have Queens in England other than the honest-to-God one?

At lunch there are many local politicians, and virtually everyone is applauded and gets an award except me. The fried trout is good. Fred Bear of Bear Archery is announced King of the Festival, and there is a hearty round of applause for King Fred and Queen Pat, who sit together in purple robes with bright-yellow paper crowns. Fred Bear has slain elephant, grizzly, polar bear and Cape buffalo with bow and arrow; he looks gaunt and fatigued, like a member of displaced nobility or an actual sultan at a Shriner convention.

There is an interminable speech by a state Fish and Game Department representative. He says that statistics show Americans spend more on outdoor recreation than they do on the Vietnam War. The comparison is boggling. We are told his department is doing a "yeoman's job" taking care of the resources that the "Omnipotent Being" and "mother nature" have given us.

During the Grand Royal Parade, I count fifty-six floats. Floats represent something truly inscrutable in our culture, and you may want to draw some conclusions of your own from this sampling: the Sheriff of Lake County, King Fred and Queen Pat, a state senator, a team of sled dogs, three mobile homes (just plain mobile homes), a church bus with a banner proclaiming HEAVEN or BUS-T, an old car, the National Ice and Snow Queen, a garden tractor with an STP sticker, an old plow, three marines, a large papier-mâché Holy Bible, the Kalkaska Sno-Packers (snowmobile club), the Missaukee County Dairy Princess, a posse mounted on horseback, the Liars Club.

I walk to Jack's to check on the fish entered in the contest. A Reverend Glick has entered a fine steelhead, and there are several good catches of browns, though one entry is suspiciously uniform and might have been caught at a planted trout pond. (When the dog days of August are around and the fishing is slow, it is great sport sneaking through the woods and poaching private ponds. I usually take along a bottle of whiskey for courage.) Looking at the pastor's steelhead, it occurs to me that an energetic and expert fisherman could catch in one day coho, Chinook, steelhead, rainbow, lake, brown and brook trout within fifty miles of Kalkaska.

While driving home after a fine, though terribly honky concert by Hank Snow, I begin to dream about what the caddis hatch will be like this year. I open the car window and restructure Carl Sandburg by yelling "The People, No!" into the American night. Then I become humble, remembering a few weeks before blowing a cast to a world-record tarpon that was hanging still in a clear green pool not thirty feet from the boat. This is akin to missing the TV across the living room with a shotgun loaded with No. 8 birdshot. My partner and quasi-guide screamed and threw a fit until I became a small, very warm blob of molasses on the boat seat. I would return to Big Pine Key only in a full Groucho Marx mask.

The night is unseasonably warm for April, perfect for the spring absurdity that I had just witnessed. Tomorrow Kalkaska can count its change in peace. Everything has been talked about except the lowly trout. It may as well have been a Frisbee Gala, but that is held in July in Copper Harbor.

A SPORTING LIFE

It begins very young up in the country, whether you are raised on a farm or in one of the small villages which, though they often double as county seats, rarely number more than a thousand souls. There is a lumber mill down by the river that manufactures crossties for the railroad, and the creosote the ties are treated with pervades the air. It is the smell of the town, depending on the wind: fresh-cut pine and creosote. In the center of the town there's a rather ugly yellow brick courthouse, plain Depression architecture. The village is in northern Michigan and does not share the quaintness of villages in New England or the deep South, being essentially historyless. There are three baronial, rococo houses left over from the hasty passing of the lumber era, but most dwellings are characterized by their drabness, simply a place for the shopkeepers to hide at night.

In the spring and summer the boys in the town carry either baseball mitts or fish poles on their bicycles. Two different types are being formed, and though they might merge and vary at times, most often they have set themselves up for life. During the endless five months of winter one boy will spend his evenings pouring over the fishing-tackle sections of the Sears Roebuck and Montgomery Ward catalogs while the other boy will be looking at the mitts, bats and balls. One tinkers with a reel while the other sits in a chair plopping a baseball over and over into his glove just recently oiled with neatsfoot. One reads about the Detroit Tigers while the other reads *Outdoor Life* and fantasizes about the time when he will be allowed his first shotgun. He already has an old .22 Remington single-shot, but he knows it is an interim weapon before the shotgun and later yet, a .30-.30 deer rifle.

The village is surrounded by woods and lakes, rivers and swamps and some not very successful farms. The boy wanders around among them with a World War II surplus canteen and a machete he keeps hidden in the garage from his mother's prying eyes. His family owns a one-room cabin a dozen miles from town, where they spend the summer. He shoots at deer with a weak bow and arrow. On many dawns he accompanies his father trout fishing on a nearby river; he is forced to fish the same hole all day to avoid getting lost. The same evening he will row his father around the lake until midnight, bass fishing. The boy and a friend sit in a swamp despite the slime and snakes and mosquitoes. They pot two sitting grouse with a .22 and roast them until they are black. The boys think they are Indians and sneak up on a cabin where some secretaries are vacationing. A few feet behind the window in the lamplight a secretary is naked. A true wonder to discuss while walking around in the woods and gullies or while diving for mud turtles or while watching a blue heron in her nest in a white pine.

Two decades later. Wars. Marches. Riots. Flirtations with politics, teaching, marriage, a pleasant love affair with alcohol. Our boy, now presumably a man, is standing in a skiff near the Marquesas thirty miles out in the Gulf from Key West. He's still fishing with a fly rod, only for tarpon now instead of bass, bluegills or trout. He wants to catch a tarpon over 100 pounds on a fly rod. Then let it go and watch it swim away. Today, being an open-minded soul, he's totally blown away on a triple hit of psilocybin. A few numbers rolled out of Colombian buds add to the sweet stew. It's blissful except for an occasional football-field-sized red hold in the sky and for the fact that there are no tarpon in the neighborhood. A friend is rubbing himself with an overripe mango. Then he rubs a girl who is fixing a lunch of white wine, yogurt and strawberries. Where are the tarpon today? Maybe in China. They want to hear the gill plates rattle when the tarpon jumps. The overripe mango feels suspiciously familiar. Peach jokes should be changed to mango jokes.

An osprey struggles overhead with a too-large fish. Ospreys can drown that way, not being able to free their talons in the water. The flight slows painfully. Between the great bird's shrieks we can hear the creak and flap of wings and the tidal rush through the mangroves. Lunar. The bird reaches the nest and within minutes has torn the houndfish to pieces. A meal. We watch each other across a deep-blue channel.

Barracuda begin passing the skiff with regularity on the incoming tide, but no tarpon. We rig a fly rod with a wire leader for the barracuda's sharp teeth. And a long wonderfully red fly that matches the red holes that periodically reappear in the sky. The fish love the fly and the strike is violent, so similar to touching an electric fence it brings a shudder. The barracuda dashes off across the shallow water of the flat, is fought to the boat and released.

The midafternoon sun is brilliantly hot, so they move the boat some fifteen miles to a key that doubles as a rookery for cormorants, pelicans and man-of-war or frigate birds. They watch the birds for hours, and the sand sharks, rays, bait fish and barracuda that slide past the boat.

Why get freaked or trip while you're fishing? Why not? You only do so rarely. You're fishing in the first place to avoid boredom, the habitual, and you intend to vary it enough to escape the lassitude attached to most of our activities. If you carry to sport a businesslike consciousness, it's not sport at all. Only an extension of your livelihood, which you are presumably trying to escape.

But how did we get from there to here across two decades? In sport there is a distinct accounting for taste. That corn pone about going through life with a diminishing portfolio of enthusiasms is awesomely true. We largely do what we do, and are what we are, by excluding those things we find distasteful. You reduce your life to those few things that you know are never going to quit. And when you reach thirty-five, your interest in these few things can verge on the hysteric: a freshly arrived single white hair in a sideburn can get a book written or instigate a trip to Africa. What energy you have left becomes obsessive and single-minded. When I am not writing poetry or novels I want to fish or, to a slightly lesser degree, hunt grouse and woodcock.

But this is to be an idealogue about something that is totally a sensuous, often sensual, experience. We scarcely want a frozen tract by Jerry Garcia on just why he likes "brown-eyed women and red grenadine." Visceral is visceral. Always slightly comic, man at play in America has John Calvin tapping him on the shoulder and telling him to please be serious. For beginners, you have to learn to tell John to fuck off. And if you're a writer, many of your friends in the arts look at you with an "Oh, the Hemingway bit" tolerance, as if that stunningly arrogant doctor's son had forever preempted hunting and fishing. They might better ask why someone who wanted to paint like Cezanne would find so much that is memorable and durable in fishing and hunting. My own life is so largely an act of language, I've found that I survive only by seeking an opposite field when not actually writing. When it feels as if you're typing with sixteen-ounce gloves, you have to get out of the house, sometimes for months at a time.

Twenty miles off the coast of Ecuador, near the confluence of the Niña and Humboldt currents, it's not all that far after dawn and already the equatorial sun is shimmering down waves of heat. I count it lucky that when you skip bait for marlin the boat is moving at eight to ten knots, thus creating a breeze. The port diesel is fluttering, then is silent. We rock gently in the prop wash, then are caught in a graceful Pacific swell. It wasn't the port engine. Or the starboard engine. It was the only engine. The pulse quickens. My friend smiles and continues photographing a great circle of man-of-war birds hovering far above us, far more than we have ever seen in the Florida Keys. It must be hundreds of miles to the closest pesticide. The birds follow schools of bait as do the striped marlin, and are considered a good sign. The captain looks at me and shrugs, the universal language of incompetence. He speaks no English and I no Spanish. My friend, who is a French count, pretends he speaks Spanish, but in a week down here has yet to make any significant contact except with some Braniff stewardesses who speak fluent English. My room overlooks the pool and I saw him flat on his back with camera poised: he had arranged a circle of stewardesses around him with the prettiest in her bikini directly over his head. The magic of photography. Either a camera or a guitar works, but you never point a typewriter at a girl. I ran down to the pool hoping to catch the camera's aura of snazz.

I stretch out along the gunwhale trying to convince myself that I am relaxed, but paranoia comes in surges. They'll never get the engine started and we'll drift to Australia, missing the Galápagos in the night by a helpless few miles. I can't even see land. We don't have any water, which anyway is undrinkable hereabouts. A lot of foul-tasting Chilean soda pop. In a shrugging fit, one of the two mates hands me a plate of fresh pineapple. It is ripe, cool and delicious. Feed the fearful bear. I toss a chunk at three passing sea snakes, who look terribly yellow in the blue water. They are related to the cobra and extremely venomous though not very aggressive. They scatter, then one swirls around to check out the pineapple. I've been assured that they never bother anyone but the wretchedly poor Peruvian fishermen who deep-jig from cork rafts. Good ole swimming hole. Sharks. Snakes. Even whales. Often in nature you get the deep feeling you don't belong. This is especially true of the Pacific and the Serengeti.

Hours pass, and they are still tinkering with the engine. I glance into its guts and regret not knowing anything about them. The day before the engine had quit while I was fighting a striped marlin. It is a difficult and exhausting job from a dead boat, especially after the spectacular jumps are over and the fish bulldogs. You can't follow the marlin on its long runs. You have to pump him back. And I had hooked the fish out of vanity on twenty-pound test. It took over two hours in the ninety-degree sun and I felt murderous. Now I was pretending the boat had a marine radio, which I knew it didn't.

But it had been a fine week's fishing so far, though we had failed to catch a striped marlin on fly rod, something that had only been done twice before. My friend had teased a marlin to within forty feet of the boat with a casting rod and rubber squid. When my streamer fly hit the water, the marlin rose up and slashed with his bill then took it firmly in the corner of his mouth. I was thinking numbly about how beautifully blue his body was and how from the side his eye appeared to be staring at us. Perhaps it was. But it only lasted a few seconds while he twisted his head and sped off in a flume of water. The leader popped. It was like fly fishing for Dick Butkus or a Harley Davidson, I thought, while trying to sleep on a sunburn that night. We had been getting a lot of sleep, having been warned by the hotel manager of the endemic shanker problem in the local villages.

You have a great deal of time to think between fish, and you wonder why you are never bored. My friend the novelist Tom McGuane has fished for months in a row in the Keys, particularly when he was learning saltwater fly casting. When I was learning from him there were moments of doubt until you have your first big tarpon in the air. Before that you had been quite pleased with a two-pound rainbow. And still are, though the true maniac deserves a tarpon. Such sport is a succession of brutally electric moments spaced widely apart. Someone with McGuane's quantum energy level quite naturally applies the same effort to fishing.

There is doubtless the edge of the lunatic here. In Ecuador, the crew was enormously alarmed when my friend went overboard to get underwater photos of a fighting marlin. Billfish have been known to charge a boat out of generalized ire. I was supposed to control the fish. I was sure my stomach wall would burst and spill its contents—an even quart of Añejo. But dangers in nature are vastly overrated, though while backpacking I tend to think of grizzlies as 700-pound Dobermans that don't respond to voice commands. In Africa, you are more likely to get bit by a snake than attacked by a mammal. Comforting thought.

There are unquestioned flops. We try to see the brighter side of our flops, telling ourselves we haven't wasted our time. And we are dolts if we aren't comfortable in a world outside our immediate preoccupations. A sports bore is far more deadly than a krait or a Gaboon viper. A true NFL freak can make a more casual fan pine for opera. A real quadra or stereo buff makes you want that Victrola the big white dog was listening to.

One of the reasons I wanted to go to Russia was to scout the possibility of an extended trip for fishing and hunting. How splendid to shoot grouse where Ivan Turgenev had hunted, and I had heard that there was good steelhead and salmon fishing on the Pacific coast of Siberia. As a poet, I have a tendency to imagine conditions and pleasures without precedent on earth. When fishing is bad, you can't tell but that just around the next green island there might be a nude fashion model on a mohair chair on the water.

Once reaching Russia, my ideas seemed clearly impossible except for an important official visitor or on an established tour, a loathsome prospect. Red tape is a euphemism. And my first morning in Moscow had been encouraging, watching old men fish the broad Moscow River, which runs through the middle of the capital. They were sitting on an embankment below the faded red walls of the Kremlin, the mid-October sun catching the gold of the minarets as a backdrop. But I never saw anyone catch a fish, just as I had gazed at other fishless afternoons on the Seine in Paris. It is enough to have a river in a city.

After several days of badgering I managed to get to a horse race. But the weather had turned bad and the horses passed all but invisibly in what must be called a howling blizzard. The tote board said that Iron Beauty beats out Good Hoe, our plump female guide translated. Her pleasure was to wander aimlessly in great halls filled with the machinery of progress. It's hard to explain to someone so adamantly political that you see enough progress at home, and that to you, progress meant motors that quit rather captiously far out in the ocean. Or the shotgun that misfired when you had a good chance at a double in grouse. No matter that it was the first time in your life that a shotgun misfired. It brutishly picked the wrong time.

The climate of inquiry was pleasanter in Leningrad, where a black market is active and there are more creature pleasures. I found a sporting goods store on the Nevsky Prospect where the clerks were affable. An electrical engineer I met there joined me for a number of drinks and explained that fishing in Siberia would be difficult. Permissions were necessary. Bird hunting would be difficult but not impossible. Since I find even mild queues a torment, I checked Russia off my list. It was sad, as I had visions of sitting at the edge of a swale taking a break from grouse with a chilled bottle of Stolichnaya and some blinis on which I would spread large amount of Beluga caviar, rolling them up like miraculous tacos.

I had another interesting failure down in Killarney, with wet May weather, on the banks of not even a secondary Atlantic salmon river, with a gillie whose language, ostensibly English, I couldn't understand. In the ceaseless rain I became convinced that he had been invented by someone who taught Irish literature. I admit I was dizzy from the dehydration brought on by a raging case of *turista*, an infirmity I pick up on the road, even in Tucson, Arizona. On one of my frequent trips to the bushes a lovely lady rode by on a horse, but in my position I didn't feel up to greeting her. So the gillie and I sat under a tree, mumbling and watching the rain. Then a hotel waiter appeared in a parka and asked what I wanted for lunch. The shock was so sweet that I ordered a six-pack of Guiness Stout and a bottle of Jameson. And watercress sandwiches in honor of the water. Booze is a sure tonic for any colitic problem. You can always get well when you get home and don't have anything else to do. Anyway, the language barrier dropped and the gillie invited me to go fox hunting with clubs. But I got up too late the next morning and missed the show. I could imagine them out there on a rainy hillside, a hundred fictional characters trying to club a real fox to death in the mud.

Outdoor sport has proven fatally susceptible to vulgarization based mostly on our acquisitiveness. Fishing becomes the mechanics of acquiring fish, bird hunting a process of "bagging a limit." Most sportsmen have become mad Germans with closets full of arcane death equipment. To some, an ultimate sport would be chasing coyote with a 650cc snowmobile armed with an M-16. And some have found that baseball bats work as well, as a coyote can't run more than twenty miles and a snowmobile has a superior range.

You suspect that the further hunting and fishing get away from our ancient heritage of hunting and gathering, the better. And I don't mean the native Americans, the Indians, who had the mother wit to understand that "the predator husbands his prey." Hunger causes the purest form of acquisitiveness, but our tradition always overstepped hunger into the fields of hoarding and unmitigated slaughter. The saddest book printed in our time is Peter Matthiessen's *American Wildlife*, where the diminishing and disappearance of many species are minutely traced to our greed and game hoggery. Sporting magazines still publish those obscene photos of piles of trout, though there does seem to be a change in the air. The dolt who stands smiling before the 100 crows he shot should be forced at gunpoint to eat them, feathers, beaks, feet and offal. The excuse is that crows eat duck eggs, as if crows were supposed to abandon a million-year food source because some clown has taken Saturday morning off for a duck hunt.

Any sense of refinement seeps slowly into the mind of the sportsman, and every advance made to improve the ethics of sport by organizations such as Trout Unlimited or the Grouse Society is countered by thousands of examples of boobery, murder and exploitation. Each state has a professional natural resource staff, but so often their efforts are countered by what are called the beer-bottle biologists in the legislatures, who think of hunting and fishing as some sort of patriotic birthright, something they know intimately by osmosis. You see the same thing out west with townspeople who've never been on a horse assuming they are all-knowing because they are Westerners.

I know a plain of about 500 acres near the Manistee River. We often begin a day's hunt there, and my image of grouse and woodcock shooting is inextricably tied up with this great, flat pasture, cut near the river by a half-dozen gullies choked with thorn apple and cedar trees. On our long walk to the grouse cover near the river, we hunt a small marsh that invariably yields a few woodcock and snipe. You are lucky if you connect with one shot out of five. It is always early in the morning: cold, often wet, with the shotgun barrels icy to the fingers. The same location means nothing to me in the summer before the frost has muted the boring greenness.

Part of the pleasure of bird hunting is that it comes after the torpor of summer: beaches, the continuous sound of motorboats, the bleached air of August, a tendency to go to too many parties and to experiment with drinks an honest bourbon addict finds abominable in the winter. (A drink of my own devising I call the Hunter Thompson Special; take juice left over from four stewed figs, add ground lime rind, a jigger of bitters and eight ounces of cheap tequila, one gram of hash, powder from three Dexamyl spansules and a cherry bomb for decoration to an iced mug, stir vigorously with either end of a cue stick. This is the only aphrodisiac I've ever discovered. It will also remove warts and give you an interior suntan.)

And there is the color, the hardwoods sinking their juices into the ground before the horror of a Michigan winter. This stunning transformation of leaves creates colors that would look vulgar on a woman. It looks good on trees, and with the first cool days of autumn you find yourself hunting grouse and woodcock. You have given up duck hunting as too sedentary. Besides, you have to get up at dawn, while mid-morning is plenty early for grouse. So you walk around in the woods for a month and a half. Unfortunately, the steelhead fishing is good during the same period, but you can't afford to divide your attention. An obvious boon in a writer's life is that he can concentrate his work into the months when no suitable sport is available. Surely it is a dream world; the nearly thundering flush and the always difficult shot. Grouse are very fast and the cover is heavy. If your shooting isn't trained as a gut reaction you simply miss, and when you miss a grouse you lose a very good meal. I suppose I especially value this form of shooting because I lost an eye in an accident and it has taken me years to reach even average competence.

The symptoms of all the vaunted instabilities of artists tend to occur in interim periods. It is the mental exhaustion of having just finished a work, and the even more exhausting time of waiting for another set of ideas to take shape. Poetry and the literary novel are a desperate profession nowadays—they probably always were—and any satisfying release seems to be desperately energetic. You tend to look for something as intricately demanding as your calling so you can forget yourself and let it rest.

Fly fishing for trout offers an ideal match of the exacting and the aesthetically pleasant: to sit by a stream during the evening hatch and watch what trout are feeding on, then to draw from the hundreds of variations in your fly boxes a close approximation and catch a few trout. It's easily the most hypnotic of the outdoor sports. Once we began fishing in the Middle Branch of the Ontanagon at dawn. I was numbly depressed from having finished my second book of poems and had been sleepwalking and drinking for weeks. My friend, who is equally mani-acal and has no pain threshold that is noticeable, insisted we eat a pound of bacon, refried beans and a dozen eggs for strength. We fished nonstop then from dawn to dark at ten in the evening. It was a fine day, cool with intermittent light rains and enough breeze to keep the mosquitoes away. I remember catching and releasing a half-dozen good brook trout from a pool where a small creek entered the river. We saw deer and many conical piles of bear shit that gave us pause, but then our local bears are harmless. We watched the rare and overwhelming sight of two adult bald eagles flying down the river course just above our heads, shrieking that we didn't belong there.

To perhaps lessen the purity of the day, I admit at nightfall we drove 100 miles to a whorehouse across the Wisconsin border. The next night a local bumpkin of the *Deliverance* sort was waving an axe around at the edge of our fire, warning us not to steal any of his logs. We felt at ease— rather than a bow and arrows, we had a rifle along.

This is a peculiarity of trout fishing—you can lose yourself completely for days at a time. If you feel your interest in women and the not-so-ordinary simplicities of sex waning, try getting on a horse and spending a week or two fishing up in the Absaroka Mountains of Montana. There are no women up there. Not even a little one. When you get back down to Livingston, a barroom tart invariably reminds you of the Queen of Sheba or Lauren Hutton. Unless you're careful, you can manage to get into a lot of pointless trouble. Of course, the same conditions can be imitated by going off to war, but it's not as much fun.

There is something about eating game that resists the homogeneity of taste found in even the best of our restaurants. A few years back when we were quite poor, lower-class by all the charts, we had a game dinner at our house. There were about twelve people contributing food, and with a check for a long poem I bought two cases of a white Bordeaux. We ate, fixed in a number of ways, venison, duck, trout, woodcock, snipe, grouse, rabbit, and drank both cases of wine. I doubt you could buy the meal on earth.

The French, however, are marvelous at game cookery. Two years ago I spent a week up in Normandy covering a stag hunt at the invitation of a friend, Guy de la Valdene. His family has a château near St. George and a breeding farm for racehorses. You do not go to Russia to eat, and I had just returned from a hungry trip to Moscow and Leningrad. Other than the notion that stag hunting seemed to me the pinnacle of stylishness in mammal hunting, the memorable part of the week was the eating, a vulgar word for what took place nightly in a local auberge. Despite my humble background I found I enjoyed saddle of wild boar, or a 1928 Anjou with fresh pâté de foie gras in slabs, trout laced with truffles, *cotelettes* of loin from a small forest deer called a *chevreuil*, pheasant baked under clay with wild mushrooms. It all reminded me of the bust of Balzac by Rodin at the Metropolitan in New York, the evidence in his immense, bulbous face of his legendary interest in food and wine. But moderation only makes sense to those whom such food is continually available. The stag hunt itself began after dawn, and the animal was brought to bay by the hounds at twilight, when the master of the hunt dispatched the stag with a silver dagger after the manner of some six centuries. All day we had been sipping Château Margaux straight from the bottle and not feeling even vaguely boorish.

I suspect that many of the misunderstandings of sport are caused by those who write for the outdoor magazines, not the best of the writers, but by the generally venal texture of the majority of the work. Most of it is simply dead, full of fibs and outright lies repeated in hundreds of variations of the same story. There is the usual tale of the grizzly hunt where we are led to assume that the bear had spent its entire life hell-bent on murdering the author, rather than merely walking around in the woods looking for lunch. And no matter that the animal is shot at 200 yards, before it can see the hunter. I can remember an account when the grizzly was asleep, something to the effect that "I poured hot lead into Mister Dozin' Bruin. It was the surprise of his life!" Certain macho aspects can be funny—a story titled "Bulls of the Midnight Pond" conceals an inflated account of an ordinary frog hunt.

The best outdoor writing is on the periphery of sport, in such writers as Edward Abbey, Peter Matthiessen, Ed Hoagland, John McPhee and a very few others. These writers are first of all artists and they deliberately avoid even a tinge of fakery. You learn slowly that to the extent that there is any pretension of expertise you don't own, or willful snobbishness, you lose it all and are simply another of millions of incompetents whose outdoor activities are very probably an extension of their sexual neuroses. It seems odd, but I know only one good writer who is truly a first-rate angler and wing shot, Tom McGuane. I hear Vance Bourjaily is good but have never met him.

After I'd been reading about African hunting for twenty years, it took a trip to Kenya and Tanzania to cure me permanently of any notion that I might hunt there except for duck and grouse. And it's not that a great deal of the hunting there by outsiders lacks validity, excepting the endangered and diminishing species. It's simply that my time there more closely resembled a religious rather than a travel experience. In the Serengeti you get an eerie conviction of what the American West was like before we got off the boat. Perhaps I could have hunted there in the twenties or thirties, before it became apparent that the natural world was shrinking in direct proportion to our insults against it: almost as if this world were a great beast herself and she had demonstrably passed the midpoint of her life and needed the most extreme and intense care not to further accelerate her doom.

The problems of East Africa have been talked about and publicized to the saturation point, which has not in the least slowed the unnatural predation of new farms, overgrazing, poaching for skins, the tide of population, ivory smuggling for jewelers and to the Orientals who have the silly notion that ground ivory gives them hard-ons. Think of the boggling sexual vanity involved in killing a seven-ton beast for hard-ons. And it is not at all sure how long we can expect native populations who smarted under colonization to maintain game parks for wealthy Westerners, no matter how beneficial.

I came to the point rather early when I realized I was not much interested in shooting mammals. This does not mean I disapprove of others doing so. Maybe it's my squeamishness over gutting and cleaning a large animal, though I suspect my qualms would disappear if I needed the animal to feed my family. And deer hunting as opposed to bird hunting is difficult to do cleanly. We mammals are more sturdy than we assume. While a single pellet can bring a grouse tumbling down, both man and deer can crawl on for hours after Claymore mines, .357s, a half-dozen badly placed rifle shots. When they were butchering, it took seven unlucky shots for my neighbors to bring down their Holstein cow.

Last Thanksgiving Day during deer season we heard loud bleating, then barking from up behind our barn. Our horses were frantic and stared in the direction of the woodlot like pointing dogs. The bleating was from a deer dragging itself through the snow by its forelegs. The deer had been wounded in the spine and a hind leg had been shot nearly off, barely hanging by a tendon. A large collie had been harrying the deer and had torn much of the deer's ass off. It was red as a baboon's. The game warden came and put it away. The deer was a young buck and lacked legal horns. Someone had shot the deer, then discovered it lacked legal horns. Before the game warden dispatched it, the deer in deep shock stared at us, seemingly well past caring, some kind of runaway slave that had fallen victim to our fatal hobbies.

It is finally a mystery what keeps you so profoundly interested over so many years. The sum is far more than simply adding those separate parts. In the restorative quality there is the idea that as humans we get our power from the beauty we love most. And the sheer, unremittant physicality makes you lose for a while those fuzzy interior quarrels your head is addicted to, sitting as it does on the top of a Western man. It is also the degree of difficulty: to outwit a good brown trout with a lure less than the size and weight of a housefly or mosquito, to boat and release a 100-pound tarpon on a 12-pound test leader, to hit a grouse on that long shot between the poplar trees. It could be very sporting to hunt a lion if you had the balls to do it as the Masai do—with a spear.

The beauty and sensuosity of the natural world is so direct and open you often forget it: the tactility of standing in the river in your waders with the rush of water around your legs, whether deep in a cedar swamp in Michigan, or in Montana where you have the mountains to look at when the fishing is slow. With all of the senses at full play and the delicious absence of thought, each occasion recalls others in the past. It is a continuous present. You began at seven rowing your father around the lake at night, hearing in the dark the whirr of his reel as he cast for bass, the creak and dip of the oars and the whine of clouds of mosquitoes around your head. You might have been lucky enough to hear a loon, surely the most unique birdcall on earth, see heat lightning silhouette the tips of the white pines and birch.

You think of this thirty years later in Anconcito, a small, shabby village on the coast of Ecuador. You're taking the day off from fishing, with heat weakness, vertigo, sore hands and the fear of death that being sick in a foreign country brings. You are sitting on a cliff next to a pile of refuse and a small goat. The goat is pure black and when it stumbles close you see that it can't be more than a few days old. The goat nuzzles you. Not thirty feet away a very large vulture sits and stares at you both. You stare back, idly listening to the Latin music from the tin-shed café in the background. A piglet scurries by. You, the goat and the vulture watch the piglet, and the goat takes chase. Far below you, so far that they are toys, there are fishing boats in the harbor powered anciently by sail. It is the hottest day you can remember. Beyond the harbor is all the vast, cool, deep-blue plenitude of the Pacific.

ICE FISHING, THE MORONIC SPORT
A Michigan Journal

There are strange things done 'neath the midnight sun.
                    —Bob Service

We're not actually *that* far north. Yes, a small church in the Upper Peninsula had a Blessing of the Snowmobiles, and not a trace of irony was noticed. But the sense of the Arctic does pull on us: days shorten, men mumble, the euchre games at the tavern grow extended and violent. There is much talk in December and January of just when the bay will freeze over. It is the west arm of the Grand Traverse Bay they are talking about, a very grand bay indeed, containing some five by thirty miles of Lake Michigan's water. The east arm (they are separated by the forefinger of Old Mission Peninsula) usually freezes first, but the lake trout there, for unknown reasons, run smaller. Some years the bay doesn't freeze, but this is rare. And some years an oil tanker is brought in at an inopportune time, say if there is a steady offshore wind and a warming trend, and the ice breaks up and blows out of the bay. Until February 15, the date on which the ice is usually safe, sportsmen must be content to fish on smaller lakes for perch or crappies, or some of them take up the ancient art of pike spearing. But these activities locally are only considered as warmups. On inland lakes, many consider these forms of ice fishing adequate and cases are made for chugging bluegills with corn borers, a small obnoxious worm found in cornstalks. Houghton Lake, a resort area drawing much of its traffic from Hamtramck and other posh Detroit suburbs, throws a gala every winter known as Tip-Up Town, the "tip-up" referring, of course, to the crude rig positioned above the hole in the ice.

Years ago, when I was a temporary prisoner on Long Island and dreamed of a return to Trout Country, I thought of those hallowed winter nights that resemble Christmas cards, with large jeweled flakes of snow falling softly on humble farm animals and peasant faces upturned in wonderment and looking not a little bit like my relatives. But reality is a different pudding. BRAAAOOWILL is what we have, my transcription of what is called a snowmobile "safari." Safari is when a dozen or so machines strike out in the night cross-country for another tavern. Let's have it once more: BRAAAOOWILL, as if a dozen burly chain saws were mating under a single tympanum cowl.

Walking out on any large expanse of ice has always been dramatic to me. After not many steps I tend to stumble involuntarily, as if I were an exhausted survivor of the Byrd Expedition. I frankly expect seals or polar bear, perhaps a wolf loping along the farther shore. But if I fall and roll over I can maybe see a '69 Camaro passing on the road or a guy and gal in his 'n' her purple satin overall suits just cattin' around on their throaty Skidoo. This brings me swiftly back to reality. Here are a few reality facts from the Great North: our unemployment rate this year is sixteen percent, giving many some much unwanted time off; snowmobiles, mobile homes and motels each outnumber the total population in '77; most of my friends are unemployed and if I *did* have any money they would try to borrow it! I am led, though, by many people I meet to believe that they are mainly worried about the Communist Threat and how the "radicals are tearing apart the country." They tell me that they "worked for what they got" and "nobody gave them nothing." In periods of high unemployment the Great Depression again becomes a ruling face of life. Yet many people up here strike me as more populist than conservative, and there is the kind of generalized suspicion of Big Government that one finds in nonurban Arizona. They are angry at Nixon for selling them that '52 Buick, but then they hated Johnson, who is still blamed for everything but the tight-money policy, which is especially hard on a resort area, the only other large local industry being a state insane asylum.

Oh boy! I have been invited to go ice fishing by two of my friends, Richard Plamondon, who is a bartender, and Pat Paton, a carpenter and machinist and block layer. As I dress before dawn, I feel somehow patriotic wearing Air Force surplus arctic balloon boots and bib overalls over other trousers and thermal underwear and various sweaters and a goosedown vest and an outsized quilted coat from when I weighed 225 pounds. Eighteen articles of clothing in all, and when I got out of my car I found I could scarcely walk. I fell on the slippery ice with padded impunity, a big helpless doll of a trout slayer. The early morning air was bluish with cold, and as I waddled along I thought of the promised steak to come in the afternoon and the whiskey I would use to wash it down. But there I was being asked to spud some holes in the ice. One cannot refuse. Chores are shared. Pat and Richard were organizing the chuggers and tip-ups. Everyone spuds their own holes, a rule of the Big Ice. I felt the spud was too heavy after only a few chops. I wanted the ice to be very thick for my safety but thin for the spudding. It became apparent that we could have fished from the security of a railroad car. Over a foot thick, and I was wheezing and steaming and my shoulder ached. I knew then why construction workers liked the sport: they were able to spud the holes. Anyway, Richard tested the depth: 170 feet. A lot of dark down there. I peered in the hole and saw the reflection of a moon face, my own. Richard set a tip-up for me and told me to spud another hole to chug in. I couldn't believe it. I thought whatever happened to the tradition of the gun bearer who in this case might be put to work, or some sallow, nasty teenager might be brought along for a pittance. But I spudded on. Finally I attached a Swedish pimple (surely the most elegant name for a bait) to a line, dropped it to bottom, raised it five feet as instructed by Pat and Richard, who watched my motions critically, and began chugging. Sort of ghastly. No question about it. I have become a Chugger! A brutish act, and it is so cold except for my toasty feet in their big white warmonger boots.

Within an hour I had eaten both my sandwiches, roast beef with thick slices of onion. I had also begun drinking my apple wine. After the second bottle I felt quite happy. I was probably cold but I couldn't feel it. The ice had become a mattress against which I snuggled prone, still chugging. No nibbles. Then Richard's tip-up flag went up and we ran over to the hole. He let the spool run freely for a minute to make sure the fish swallowed the minnow, somewhat similar to the way you hook a sail or a marlin. But not too similar. Pat contended that the fish was large, as only a large fish made a long run. I watched the red plastic spool steadily unwind until Richard picked it up and lightly reefed the line. Then he began to slowly draw it in hand over hand as if he were retrieving an anchor or a used kite. I was jealous. Why didn't my flag go up? Perhaps I wasn't "living right," as they say. Richard was gaining steadily on the fish. He announced laconically that it wasn't large. We stood peering down the twelve-inch hole until, shockingly, a trout popped out with the tail of a minnow sticking out of its mouth. Then, horrors! It flopped on the ice and gave off with a prolonged BELCH! a sort of berserk flatulence. I was deeply shocked.

"That pressure sure gets to them," said Pat sagely.

"You're not just a ———," replied Richard.

The point was that the fish had been pulled up precipitously from 170 feet and the variance in pressure was explosive in a minor sense, somewhat like the gas released by a semi-impacted bucking bronco at a rodeo. The trout weighed about three pounds, a good eating size. His eyes bulged and quivered in utter defeat, the ultimate tummyache and bends. I went back to my chugging hole after breaking up the thin ice that had gathered in the cold around my tip-up. I wanted to catch a fish and bring it home so that my daughter wouldn't peer over the top of her Wonder Woman comic and say "You didn't catch any!" and my wife wouldn't ponder "Did he go to a bar and play pool or did he really go fishing?" To no avail did I chug until I got tennis elbow. I grew bored and cold and began playfully throwing chunks of ice at Pat and Richard. They were not amused.

We finally quit by midafternoon and drove to a restaurant where the waitress giggled extravagantly over my balloon boots.

"Are your feet *that* big?" she asked.

"I'm an American Ice Fisherman, bring me a drink," I shouted wittily. The jukebox was playing a merry polka.

When she brought the drinks she rolled her eyes again at my feet. I told her then that I was a veteran of many polar expeditions and had tracked the wily seal to his air-conditioned lair. She asked if seal meat was good and I said yes if they take the ball off their noses har har har. Richard and Pat were sullen as the pretty waitress wasn't interested in them but in my feet. *Tuff* I said. So it goes, this sport of the north, fit mostly for the hardy unemployed, those who dare thin ice with their snowmobiles and often plunge (eight last year) to a gurgly death amidst the very fishes they sought with pimples and cornborers, red worms and dead smelt (two for a quarter).

A few days later I got a call from Richard saying that a group of locals were going out the next morning and I could meet them on Route 22 about 300 yards south of Chervenko's Rung & Bung Works (coopers to the fruit-orchard trade). I was several hours late due to sloth and invented errands. I spotted them with my binoculars a mile or so out on the ice. But farther up the bay a Coast Guard icebreaker was leading in a tanker with a rather eerie succession of resounding crashes, like hearing a battle from a distance. The ships were well beyond the fishermen, but I decided that the ice looked a trifle soft. Definitely unsafe. Perhaps I would go home and treat myself to an extended nap.

I began to think of ice fishing in the old days. It is, after all, no modern invention. I have a Currier and Ives print of some pilgrim types hauling shad from the ice. In the 1930s great cities of ice shanties were erected on large northern lakes. Even electricity was available. Recently I was in Minnesota, a state that along with Wisconsin can readily be confused with Michigan, chauvinists notwithstanding. In St. Paul an old-timer told me many yarns. He said that entire cottages especially built for the purpose on skids are pulled onto the ice by diesel tractors. From the comfort of kitchen, bedroom and the living room the fabled walleye is fished for. Imagine your own living room with a big hole in the floor. You're lolling in an easychair fishing through the hole, with a couple of lunker wall-eyes on the floor beside you. Maybe you have the TV on, and Jack Nicklaus is grinning his Ohio grin on an eighteenth green somewhere. You will cook the walleyes for dinner. They taste better than any fish I've eaten, better than mountain cutthroat, Dover sole, swordfish, lake trout or pompano or lungfish. Perhaps Myrna in her tattersall negligee is bringing you a cold one or just plain Mom is across the room knitting. It is imperative for obvious reasons to have your cottage dragged off the ice before it thaws. I might add that the "walleye" got its name from its particularly weird stare, but then you don't have to eat the eyes.

In my own "old days" we knew none of these sybaritic pleasures. I suspect my father thought if comfort were involved it wasn't sporting. So we would get up before dawn, drive out through the snowdrifts along a log road and fish all day long in the bitterest cold for a mess of bluegills and perch. Nothing sentimental here. It appeared fun because it was supposed to be fun. Kids are doggish, and if you say "come kids, let's pick the dump" they will jump at the chance.

Earlier in January I sat with Richard for three days in his shanty on Lake Leelanau looking down through a hole at a foot-long live sucker minnow dangling from a line. The shanty is kept totally dark. The hole in the ice for spearing is usually about three feet square. The visibility is amazing—a window on the fresh-water netherworld, which, though the life doesn't compete with the multitudinous saltwater variety, is nonetheless a lot better than staying home and waiting for winter to go away. Anyway, the sucker minnow was supposed to attract the great northern pike, or Mister Big Teeth as he is known in some quarters. When the imaginary pike drifted into our rectangle of vision for a sucker supper, the spear would be thrown at him. The spear was somewhat larger and certainly more cumbersome than the tuna harpoons used off Gloucester and Block Island. Poor pike. But only one appeared in the three days and we were caught unawares, and when Richard lunged with the spear the pike was driven against the bottom and squiggled out between the spear tines. So much for pike spearing, which is in danger of being outlawed. But it was pleasant sitting there in the dark shanty, warm with a propane stove and copious supplies of food and drink. We would occasionally chug for perch with small minnows while we watched our decoy. In addition to the meat of the fish, perch roe lightly fried in butter is delicious. I suspect that it is healthy, too, though I have no evidence. But some I know who eat it are huge, a trifle fat, in fact, and can drink fifty glasses of draft beer in an evening. It's never boring in an ice shanty. You talk idly while your head sweats and your feet freeze. There is all the husky camaraderie of the locker room. A sample:

"Do you know *that* girl in Sutton's Bay? You know the one I mean."

"Yup."

"Well I would —— —— ——."

"She's built like a rain barrel."

"Pass the wine."

I would like to make an elementary contention here about expediency and sport. In this locale, winter began in late October and ran unremittingly until the end of March. My friends in warmer climes won't believe we we had sixteen-and-a-half feet of snow this year. After a while you no longer believe there's any earth left under the snow. The ground is a fib. It was still possible to fish on the part of the bay nearest Traverse City in early April. In fact, a large school of young coho salmon running

176

between two and three pounds were discovered in the shoal water near the power plant. A healthy adult with an interest in the outdoors had to *do* something during these five months. The snow was almost immediately too deep for rabbit hunting—the beagles floundered on their short legs. Even an instinctively arch and lazy whiner like myself doesn't want to spend the entire winter looking out the window dreaming of Cozumel, Cabeza de Vaca, Belize. And you worry too much: a night when it is below zero and the wind off Lake Michigan is at forty knots and the car is buried in snow, and you count and time the weird thunks and squealings from the furnace, which inevitably broke down. The weather seems to lose its threat when you spend time out in it, and if you're not geared temperamentally to skiing or snowmobiling, you're left with nothing to do but fish.

The true force behind ice fishing is that it is better than no fishing at all. In extremis, an addictive fisherman will shoot carp with bow and arrow, set up trotlines for carp and suckers, spear dogfish on Pig Trotter Creek, chum nurse sharks within rifle range. He will surround the crudest equipment with a mystique and will maintain to the uninitiated that there's no sport quite like fishing rainbows with bobber and marshmallows.

And ice fishing has its strenuous converts. Pat told me that a year ago in April, just before the ice broke up, he was chugging out on the bay when a Coast Guard helicopter came over low and motioned him off the ice. He stayed until he got three fish and the helicopter returned. Then he noticed that the ice beneath his feet was sinking a bit. He grabbed his fish and ran and the ice for a mile around began wavering and rippling and heaving. The groans made in this situation convince one that there are prehistoric monsters under the ice trying to get out. It is chilling.

One day I drove up along the water through Pshawbetown, a small enclave of Chippewa Indians who are much the worse for wear. Naturally at one time they owned all the land around here. Now there is little or no running water, few indoor toilets, a ghetto shabbiness if it weren't for the fact that there is space to roam. Most of them are kept busy in the winter cutting wood for their stoves. An uninsulated shack can use an astounding amount of wood. I glassed a small cluster of fishermen about a mile out. In the tavern the night before someone anonymous (I must protect my sources) had claimed he had taken seventeen lake trout with a combined weight of over 100 pounds in just a few hours. This is well over the legal limit, but there is simply too much ice for the game warden, Reino Narva, to cover adequately. Concern is minimal, however, as the lake trout population is approaching the vastness of earlier in the century through concerted plantings, lamprey control and stringent but perhaps unfair regulation of commercial fishing.

I cut across the peninsula to Leland, a beautiful little harbor town. People here are upset over the government's acquiring 70,000 acres of local land for a National Seashore. Of only slightly less concern is Bill Carlson's attempt to regain some of the commercial fishing waters taken away by the Department of Natural Resources. An additional severe irritant is the state and federal DDT regulation: most varieties of Great Lakes fish have close to ten parts to the million, which is above the legal allowable limit for shipping. I eat all the fish anyway because I am young and fat and reckless and love the forms of danger connected with eating. I feel sad, though, when I watch the magnificent steelhead leaping against the dam in Leland: all subtly poisoned, though expensive equipment is needed to determine the fact. They still *look* like steelhead. The breakwater is mountainously covered with ice, but still some waves break over the ice, pushed by our third gale of the season. Bill Carlson is a fourth-generation fisherman. The nets around his shack remind me of Cape Ann. But far out beyond Cape Ann the swordfish are gobbling mercury below waves dotted, according to Heyerdahl, with eraser-sized gobbets of oil. And then above them a storm petrel or sooty shearwater or plain old herring gull wheels in ordinary gyres carrying a special freight of poison. There is a certain boredom in anger.

I was down on Good Harbor Bay when the ice was breaking up. The bay is about five miles wide and the equal of any tourist-photo bay I know of, though ungraced by Noel Coward and suchlike who go to Montego. A few days before I had walked out two miles on the ice to see Richard and his father Dick and Bruce Price. I followed Bruce's footprints as he weighs nearly 300 and I wanted to feel safe. I stepped over a two-foot-wide crack and peeked for a moment down into the dark clear water. They hadn't any luck. And Richard was angry. He had dropped a twelve-dollar augur while spudding a hole, and there it would rest permanently 100 feet below us. I said that I had stepped over a crack and they said the crack hadn't been there in the morning. But there was no offshore wind that would drive the ice out toward South Manitou Island. I felt edgy and got the creeps as if Lon Chaney were under the bed, turning into a man-wolf hybrid. I neatly tiptoed back to the car, listening for any rumbles or giant sighs that would announce my death by cold water. POET DROWNS, the local paper would read. Or probably MAN DROWNS, as there is a prevalent notion in the upper Midwest that poets are invariably "dead people."

Back on shore a man was whistling hopelessly at his Labrador, who was busy sniffling around the juniper bushes that abut the shore. Dogs. I had recently apologized to a neighbor about my male Airedale Hud "covering" his own dog, but he said it was okay because his dog was male, too. Nature! Then the Labrador came over and sniffed my leg, smelling my penned bitch Justine. He looked at me soulfully and I quickly removed my leg to the safety of the car.

I drove to the tavern in the evening, and Richard said he had called the Traverse City Chamber of Commerce and asked about a petition that would attempt to keep the oil freighters out of the harbor during the prime fishing months of February and March. An unnamed party suggested that the malcontents should be out looking for work. Bumpkin vigilante action has been talked about—say a string of snowmobiles in a freighter's path. Count me out. The ice fisherman is low on the economic totem ratings for logical reasons. One can equip oneself for five bucks. And ice fishermen aren't big spenders in the tourist operations. A five-dollar frozen steak is for Detroiters.

I got up at 5:00 a.m. to go steelhead fishing, but when I got there my rod guides kept icing up and the line wouldn't move freely. But a week before I had stood on the discouragingly thick ice and cast my fly, a mylar dace, and lost it to a floating iceberg. Oh well. Last year I had broken a rod trying to cast strongly in the bitter cold. Will real spring never come? I said to myself, echoing the poets of yore. I meditated on the difference between a fly rod and a chugging paddle, which resembles a fraternity (or sorority) paddle with no initials carved on it. Pulling a fish in hand over hand has an atavistic glee to it; the fish imparts directly to the senses his electric struggle far below. Meat on the table! The provider! The "little woman" will be right proud of her jolly though indigent hubby. Pull that lunker out on the ice and cover him with snow to prevent the effects of dehydration in fish sunburn. I wandered around the creek estuary until I tore a foot-long hole in my waders. The water pouring in was horribly cold. I walked up the shore to an empty cabin, and a thermometer on the porch read twenty-four degrees. How stupid. I built a small fire out of driftwood and warmed my foot, watching some buffleheads circle above. From out in the bay, the birds were barely visible. I could hear the tremulous cry of two mating loons. I was frankly tired of cold weather and I imagined that the loons were also tired of running into icebergs, and the steelhead were tired of dozing in the cold water with their brains asleep to the spawning run.

Now the ice is gone and the snowdrift on the hill across the road shrinks daily. I have had two fair weeks of steelhead fishing and am gathering my equipment for a trip to Key West. Fantasies of a record tarpon are rife, though as unlikely as a record starlet. I feel somewhat benign about the preposterous winter I have endured. A crocus has appeared in vulgar purple glory. I will avoid hammerheads and moray eels and rattlesnakes and other imagined dangers, and go through more winters not unlike this one, where the depleted imagination narrows to a singular point. Fish. Anywhere and almost anytime. Even when trees split open from cold and the target is a bowling-ball-sized hole in a lid of ice.

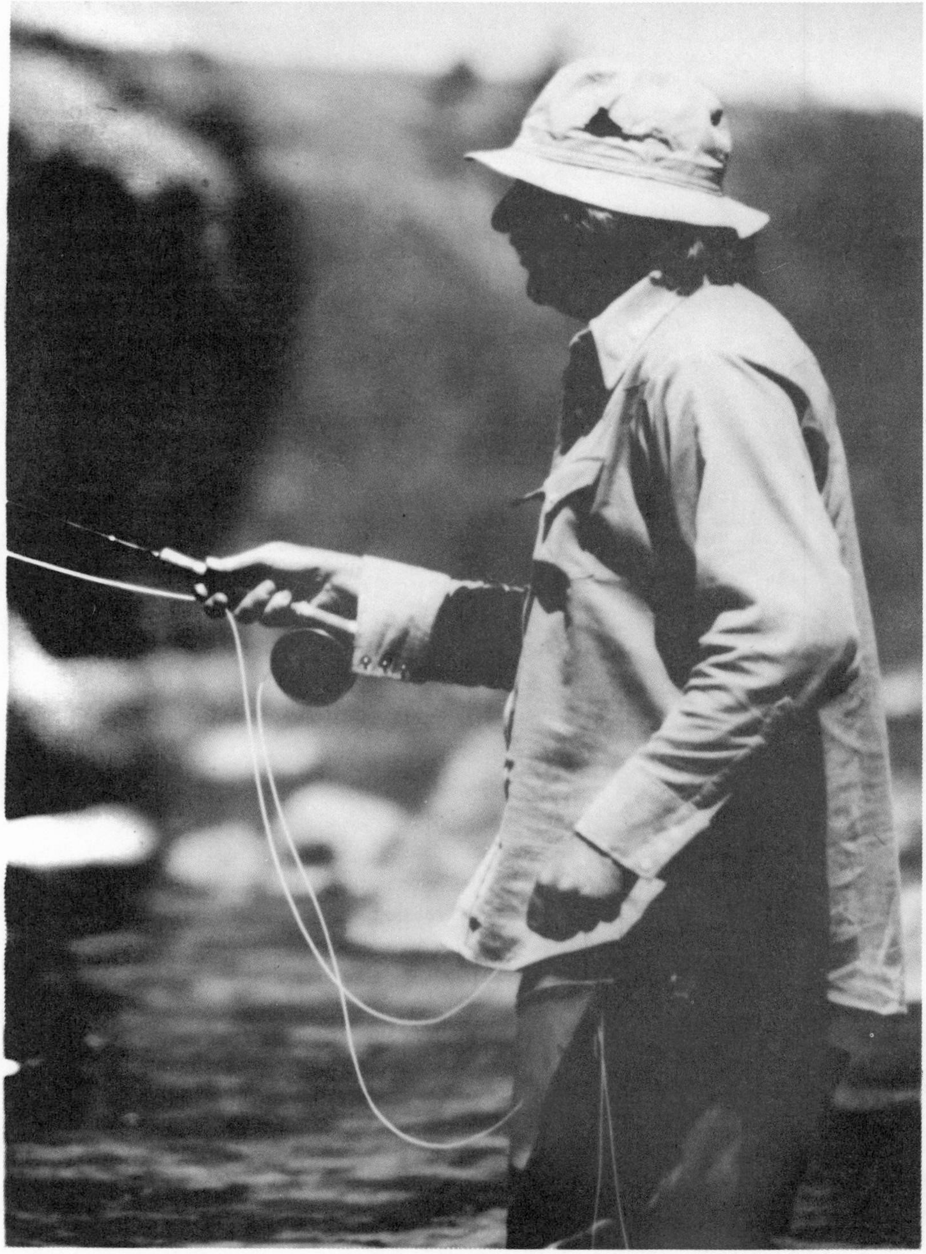
HAL LAURITZEN

RUSSELL CHATHAM

Some of us went quite crazy over fishing at a pretty tender age. I think those like myself were at first seeking a kind of refuge away from the erratic and sometimes frightening behavior of our young peers. Or, in other cases, our parents.

Fishing at its most rudimentary level is essentially solitary. Not only that, but its components, outside the particular baggage one brings to it, are entirely trustworthy. I mean, what creek ever teased you about your pimples; what breeze ever ridiculed you in front of your friends?

So then, some of us found something we could count on, a world in which we could participate without having to own the right brand of bicycle or have the same pug nose as the class president. In my own case, that world expanded into many other things, the most important of which were friendships, at first limited, it's true, but later expanded, deepened and broadened.

For some, fishing was a momentary distraction soon to be replaced by cars, sports and a teenager's natural attraction to the opposite sex. For others, change came more slowly and painfully. Some of the results of the latter were an expansion of real knowledge about fishing, development of finely tuned skills, and a more mature understanding of just how reliable the natural world really is, something only sensed earlier. It then becomes clear that not playing it straight is to cheat yourself at solitaire.

Like all kids, you find the literature. The first of it is right there on the stands alongside Donald Duck and "Tales from the Crypt": *Field & Stream, Sports Afield* and *Outdoor Life*. If we were easily seduced by the outrageous declarations of some largely suspect authors, that only served to hold our interest until, finally bored, we turned to the more rational and poetic contributors. You learned to look for heroes that would stick.

In a word, the thread which held almost all outdoor writing together was Challenge. In that aesthetic you hunted, killed, outsmarted, outwitted, bagged, fooled, trapped, beat and otherwise murdered fish and game. Often there was even the threat of personal injury from the likes of alligator gar or barracuda. The idea was to overpower and take.

Unfortunately, these notions have not yet completely died out. Any day you like you can stroll through the Safeway and see headlines on the sporting magazines proclaiming NEW WAYS TO MURDER BASS IN YOUR AREA! It could be that these writers never made the football team or couldn't get into a Green Beret unit. Maybe they made both, and when it was over the habit of fighting still stuck, I don't know.

I do know that it is inappropriate, especially in our era, to compete with nature and her creatures. This is not to say we shouldn't hunt or fish, quite the contrary. Properly pursued, these activities are the best ways we have of understanding nature. What we need more of is an abiding and governing love for animals and their environment. With respect to that premise, then, I feel Irwin A. Bauer should be placed in the penitentiary, and Roderick Haig-Brown should be required reading in every school.

SUMMER, AND OTHER
SMALL THINGS

Black bass season on the Russian River got underway about the time they put up the beach umbrellas. I regretted that because it meant you couldn't really fish during the day with much concentration or detachment. I mean, the teenagers would swim out and tip your canoe over just because you were dressed.

The truth is, the fishing wasn't much during the day anyhow. If you were going to go for smallmouths, you started at dawn. The gray squirrels woke you, or the bluejays. By that time particles of sunlight already colored the tops of the redwoods and you had better get down to the canoe before the best part of the morning was gone.

If we didn't have any eels for bait, we usually started by trolling airplane spinners along the slow stretch out from the beach where the umbrellas stood in the morning shade, closed up like so many flowers. We usually caught one or two small fish near the diving board.

After that, we had to decide whether to go upstream and fish the cliffs and the rain-gauge hole, or go down, past Badman's Beach to Hilton, and then on to Oddfellows Park. It depended on how early a start we'd gotten, and whether we felt like paddling upstream when the fishing was through, or drifting lazily downstream.

But when we had eels, the fishing achieved a considerably more important stature, one characterized by earlier starts, more concentration and a lot more fish. Baby lamprey eels are a bait a bass can't refuse.

The reason we were sometimes without them is that they can be tricky to locate. Adult lampreys ascend coastal rivers during the spring months to spawn. By summer, the babies are from two to six inches long, and live buried in the mud wherever the currents are not overly strong. This usually turns out be a backwater or the mouth of a small feeder stream.

185

What you did was to wade along, stopping now and then to dredge up great handfuls of mud, hoping to capture an eel or two as it wriggled back toward the river. You could keep the eels alive in a bucket for a week or so.

Our way of fishing them was to lower our lines over the side of the canoe and drift with the current. It was a magnificently silent and compelling way to fish: like fishing a still pond if you watched only line and water, but one where subtle folds and boils in the current bespoke movement, like a thin film of oil on water. Sometimes there was the sudden appearance of gravel rushing by, the too-late realization that the pool had become rapid. We learned that seldom will a look of astonishment keep a canoe out of the underbrush.

On our section of river, which centered at Summer Home Park, only one other person fished for bass. We knew Earl to be a serious fisherman. You watched Earl as keenly as you watched the river. Earl knew eels were the best bait, but when they were hard to come by, he worked the rapids with a screen and caught small soft-shelled crawfish.

Once, on the Fourth of July, right during the two o'clock swimming races, Earl and his wife anchored their rowboat in the deepest part of the Summer Home Park Hole, lowered crawfish baits to the bottom and caught one bass after the other. No one paid the slightest attention, right up to and including not tipping them over.

The fifties was no time to be a loner, especially a shy one. I think there is nothing camp, let alone amusing, about gang consciousness. Rock 'n' roll was visited upon the redwood country along with the summer hordes. At beaches like Hilton, Rio Nido or Guerneville, groups of teenagers roved the evening, looking for such as the innocent camper asleep on the sand. Finding same, they would circle, and gaily micturate on him and his belongings.

One evening I was walking along the road near the Korbel Winery. A candy-apple-red Mercury screeched to a stop and a picture-book greaser rolled down the window.

"Hey you, yeh, you big hero. Where's Squaw Rock at?"

"I think it's up around Cloverdale. I'm not sure. It's a long way."

The driver threw a beer can out onto the highway, the guy on my side flipped his cigarette butt at me and they fishtailed away. At the top of second gear, just before getting out of sight, they took out a guardrail and went into the river. I wondered if they killed any bass.

About the time we were old enough to complicate the fishing by taking up the fly rod, the Department of Fish and Game decided to rotenone the river and rid it of carp and other trash fish forever. What they forgot was, you can't do that.

Most of the smallmouths, being somewhat less tolerant of poison than carp, simply shrugged their fins and went belly up. The carp, on the other hand, suffered only mild nausea and occasional fainting spells, during which they drifted downstream to revive at, say, Monte Rio or Villa Grande.

After that, on the broad inside shallows of bends in the river like the one at Bridgehaven, you could see shoals of carp foraging as if the bottom itself were alive. I thought of this the other day when a friend of mine said to me, "You know why there are so many whitefish in the Yellowstone River? Because the Fish and Game people have never done anything to help them."

Having understood the tenacity and surprising quickness of river smallmouths firsthand, when it came to lakes I was suspicious from the start. There was one about three miles from where I grew up, not large, but certainly not just a pond either. It lay on a private estate, which necessitated sneaking in. Every kid in the community had done it for years; in fact, the primary angling skill involved in fishing Hollowell's Lake was knowing how to sneak in. When you got there, you could look into the clear water around the shoreline and see these overweight largemouth bass placed among the tules and weed beds rather like old people sitting in a hotel lobby.

Before long you would hear the caretaker coming, and then fishing became strictly secondary to keeping the lake between you and him. He drove a green convertible Model T Ford with wooden-spoke wheels which you could easily hear for half a mile. When he got to the lake, he would shut the car off, get out and stand there for several minutes. Then he would start yelling. I was never able to make out a word he said. Years later I learned he didn't speak English.

Sometimes we actually caught a few fish. One kid in particular, whose family did a lot of sailing and playing of polo, had a new kind of fishing outfit called *spinning*. With it he could cast lures a mile out into the lake, and as a result he always caught the most fish. Almost all those we caught succumbed blithely to their fate like rabbits being removed from their cages.

Sometime after that, one of the neighborhood kids told me that the owner of the lake had died, his mansion had burned to the ground and now they were draining the lake. I sneaked in to see, a pointless caution, since the old caretaker had long ago disappeared as well. A brown puddle no larger than a tennis court remained. I walked out on the cracked and separated ground that had once been lake bottom and pitched a Colorado spinner into the mudhole just for the hell of it. There was a great wallowing strike and several minutes later the biggest bass I'd ever seen lay flopping weakly in the mud at my feet. It would weight six or seven pounds—astonishing because we had never seen one come out of the lake that would go much above a pound and a half or two pounds at the outside. Unreasonably, I turned it back, hoping at the very least it would lose a more dignified battle with an old boar coon.

These days there is a school for girls, flanked by condominiums and ranch-style homes, where the lake once was: the California Dream extant, in technicolor and three altogether distressing dimensions. Nonetheless, last year while in the area I scooted past the guard at the gate and parked where the feeder stream used to come in.

On the hillside some of the old oaks still stood, beneath which I cast frog-finish flatfish to those dour old folks in the hotel lobby. I recalled how especially nice the reeds and cattails were there. Standing under those trees now, I was looking at the side of a building presumably designed by a blind man, the single interesting feature of which being that it housed young ladies. Through one of the windows, roughly forty feet above where the bass used to stare at me, a girl was hanging clothes in her closet. And in spite of the intriguing, if somewhat tacky, possibilities which that might suggest, I sat down, closed my eyes and cried.

My career as a lake fisherman came to an end the time I decided to get serious about largemouth bass fishing by driving up to Clear Lake. That was the year I turned sixteen, applied for a driver's license and bought a very used 1946 Plymouth. I convinced my cousin to go along by telling him that Jason Lucas fished for largemouth black bass in Clear Lake.

We went during our Easter vacation. When we arrived, it was hailing and snowing and a wicked wind was shrieking across the lake. The campground was deserted.

"Boys," the owner of the store said to us, " 'fraid it's a bit on the chilly side for bigmouth. Best bet now is cats."

"Oh?"

"You boys like a nice mess a fried catfish, dontcha?"

"Uh, sure. How do we fish for them?"

"Nightcrawlers. Nothin' a cat likes more'n a big fat 'crawler. 'Less you got chicken livers. You got chicken livers?"

"You don't think we might catch some bass on Hula Poppers?"

"Do a snowball stay round in the oven? Here. Two bits an' I'll give ya' a carton a crawlers 'n you go on give 'er a rattle."

"How do we know where the catfish are?"

"Don't. S'why ya fish at night. Jus' go on out there, fix yer Coleman light so's it'll stay by the gunwale, 'n start fishin'."

I had brought along a used Mighty Mite engine that I bought for twenty dollars. We decided if we were going to do this catfishing we better try out the motor, so we rented a rowboat for a dollar and a half and shoved off into the choppy lake. Less than fifty yards out the engine seized up and the wind blew us back to the dock.

"Hey mister, think we can catch any catfish off the dock?"

"Nope. Crappies maybe. 'Bout a month from now."

"I don't know." I looked at my cousin. "What would Jason Lucas do?"

It was too far to drive home that night so we put up our nine-by-nine canvas umbrella tent. After supper we were sitting on our cots when a car pulled into the campsite next to us. We peeked out and saw a man and woman unloading gear. The wind had eased a bit, but it still moaned through the trees above. We went to sleep to that sound and the bickering, cursing voices of our neighbors.

Not long after we had fallen asleep, a voice awoke us.

"You awake in there?" A man stuck his head in. "How the hell do you put these things together?"

We could smell bourbon as the man played his flashlight around the interior of our tent like a building inspector looking for dry rot.

"Well, you see," my cousin explained, "you just stake out the floor first, then you raise the center pole, extend the four arms and it's up."

189

"Unh. Think I could borrow your axe? See, this tent ain't mine. I got a weekend pass from the base and my girl and I decided we'd like to camp out, so I sort of borrowed it from my sergeant. Ha ha. I mean, he wasn't home, you know?"

In the morning when we woke up, my cousin sat up on one elbow and said, "That guy burned up his tent last night. You slept right through it."

I stuck my head out and there it was: a pile of ashes. The woman, rolled up in blankets, was asleep on the ground. The man was standing with his back to me, one hand on his hip, the other holding a bottle of Early Times. He took a long drink, then lay down on his back. In a few moments he addressed the sky: "Son of a bitch."

We took down our tent and packed the car. The man and woman were out cold, the bottle lying askew close by. I remembered the Mighty Mite was still on the rowboat, so I walked out on the dock. When I'd loosened the clamps, I simply eased the thing off the transom and let go. It disappeared at once in the murky water. Jason, I thought to myself, she's all yours.

Melvin was my best friend all through grade school and on into high school. We went trout fishing together often. Melvin had what I guess you would call a very repressed personality. You never saw him in wrinkled clothes and he washed his hands a lot.

He wanted to be an engineer, and had certain technical and mechanical curiosities and abilities. About these, he was a bit eccentric. For instance, after developing an interest in hot rods, he spent $3,000 disassembling a 1949 Ford convertible, only to reassemble it using factory-new parts, a Cadillac engine, a La Salle transmission and a hundred other bizarre modifications, the names of which I could never remember. When he was finished, he never took it out of the garage. Those who wished to view the automobile were given a tour, with strict instructions not to touch.

About this time, record players were becoming known as high-fidelity equipment. Melvin, his imagination fired by the notion of stereophonic sound, built an enormous set. Thing is, Melvin actively disliked music, as did his mother and father, so the only record he owned was the one where the two trains crashed.

"Want to hear my stereo?"

"Sure, Mel."

"Okay. Sit right here in the middle. You've got to sit *exactly in the middle!*"

I think though, that Melvin's most cherished possession was his Sila-flex spinning rod. I coveted it, too. It had what seemed to us a perfect action, and it was handsome as well. One time I was invited by some people to go with them to a private lake which was reputed to have legendary fishing. I asked Mel if I might possibly borrow the rod since this was a special occasion.

"Hmmmm. Well . . . uh, how big are the trout in this lake where you're goin? I mean, this is a delicate rod and I don't want you snapping it in half on a fish you don't know how to handle."

"They're not trout in the lake. It's bass."

"Bass! *Bass!* You've got to promise me you're joking. You want to use my Silaflex rod on . . . bass?" He careened around the room clutching his throat until he fell moaning on the bed.

"Geez, I'm sorry Mel. I didn't know . . . why don't we go listen to the stereo some more?"

After high school Mel went on to college and after that, got a top-secret job with the Atomic Energy Commission. For months at a time he worked at a lab in the Nevada desert and he never spoke about it at all.

A few years later, a mutual friend called to say that Melvin was missing and that they'd found his car parked near the toll plaza of the Golden Gate Bridge. A Coast Guard search turned up nothing.

I went by to see his mother. "I wish you'd take all that fishing stuff of Mel's. That's all you boys ever did was fish all the time. He talked about it last month when he was home. He said he couldn't stand his work anymore. He said he wished he could go fishing again like when you were in school. He said something about the Klamath River. That's one of the places his father used to take him."

I looked in Mel's closet and there were some odds and ends there: a worn-out pair of boots, an old canvas creel. But the Silaflex rod and Mitchell reel he used with it were gone. I smiled and wondered how he was doing.

It was decidedly possible to develop real affection for river small-mouths. Their vigor and aggressiveness let you work up an enthusiasm that involved, on the one hand, the river with all its marvelous vicissitudes and, on the other, a fish with many of the characteristics of trout, only a good deal broader in the shoulder.

I once told Melvin if we could tie a rainbow trout and a river smallmouth of equal size, tail to tail, the bass could tow that trout clear up to Healdsburg. Mel drew himself up, closed his eyes and pointed to the door. He didn't speak to me for days.

In particular, what fishing the Russian for bass did for me was to lead me, in blueprint form easy to read, to a life fully concerned with the natural world. Each joist and beam suggested a new connection, a renovation here, an addition there.

"Look," my cousin said excitedly one evening. "Shad!"

"Shad? What's a shad?"

"I don't know. But my dad told me when you see those wakes on the river just before dark, that's them."

"How come we never catch any when we're bass fishing?"

"I don't know. I think they only get them in nets."

Much later we learned how to catch shad, hundreds at a time, all of which we released back into the river.

"Hey mister, what kind of fish are in here?"

"Shad."

"What was that big silver fish you just caught and threw back?"

"Shad."

"What kind of fish are you trying to catch?"

"Shad."

By ten o'clock, or maybe noon if it was an overcast morning, bass fishing was over for the day and it was time to go back. By now perhaps half the beach umbrellas were open and you could hear screaming and laughter borne toward you intermittently on a light breeze. You checked to see that the rods were tied securely to the thwarts in case you failed to outpaddle the teenagers.

When you got near the footbridge, opposite the raft, a bunch of the kids would be sitting there rocking it back and forth. All were at least acquaintances, but you looked for one special face, a girl's.

Yesterday while swimming you played a game with each other where you kissed underwater. Last night in bed, you thought of it again and again. Unfamiliar nerve ends prevented sleep, and thoughts of playing the same game again tomorrow crowded out the usual excitement of the next morning's fishing.

If the bass had only known, they could have swum over and watched the children pressing against one another, alien monsters locked in unfulfilled embrace. Had the bass known to do this, they might also have considered a certain measure of their own safety; for many years would pass before the questions those underwater kisses raised were answered. During that time they would have only Earl to deal with.

Later, their troubles would start again.

STERLING SILVER

The elemental flatness of the Florida Keys is compelling and mysterious in its thin plane of reflective brilliance. Within their own horizontal galaxy, the flats are as inscrutable as the empyrean-blue water of the Gulf Stream itself, far outside the shoals where you look down along sharp, beveled shafts of light that narrow into blackness thousands of feet above the ocean floor.

Inshore, and out of sight of the Atlantic's barrier reefs, among the very Keys themselves, the horizon is often lost somewhere behind refulgent bands of light and shimmering heat waves. On certain hot, humid days without wind, distant mangrove islands are seen only as extraneous tubes of gray-green, lying inexplicably in the silver atmosphere like alien spaceships.

Over in the backcountry, the Gulf side of the Keys, long plateaus of uneven coral stall the tide and agitate it so the waterscape vibrates and sparkles. The whole of this inside territory is an unfathomably complex tapestry of radical design.

Few people understand that this vast district is one of the great wildernesses of North America. Travelers, as they fly between Marathon Key or Key West and Miami, are temporarily enthralled by the complicated pattern of lime-green channels and basins, the ochre and light-sienna coral and sand flats, the islands. But almost no one ever *goes there*.

Most of those who do have occupational reasons: sponge, lobster and conch fishermen, shrimpers, and fishing guides. Groups of bird watchers sometimes visit certain special keys. Skin divers occasionally get out and poke around old wrecks. And lastly, there are sportsmen.

Even within this last category is bracketed yet another minority within the minority: a fisherman who, in the opinion of some, carries it too far, bringing with him restyled nineteenth-century attitudes, seemingly inappropriate equipment and a full-on desire to proceed without secondary motives. Sometimes alone, sometimes with a close friend or perhaps a sympathetic hired guide, with benefit of only a small open skiff, a pole to push it, a fly rod and a perverse desire to be out of fashion, he goes out there to fish for tarpon.

It takes leisure time and a nature disposed toward contemplation, and sometimes contradiction, to develop passion for pastimes with surface pointlessness. In the instance of fly fishing for tarpon, a certain quantum of cash on hand is also required, although in no way is this an endeavor suited to the idle rich, or, for that matter, to anyone else slightly dotty. You need all your faculties.

Suppose you have the time, the money and the faculties. Assuming you want to expend them all on exotic fishing, why would you choose to go for tarpon rather than, say, marlin, a historically much more glamorous quarry? Enter your aforementioned contemplative, sometimes contradictory character.

If you think about distilling *fishing* down to *angling*, then further, to angling's diamond center, you can scarcely come to any conclusion other than this: as the time immediately preceding that point at which the fish actually becomes hooked grows more difficult, intense and all-absorbing, the quality of the fishing improves.

After that, you want the take to be hard to manage—fascinating in and of itself—and the ensuing struggle to be, above all, noble. Now, these moments may follow so closely upon one another they seem as one, yet there remains a hierarchy, however blurred. Then, way down there at the bottom of the list, is the dead fish on your hands.

To catch a marlin you must troll. Say the word over and over again to yourself, drawing it out as if it were spelled with lots of *o's* and *l's*. There may be nothing on earth, except perhaps an unsuccessful bridge-club luncheon, quite so boring as trolling. Trol-l-l-l-ing. Several hours of it should be enough to dull your senses so that when the captain or mate or speed of the boat, or whatever it is, finally hooks a fish and you are faced with the appalling prospect of an hour in the fighting chair, you simply would rather have a beer.

On quite another hand, nowhere else in the spectrum of available angling can there be found a more profoundly thrilling prelude to the hooking of a fish than in the stalking of tarpon in shallow water. The fly rod ups the ante considerably, too. In short, it's at least twice as much trouble as any other tackle you could use.

On the flats, where you must *see* everything, the search becomes an alarmingly patent and suspenseful intrigue. This game calls for a blend of refined skills, those of the hunter as well as the fisherman. It is a process, an experience, to which few, if any, ever really become fully initiated.

This is one of those spring mornings you always hope for; still, humid and already warm, so that the guides at the Sea Center on Big Pine Key feel the air and call it a tarpon day. As you ease out of the cut, enormous clouds are stacked around the horizon, nacreous and pillowy. Later a breeze may rise out of the southwest, but now the water is slick as mercury, its pastel patina reflecting the tops of the tallest clouds.

You are two days into a series of spring tides. This means you will be able to fish places that have been neglected during the preceding weeks, when there was not enough of a flood to bring the tarpon in. The plan will be to stake certain corners, then later, pole out some other banks.

When you shut down at your first stop it is suddenly as still as a room. The pole is taken from its chocks and your companion begins moving you into a higher position. It is still early, the sun at too oblique an angle to give real visibility yet.

Already it is getting hot, the high humidity causing a haze to form. It is impossible to see anything of the bottom beyond a few yards and you wonder how your friend knows where to stake. He is looking for the *corner*, he says, but you can notice no variation whatsoever in the even carpet of turtle grass.

Shortly, he pushes the stake in and ties off. You get up on the casting deck. Fish will be coming up the bank on your right, then cutting across where you are staked.

You pull off enough line for a throw, make one, then coil the running line neatly at your feet. You hold the fly in your hand, leaving a loop of fly line in the water long enough for a false cast. Now you wait and look.

There is plenty of time to think about the shortcomings of your fly casting, the different ways you might blow the chance when it comes. Your feet start to ache and you shift them a little so that later when you look down to make sure the fly line is not tangled, you see you're standing on it. You cast and recoil it carefully.

"Rollers. Hundred yards."

You look with extra intensity at the indefinite sheen as if the harder you stare the more likely you are to see something. Then they glint in unison, closer, and are gone again. The first wave of fright settles into your abdomen.

They're coming just as we thought. This way. Up the bank. Where are they? Where are they! It's not too soon to false cast. Get going. Oh no. No! They're right here. At the boat. Flushing.

The frightened fish are scooting away, back into the sheen. There are marl muds everywhere around the boat, and the boils the fish make as they depart seem to send a shiver beneath the skiff you can feel on the bottoms of your feet. You wish you had your blanket and a bottle of Jergens Lotion.

Several other pods of tarpon work their way up the tide. Always, though, their trajectory takes them past the skiff out of range. In an hour the surge of fish seems to have passed, gone on to Loggerhead or wherever they were going. You decide to pull the stake and pole out the bank.

As your companion begins to pole, you wish the sun would climb higher, the haze dissipate. You offer to take the pole, are turned down.

The drab grasses tilt in the slow current like a billion signposts gone wrong. Poling, you will be obliged to concern yourself with trigonometry; moving tide, moving boat, moving fish, degree of intercept.

Without notice, basins appear, deep and crisply emerald over their white sand bottoms. Sometimes there are barracuda arranged in them like dark lines of doom.

Small, tan sharks glide past the boat; rays, too, moving over the flat as the tide floods. The bank is 1,000 yards long. Somewhere on its easy slope there must be tarpon. You surge smoothly forward, transom first, that gentle sound being the only one you hear. Three hundred, 400 yards. Nothing.

What a strange way to fish this is. You might be out here for eight hours, running the boat ten, maybe twenty miles, and you never lose sight of the bottom. A drastic change in depth, one that might mean fish instead of no fish, or an easy pass through a little green cut rather than a grounded skiff or sheared pin, is twelve inches. Coming down off a plane at thirty knots at the wrong moment can mean settling into the grass so you will have to get out and push the heavy skiff until the bottom slopes away enough to get back in and pole your way out of it.

Down here they always tell you, if something goes wrong with the engine, just get out and walk home.

"Twelve o'clock. Way out." Quite far ahead, you see the chain of sparkles as tarpon roll, gulping air.

Tarpon on the bank. Hundred and fifty yards? Hundred? Can't let them get too close. Stay in front of the first fish. Are there two? Six? A dozen? Nothing. Sheen. Reflection. Haze. Useless glasses. Boat's closing. Fish coming on. Remember. Fly in hand. Ready. Loop of line trailing. Glance to see it's not back in the way of the pole. Fly line still coiled. Loose. Strain your eyes. Look. Wakes? They're colder gray. Light. And dark. Not warm, not tan like the bottom. Movement will tell. Long. They're long, cool gray. Temples pound. The glare, relentless. Sheen. No shapes. No gray. Another wake. Still farther out than you thought. Never mind. Roll the line. Think about it. Streamer gone, in the air. Back loop flat . . . not so tight! Slow down. There he is, within range, rolling, enormous scales catching the light. Your friend is urging, warning. Now! Wait out the backcast. Don't dump it. Wait. Drift. Know the intercept. Correct. Don't change direction too much. Not too much drive. Ease the cast off. Strip hard. Get his eye. Strip. A wake. Water rushing, churning. A take! Stay balanced, feel the turn, the tension. Now strike. Again, to the side. Again. Don't look up. Watch the line clear itself. Tarpon's in the air. Eye level, upside down, twisting, rattling. Push slack. Running. Too fast. Another jump. Gone.

Tarpon are not used as food. You would think there must be some way they might be thus prepared, but they just aren't eaten. Nor are they taken for other commercial reasons. At one time there was a scheme to convert them to pet food or fertilizer, a plan fortunately abandoned. In any case, there is no price per pound for tarpon, and no diners sit fidgeting with their utensils while their tarpon fillets are being broiled.

On the other side of the ledger, this has come to mean a lack of sound information about the fish and its habits. Tarpon are thought to be migratory, moving from south to north and from salt to brackish or fresh water as part of their spawning cycle. They also travel from deep to shallow water, ostensibly to feed. However, a true species pattern is not clearly known.

To the fish's broadest advantage, this also means there is no wholly justifiable cause for anyone to kill one. Those slight reasons used center entirely around man's own vanity. Fishermen may cart them to the dock, but the only one truly bringing them home is the Southernmost

Scavenger Service. The flimsy excuses, then, for killing tarpon rest in that zone somewhere between the charterman's only ad a tourist will buy, and the Kodak dealer.

It's possible to intrude upon the larger spirit of fishing in any number of ways besides pointlessly killing the animal. No the least of these is to destroy the privacy. For example, hardly anything can ruin the tranquility of a day's fishing like a good tournament. The reason keeps turning out to be greed in one form or another, with slices of unresolved ego gratification thrown in for good measure.

It's becoming practically un-American to disapprove of fishing tournaments these days. But if you take an affable, essentially non-competitive, harmless activity, the principal attribute of which lies in the quality of the time spent pursuing it rather than in the grossness of the last results, and you begin giving large cash prizes for the grossest last results, suddenly it's all gone.

Some negate the magic of angling by approaching it from a standpoint of overt, even bizarre practicality: equipment specifications, a humorless concern over questions that have only numbers as answers.

What hook size to use? What percentage of the point should be triangulated? What pound test should the weakest leader section be? What pound-class world record do you want to qualify for? How long should the whole leader be? The butt section? What size line? What's its diameter in thousandths of an inch? How long are its tapers? The belly? How thin is the running line? How much of it is there? How long is the rod? How heavy? How many yards of backing on the reel? What pound test? How tight do you set the reel drag? How long is the boat? How much does it weight? Its beam? How much water does it draw? How fast does it go? What horsepower is the engine? What's the capacity of the gas tank? How long is the push pole? How many knots can you tie? How far can you cast? How high is the tide? What time do you start fishing? What year is it? How many points do you get for a keeper in the Islamorada Invitational Fly Championship? How much do Minimum Qualifiers count per pound? How much do releases count? If you caught a 73-pounder, a 104½-pounder, three releases and a 90¼-pounder with cheese, what would you have? A large hamburger?

Everyone addresses a certain number of technical questions, but it seems this can be done cursorily, and as a matter of light concern. Attention to facts and figures as if they were really important often obscures the things of real importance, things that cannot be counted, recorded or even clearly explained. In the final analysis, those things will appear as states of mind, wordless, indescribable and of a dimension altogether intangible.

If you are going to replace the essential quietude of fishing with semi-industrial or businesslike considerations, it might be more sensible, simpler and certainly cheaper never to leave the office.

It is now early afternoon and you are being poled downlight over a brilliant, white-sand bottom. Much of the earlier haze has cleared and visibility is now extraordinary. Actually, you're just offshore from a low, tropical-looking key which shimmers in the heat, its long beaches curving nearly out of view.

Swells from the Atlantic roll the skiff so that it is important to remain keenly balanced. You are in about eight feet of water, somewhat on the deep side for fly casting to cruising fish, particularly if they are near the bottom. As you shift your weight with the motion of the boat, the Cuban-mix sandwich and the three Gatorades you so hastily challenged for lunch press heavily against your tee shirt.

You are in the middle of a long corridor of stark, bright bottom. On your right is the island; to your left, perhaps 100 yards away, the sand abruptly ending against low coral; there is a thin, irregular line of green, breakers and then blue water. Once, you see an enormous hammerhead cruising the edge.

Visibility is so perfect there is no need to be on the alert for the surprise appearance of tarpon anywhere within a 200-foot radius of the skiff. If it came within fly casting distance, a three-pound barracuda would look like a Greyhound Scenicruiser.

It is troublesome poling in the deep water, not only because of that very fact, but because the bottom is quite hard, so the pole makes a clunking sound when it's put down. The foot of the pole doesn't grab well either, slipping off ineffectually behind the boat.

You and your companion see the dark spots at the same time. There is a moment of hesitation, then it suddenly becomes clear they are tarpon even though they are still very far off. You will have a full three minutes to try and get the upper hand on your mounting nervousness.

Were we wrong? No, they're tarpon all right. Eight, maybe ten. All big—seventy, eighty pounds and better. Still very far. Funny how the school changes shape. They string out, bunch up. Fish must be very foreshortened at this distance. So clear. Almost like watching birds flying. Watch footing. Is the fly line tangled? School's turning. Traveling closer to the key. Boat's turning. Good. Must make the intercept. Must take them head on. Too deep for a side shot. They'd see the boat. It's going to work. Looking at them from in front.

"I'm down. Anytime." You look back and your friend has the push pole flat across his knees. "Go." He insists, never taking his eyes from the tarpon.

How far now? Hundred-fifty feet. False casting. Hold up all the line you can. Fish coming on, almost single-file. Watch. You want thirty feet on them. No slips. Loops open. Controlled. Cast. Wait. Fly settling. Two, three feet. Tarpon at six. Or eight. Closing. Is the lead fish close enough? Start bringing it back. He sees it. Accelerating. Elevating. Growing silver. Face disjointing. Dark. Has it. Turning back down. Tension. Hit hard. Again. Again. Again.

He is already going another way and the strain disorients you so much the fly line is suddenly gone from your left hand. Whirling, it jams its way through the guides. You hear the sound of the power tilt as the engine goes down, starts. Slowly, you begin to follow.

SEASONS
THEN AND NOW

The Gualala Hotel is one of those uninstitutionalized landmarks that still remain to remind us of a time when California belonged to the Spanish and Russians, or later, the Swiss who came to live and farm so peacefully. Not that these people had anything in particular to do with the hotel, but when you see the rather chaste two-story building washed in warm afternoon light, you are reminded, if abstractly, of an Andrew Wyeth painting, or if you were born here before about 1940, of all places and people out of your childhood.

Gualala is a tiny town lying on the northern California coast about halfway between Jenner, at the mouth of the Russian River, and Fort Bragg. Pronounced with a silent G, the name appears vaguely Spanish though it was the Russians who used this territory. Some historians believe the word is the Spanish version of Valhalla, while others maintain it comes from the Pomo *Walali*, "Where the waters meet."

It works either way. The Gualala River lagoon stretches for nearly a mile before breaking through its sandbar to the ocean, and the two flirt with each other much of the way, especially when the sea is rough. And the countryside here is abundant, the river and ocean yielding rich harvests of fish and shellfish, the forest full of game. No hero fallen in battle could contrive to have his soul rest in a more generous hall.

To those of native distinction, the word "California" is pronounced slowly in the mind, as if speaking with a modest Italian or Spanish accent, to dignify the word and make it somehow expressive of an ambience having nothing whatsoever to do with suburban sprawl, freeways, bizarre population densities and the positively lethal disregard for history Southern Californians pioneered.

You can still see some of the underpainting in places like the Salinas

Valley, where the farms don't seem to change much. The old people were uncomplicated, and along with their crops, cultivated attitudes of decency. Many ranchers and farmers grew rich, became millionaires in some cases, but few considered it a matter of consequence. When the time came, as it did to so many, that unfair taxation forced the sale of land to developers, they did not gleefully take the money and run. They despaired for loss of the soil.

The coast north of San Francisco remained largely provincial until about ten years ago, when the Flower Children decided they would rather live in the country. They showed by example that if you could manage the right blend of welfare benefits, food stamps, MediCal, unemployment insurance, subsistence gardening, checks from home and Volkswagens, the last thing on earth you needed was a job opening close at hand. You could lie back in the sun out there in the middle of nowhere and pick your nose until hell wouldn't have it.

Until that time, Gualala was an isolated North Coast community. And it has been, in fact, the last in the region to knuckle under to the pressure of the times, the first being Mendocino City, north of there, where vacationing art teachers seized control years ago.

My family began going to Gualala before the Depression for the steelhead fishing. It took at least two days to get there from San Francisco, over dirt roads that became impassable in wet weather. If you went at all, you took your fishing pretty seriously and planned on staying awhile.

Those were not years when Leisure Time lay heavily on people's hands. Backpacking and camping were for eccentrics, jogging would have been inconceivable and hang gliding hadn't been invented.

One December, my father, uncle, an old gent named Walt Mullen and my father's roommate at Stanford, Pinky Mahoney, made an expedition to Gualala to fish and hunt.

My father loathed fishing, especially where it involved a boat. His view maintained that the seat of a rowboat was harder than a landlord's heart and had only one purpose: to make you suffer in the region of your rear end. My father's opinion of the Gualala River as a fishing stream derived from a day early on, when he caught a logger's boat in the lagoon after trolling for it for five hours.

So he talked everyone into going hunting. They would take a handcar up the logging tracks and shoot some quail. The first covey they found, everyone but Pinky had shots and missed. Pinky allowed that no one seemed able to hit their hat. My father wondered aloud if Pinky would like to throw out his hat and settle the matter. No, instead they'd do this: my father would throw his hat in the air and Pinky would shoot at it, then Pinky would throw his hat and it would be my father's turn.

Pinky was from a distinguished Boston family. His 20-gauge was an elegant Parker double. His hat was made in England. My father admired Pinky for his candor, generally, but never failed to raise his British eyebrows over the fact that Pinky wrote a master's thesis severely critical of Boswell's *Life of Johnson*.

My father put a stone inside his sweat-stained Dobbs and gave it a toss. Pinky missed with both barrels.

"Your turn, Pinky."

As Pinky removed his wool cap, Walt and my uncle slipped off their safeties behind his back and stood waiting. When the hat sailed out over a blackberry bush, six loads blew it into infinity.

They took me to Gualala shortly after 1950. It was a little like leading the boy caught smoking to a whole box of cigars and demanding he exhaust his interest. Perhaps not quite that, but my parents were alarmed at the obsessive hold fishing had on me. I would have dashed through a forest fire in a flammable sweater if I thought there might be a trout on the other side.

They opted for the join 'em approach, and the next thing I knew my uncle was buying me a Pflueger Supreme casting reel and a nine-foot, two-handed bamboo rod. That winter when the weather broke, school was out of the question. We were going to go steelhead fishing at Gualala.

We fished with bait, fresh roe, which we tied into "berries," small balls wrapped in moliene, a material not unlike nylon stocking. In the lobby of the Gualala Hotel, tables were set up so you could tie your bait. This was the main function of the lobby, except when a few old-timers played pinochle in the afternoons while everyone else was out fishing.

What you did was to tumble your bait through the places where steelhead were apt to be lying. You cast slightly upstream, then followed with your rod tip as the current took the berry around below you. Whenever there would be a pause in this drift you would strike, because often the steelhead would take very gently, then let go.

You were always hanging up on the bottom, forever fixing a new rig. Someone was always talking about someone else he knew who had gone a whole season without catching a fish. As my bait swung around again and again, I wondered if that was going to be me.

Some of the real veterans claimed they pretty much knew the difference between a fish and the bottom, so naturally, they snagged up less often. I was on the bottom constantly. In that icy canyon, my hands would get so cold I couldn't work a swivel or tie a knot, so I would retreat to the beach and kneel down, where I would try to warm my hands before rerigging.

"What are you doing?" my uncle would ask with impatience. "Praying? Get your line in the water. How do you expect to catch anything kneeling on the beach?"

Then, back at the hotel in the evening at the bar, he'd tell everyone with mock concern, "He prays all day for a hit, but he never fishes. Spends more time on his knees than one of the Apostles."

My uncle was so good he could cast his bait and sliding sinker into a teacup at thirty yards. He used an old eleven-foot Leonard rod with a hardwood handle he'd made himself and a classic J. A. Coxe freespool reel. He knew where the fish would be and he could feel pickups when there was almost nothing to feel. Once, he found a school of fish near a cut bank. He was getting a pickup on every cast, hooking a fish on every fourth or fifth. He called and had me cast in there, but I couldn't feel a thing.

"You're not casting far enough," he said. "Make it about three inches more."

I'd try, and even when the cast was right I couldn't feel the pickup. He'd stand there and watch my line and see a pickup I couldn't even feel.

When fishing was really tough and he was one of the few on the river to have hooked anything, he'd let me play and land it, then up at the hotel when the men asked how it went, he'd say, "The kid got one."

I want to go back strongly enough not to care what a number of intervening years may have wrought. Few things in memory stand out quite so clearly as seasons in Gualala. Youthful enthusiasm distorted the proportion, but even in the light of later perspective, those times are rich. You know you have tasted the best there is, and somehow even if there are only leavings, they will still have a touch of that flavor.

This winter of 1975–1976 is disastrous on the coast. Hardly a drop of rain has fallen on California. It is the driest year on record. In February, when there should be six inches of bright-green grass everywhere, there is only dust.

The streams remain at summer level. On the California coast, where there is no such thing as snowfall, the precipitation is largely rain, which comes during the winter months. In the six months from May to October, only one to two percent of the annual runoff finds its way to the sea.

The Gualala River, then, like all the others, is practically dry when I see it in late February. A few fish make it over the shallow riffles at night, but the main schools hold in the big pools waiting for rain. All winter long there have been reports of masses of fish in the lower pools: Thompson, Minors, Mill Bend, the lagoon. The water is crystal clear, the fish very touchy. You have to fly fish using long, light leaders and small flies to hook anything.

Word spreads through the angling community so that these pools are elbow to elbow with fishermen. The news reaches my uncle and he decides to go up for a look. He hasn't been to Gualala for at least fifteen years, maybe longer. He gave it up when the fishing slid downhill to practically nothing in the late fifties and the crowds became intolerable. He hasn't seen anything.

"How can they do it?" He asks when I see him. "The whole fun of going fishing at the Gualala was you could get a pool to yourself. There must be twenty or thirty fishermen in every hole, all casting into the same spot."

Today, among these younger Californians, the notion of having a pool to yourself is as foreign as a ride in a Model T Ford along the coast from Jenner on a dirt road, having to stop every few miles to open gates.

It is about two o'clock one afternoon as I cross the bridge at Gualala and decide to look first at the Thompson Hole. The old river road is now paved, the turnoff unfamiliar. A sign says COUNTY ROAD 501, CAMPING, and there is an arrow.

The camping turns out to be at the Thompson Hole where there is another sign, this one rather enormous: "Gualala River Redwood Park. 4.50 per day per car, 90.00 per month payable in advance. Up to four persons. Each additional person 25 cents per day, 7.00 per month. Check-out hour twelve noon. Day rate 1.00 per car. We reserve the right to refuse admittance to anyone."

You think about the old boy who used to spend the whole winter under the dark, damp redwoods at Thompson's in a leaky canvas tent. No one could understand why he didn't die of pneumonia, because it was always wet inside. All he cared about was catching steelhead. Every so often someone would bring him a bag of groceries and a handful of candles. Today he would probably be refused admittance.

Actually, when you think about it, it gets cold enough in there to freeze the eyelids off a brass monkey, and only a masochist would want to camp in that dungeon when, for another four bits, you can get a comfortable room with maid service over at the hotel.

The road to the river, which has always been no more than two ruts you take your chances with, is now asphalt. Where it comes back out of the campground there is a sign in red letters warning you WRONG WAY. All the redwood trees are wired for lights.

At Thompson's nine people are fishing, five fly casters and four bait fishermen. One of the fly fishermen evidently snapped his fly off on the beach earlier and is now fishing without one. I wonder why he doesn't notice this while I do, since he is approximately fifty yards closer to where his casts are landing than I am.

The fishermen are directing their attention at the deepest part of the pool where, under normal conditions, you would never find a steelhead. But in this low water the fish are piled in there so thickly, if you climb the bank you can see them as a dark mass, changing shape once in a while like a huge amoeba.

The lower end of the pool, where the steelhead usually lie, is all but dry. The old redwood stump in midstream, which has been there as long as anyone can remember, is wholly visible. Ordinarily, only the tip of it shows when the river is at fishable levels during the winter.

One of the verities of fishing the Thompson Hole is that if you are the first one in the morning to roll your bait past the log, you'll have a fish. It is very strange now to be able to see the bottom all around it.

I wade across, not getting my knees wet, to the top end of Minors Bend. It is fine bait water, where the current flows against the other bank. Snags and windfalls give it a fishy appeal. Sometimes you can catch spawned-out fish on flies here if the water's not too high, but it's always a good bait spot. No one is fishing it.

Down at the deepest part of the bend, three men are fly casting from small prams. Two others are wading near the boats. On the cliff across the stream, ten or twelve people are bait fishing.

One of the men in the boats turns out to be Bill Schaadt, whom I've not seen for several years. We are happy over this accidental meeting and Bill excitedly describes how the fishing has been and how it is today. The steelhead are schooled up just off the old alder, milling somewhat, biting spasmodically.

I think of the day here at Minors about twenty-five years ago when the late Claude Kreider, then a popular outdoor journalist, came down and saw Bill fly fishing, and, taking out his spinning rod, announced that it was too muddy for flies. That day, Schaadt landed thirty-three fish, one of which was nearly twenty pounds, at the time the largest steelhead in the world ever caught by fly fishing.

In waders, it is almost too long a cast to reach the fish. I watch the other fisherman and am embarrassed for them, for their lack of fly casting ability, their dull expressions, the obvious fact they do not truly see or understand the essential life of the river around them.

I can feel all too precisely how many feet, even inches short, a certain cast is, or when a subtle surge in the current snakes it away from the fish. And it takes several line changes to find the one which sinks exactly right so the fly is down among the fish, yet never on the bottom.

When I was still learning to fly cast I would have been ashamed to be seen handling my tackle as poorly as these men fishing near me. Perhaps it's no more than Calvinistic intolerance, but it still seems a lack of pride is a sad thing. These fellows cast sloppy lines yards short of where they must be, and routinely retrieve as if just throwing it out there is enough of an act of faith to justify a reward. It is quite easy to imagine them going a whole season without ever catching anything.

Bill and I fish in silence for an hour. I look up at him, shake my head. He shrugs.

"Where are all the regulars?" I ask.

Bill is stern but matter-of-fact. "They're dead."

In the lobby of the hotel are some of the old photographs, even though the hotel has changed hands and the bar is remodeled. There is no pretense in these familiar pictures; they are clearly not intended for public entertainment, and in their simplicity, defy the falseness of brochure aesthetics. They not only record tangible evidence of good fishing, but a lack of hysteria as well. There is a curious quietude registered on the faces of these men as they squint into the winter sun.

I remember Johnny Verges, Hank Adler, Lou Villa, Allan Curtiss, Fred McMurray, Neil Gordon, Joe Panic, Gunderson. Where are these men now? A few dead, but not all. Do they still come here to drift their baits through the pools and rapids? If so, do they stay at the Gualala Hotel?

My room is on the second floor, Number 3. Merv Suitor used to stay in . . . was it 8? Merv was always here. He came in on Monday, went home again on Friday, all season long. Everyone wondered how he managed, but he did. He woke early in the morning, three-thirty or four, and read until it was time to go to breakfast at six.

He'd get out on the stream with everyone else as soon as it got light, even if he did grumble about it. But as soon as the sun came up, he'd find someone on the beach to talk to. He'd sit up there all day periodically yelling, "A good man'll get 'em," or "What would the experts do?" or "Chatham, you'll never make a pimple on a real fisherman's arse."

Joe Panic owned the hotel at the time and he often made a lot of noise behind the bar. Just after Fred McMurray married June Haver, they came up to go steelhead fishing. After toughing it out on the river one cold day, June came into the bar, took her waders off and asked Panic to please rub her ice-cold feet.

"Aw gee, why don't ya get one a these married guys to do it?"

One night, in a playful mood, while Fred was talking about fishing with some of the others, she plugged in the jukebox and started trying to find someone to dance with. I was probably about a sophomore in high school at the time, and when she got around to me I was frozen with fear. For some time after that, my name was preceded by the nickname, "No-dance."

Fly fishing was considered pretty exotic back during the early fifties. But there were some who stuck with it all the time: Curtiss, Schaadt, Joe Paul, Frank Allan, Carl Ludeman, Jim Golden and a few others.

Now nearly everyone fly fishes and you seldom, if ever, see any of the old-time bait fishermen. It is evidently hip to be a fly fisherman. Young anglers on the stream have the most stylish tackle. Many sport badges or arm patches declaring their affiliation with clubs or organizations. There is no doubt that, by and large, they aren't as bigoted or opinionated or as secretive as their earlier counterparts. And, if you can trust what you see, not nearly as knowledgeable either.

Things change. We got used to the new highway bridge even though it ruins the solitude of Mill Bend, not to mention the Racetrack Riffle, which it spans. Now, when you start up the hill into town, a large billboard welcomes you to Gualala. Among other services, you learn you now have two choices if you want to get your hair done: the Gualala Beauty Salon or Shurl's Curls. There are the inevitable real estate offices, two huge service stations and a brand new post office-bank complex that looks as if it just landed.

A bright new green-and-yellow Volkswagen bus pulls slowly to a stop in front of the hotel. A shiny canoe rests on the roof of the bus. A California Couple get out and look with interest at the quaint building. He has a perfectly trimmed beard, her hair is long and light. They are dressed in denim. They will probably have dinner at the hotel and would perhaps think it amusing to take a room for the night.

Meals at the hotel used to be potluck, family style, always hearty. The same dining room is now a popular restaurant on the coast. On weekends you can barely squeeze in, and the barroom sometimes looks like a dress rehearsal for Soul Train.

On the second floor at the east end of the hall is a window covered by a gauzy curtain. Through it you see a vertical cross section of typical coast landscape. Below, the green, uneven yard, fish house, moss-covered shed, pines, then the stark white Baptist Church, dark-green cypress and more pines against a sky bleak with the present threat of rain.

Yes, it will rain, and never was it so needed. But you can't help responding like a steelhead fisherman, and curse the weather.

You walk down the hall to the front of the building and look out at the ocean. The sandbar is dense with seagulls and the surf is enormous, crashing over into the lagoon. Breakers explode against headlands to the south. When you look that way you think of the Sea Ranch, a vast new second-home and retirement community which sprawls for ten miles below Gualala.

You have been aware that there is hardly a bit of funkiness or eccentricity left. People used to do things on the coast like decorate their barn or yard with abalone shells. These days tourists would see that and start screaming ecology, because a lifetime collection of abalone shells looks like a lot. Even more than that, most objections would be on grounds of taste.

Many point to the Sea Ranch as an example of clean, tasteful planning and architecture. Instead, is it possible that the Sea Ranch is not in good taste at all, but is rather sinister? For starters, they have cut off public access to the ocean for ten miles.

In another, more important sense, the whole development is self-conscious and self-indulgent. It is truly a realtor's dream of take-and-take-more come true. You sell the large expensive homes on the hill to the wealthy on the basis that the low slopes will remain "open space." Then, when you run out of hill, you start working your way down until you've filled all the land with homes, diminishing in size and price as the elevation drops.

Architecturally, this may be the final moment of the Bauhaus, of that Aryan insistence that you remain in step. All the buildings are alike: bleached cedar, tinted glass, triangles, trapezoids. Modular units.

The old barns and other buildings weren't designed by architects imposing their conformist notions on the countryside. The old buildings had a sense of modesty, of legitimate purpose, and they did not insult the landscape.

Even the Sea Ranch logo, hatched by some graphic designer and looking oddly pre-Columbian, is harsh and entirely out of place. Over and over again it pokes out from behind the bushes to tell you not to trespass.

Two things are no longer there which were a real part of fishing at Gualala: the mill with its rumbling and smell of smoke, and the sound of diesel logging trucks coming down out of the canyon.

Funny thing is, we all screamed because logging ruined the river and there seemed to be no stopping it. And now that it's gone, it's somehow worse because you have only this rather spineless situation left where everything is manicured and complete directions are posted.

Where you park, or rather where you are now told to park at Thompson's, there is a sign on one of the trees that says TO BEACH AND RIVER AREA. This is in case someone is not able to recognize a river or a beach even though they are both only ten yards away.

Fishing in the canyon, there is a sense of loss without the logging trucks. Yes, you will have to adjust, but you think that maybe a nice muddy, rutted gravel road plus the downright recklessness of those old drivers might have alarmed some of these denim dandies in their Malibu Classics enough so they would never venture as far as Thompson's, or ever come peering through the trees to find the crossing to the Donkey Hole.

You try to hold the bitterness at bay, but it creeps in anyway. You wonder if you are merely expressing some sort of class prejudice, but what you finally come down to is that there are just too goddamn many people.

There is an hour of light left. The day before, the lagoon had been boiling with fish. You wonder if they might move up to Mill Bend on the tide. They would be bluebacks mostly, smaller, late-run fish.

The wind is up, blowing in from the south. With it there will be rain. The sky is leaden. In a few days the season will close, and each year it is the same. One day you may stand here and fish, the next you may not.

You always regret not being able to fish in March, one of the most interesting months. You think how nice it would be if there were a special catch-and-release season. After all, the closure is to protect fish heading back downstream to the sea. Secretly you know that most people wouldn't bother to fish if they had to release everything.

The steelhead are here, rolling and splashing everywhere. The wind is fierce and that, plus the gloom of evening, will, you hope, offset the clear, shallow water. It is nearly dark when the take comes and it is a surprise, as they all are. In that moment you know, yet do not understand, why you spoiled so many years fishing for these things.

You want to say it has to do with intercepting a migratory cycle, that it puts you in touch with certain seasonal mysteries, is at least a partial definition of the cosmos, life itself.

But this has all been said before by thoughtful men, and it is true, only no matter what is said it's never enough, never really *it*. Or perhaps it's too much, because we are in that region of the senses, of the heart, where experience defies translation, ridicules explanation.

You have gone to some good deal of trouble to be here, not only currently, but through years of asking, searching, trying. Now you're banking one of the jackpots. These cliffs are dark and exquisite, the cypress so expressive they seem to be reaching, gesturing. It is as if they were imploring you to love them.

The stumps lying in the water go so far back beyond memory that they become almost like characters in a book or play. Each time you look, they are themselves and something else; memories layered thickly in the back of the brain.

Coming up tight on the steelhead is like confirming the answers to a thousand impossible questions, being admitted into secret chambers of knowledge. It is only in the moments after that you face the fact you have done nothing extraordinary.

It rains all night and you can hear the wind pushing at the window and soughing through the forest. At six you go down for breakfast. You remember those times when you came in here and fishermen were talking, eating, and you came away from the table with some notion where everyone would be on the river. If you excused yourself early, they knew you fully intended to be the first one through the lower end of Thompson's by the log. They wouldn't leap from their chairs and try to head you off; they also knew overeagerness was a function of youth.

This morning in the old dining room there are a couple of construction workers, yourself and two or three other fishermen. You are already in your waders and one of them asks if you think the river has come up during the night. You shrug.

It's still raining, so you decide it best to go down to the highway bridge and check the stream. In the first light of dawn you can already tell, by looking over toward Mill Bend, that the river's too light. When you get to the bridge the water is light brown. The sign that says No Fishing From Bridge looks strangely alone in the gray light. You wonder what kind of moron would ever fish off this bridge anyway.

You drive to Thompson's where you can determine how much the river has risen and how the flow has increased. You feel there might be a chance as the fish move over the riffle from Minors and stop here for a few moments.

At Thompson's you see the same fishermen as the day before. They are standing tentatively on the bank right where they were fishing yesterday. One of the fly fishermen nods and says with authority, "Better have your fast-sinking line on today."

You realize, not without a mixture of alarm and pity, that he fully intends to fish the precise piece of water as he had the previous week when the steelhead were forced to hold there by conditions. Now, that stretch is a raging chute barren of fish; even those swimming quickly through will do so near the shallow side where the current is less severe.

No one is paying any attention to the lower end, the only possible place you could hope to fish. As you watch, several wakes come over the riffle.

You reflect that the old boys would have that spot sewed up tighter than a surgeon finishing an appendectomy, but here it is wide open. Casually, you wade in, watching the lip as several more fish ease over. A steelhead boils right in front of you, then another. Across the river, the tip of the log is visible.

It's a long shot, with visibility in the water of less than three inches, but you tie on a large black fly and cover the rollers with short casts. In a moment of luck you have a take, but manage to hold onto it for less than half a minute.

The current grows stronger as rain keeps falling. Debris is floating past. The log is now underwater and you only know it's there by the trailing wake of disturbed current. The fishing is over.

You stroll to the car and put away your tackle, then walk over through the redwoods to where you can see the huge tree that slopes into the water at the head of the pool. That too, like all the others, has been there since anyone can remember.

As if looking for something even more primordial, you watch the cliffs, covered with bright yellow moss, then the river where it bulges against them. The redwood log is young compared with the cliff. How long ago had it come to rest there? Had the sun ever shone on that moss, even in the summertime?

The canyon is so deep here that with the darkened sky, it is like being in a cathedral. The light is dull, and you keep coming back to the mossy cliff which seems illuminated.

For me, this is a gallery of spirits, though now they are less real than ever before. I look at the river steadily for perhaps a full minute and my mind expands that sixty seconds into a century, a millennium. In my limited way of sensing things, I feel this will go on forever.

RUSSELL CHATHAM, BORN IN SAN FRANCISCO IN 1939, BEGAN FISHING, PAINTING AND WRITING AT AN EARLY AGE. SINCE THEN HIS ESSAYS ON SPORT, CONSERVATION, ART AND FOOD HAVE APPEARED IN SUCH PUBLICATIONS AS *ESQUIRE, THE ATLANTIC, OUTSIDE,* AND *SPORTS ILLUSTRATED*. HIS PAINTINGS, ETCHINGS AND LITHOGRAPHS CAN BE FOUND IN PUBLIC AND PRIVATE COLLECTIONS ACROSS THE COUNTRY. CHATHAM'S OTHER BOOKS INCLUDE *DARK WATERS, RUSSELL CHATHAM: ONE HUNDRED PAINTINGS, THE MISSOURI HEADWATERS, STRIPED BASS ON THE FLY,* AND *THE ANGLER'S COAST,* WHICH WILL BE REISSUED THIS YEAR BY CLARK CITY PRESS. CHATHAM LIVES WITH HIS FAMILY IN LIVINGSTON, MONTANA.

COVER PAINTING *SILENT SEASONS* AND INTERIOR DRAWINGS
BY RUSSELL CHATHAM
COVER DESIGN BY ANNE GARNER
BOOK DESIGN BY RUSSELL CHATHAM, ANNE GARNER
AND JAMIE HARRISON POTENBERG
COMPOSED IN BEMBO AND
PRINTED BY BRAUN-BRUMFIELD, INC., ANN ARBOR.